32.95

Dividing
WESTERN
WATERS

Mark Wilmer
and
Arizona v California

Dividing
WESTERN
WATERS

Mark Wilmer
and
Arizona v California

JACK L. AUGUST, JR.

WITH A FOREWORD BY JOHN BOUMA

TCU Press • Fort Worth, Texas

Library of Congress Cataloging-in-Publication Data

August, Jack L.
  Dividing western waters : Mark Wilmer and Arizona v California /
Jack L. August, Jr.
    p. cm.
  Includes bibliographical references and index.
  ISBN 978-0-87565-354-9 (cloth : alk. paper) —
  1. Colorado River (Colo.-Mexico)—Water rights. 2. Arizona—Trials,
litigation, etc. 3. California—Trials, litigation, etc. 4. Water rights—
Arizona. 5. Water rights—California. 6. Water-supply—Arizona. 7.
Water-supply—California. 8. Wilmer, Mark. I. Title.
  KF5575.A55A753 2007
  346.7304'32—dc22

                                        2007000844

Cover and text design by Bill Maize; Duo Design Group

TCU Press
P. O. Box 298300
Fort Worth, TX 76129
817.257.7822
http://www.prs.tcu.edu/
To order books: 800.826.8911

To my son, Sam

TABLE OF CONTENTS

FOREWORD

Men matter, and can make a difference, for good or ill. In Mark Wilmer we have a man who mattered mightily in the development of the Southwest, and in the ability of our country to achieve what many believe is Manifest Destiny, the inevitable westward expansion of our nation. Mark was a man who stood on its head Shakespeare's gloomy observation that "The evil men do lives after them, the good is oft interred with their bones." The good Mark Wilmer did certainly lives after him and will remain a monument to his skill, courage, and character for generations to come.

This volume is a tribute to Mark as a lawyer, a visionary, and a man. It was my good fortune to know and work with him as a colleague and friend. As Jack August points out in this highly readable volume, Mark and I often roamed the state in search of places in which we could fish, hunt, and—most important—just talk. He was simply good company.

In this day when "mentoring" has been raised to the top of the agenda of most law firms, it is difficult to convey how desperate new, young lawyers once were for advice and counseling from older colleagues of the "sink or swim" school. Law school may be a wonderful place in which to become acquainted with some of the tools of the trade, but only the tutelage of a wise, experienced colleague can teach the bearer of a newly minted degree how to turn those tools into implements useful to clients, the community, and the state in which we are privileged to live.

Mark was just such a colleague. Whenever I needed advice on theory or tactics in a particular matter, I could turn to Mark and count on a thoughtful, imaginative—and equally important to a youngster—courteous and respectful response. And much more. Mark not only knew what the law was, but he had a fine sense of what it ought to be, and how best to undertake the task of bringing the law more in line with good public policy.

As we look around Phoenix and Arizona today, it is difficult to remember what the city and state were like before Mark watered these seedling communities. Dr. August describes the Arizona that Mark encountered in 1931 as "a harsh and arid environment." Phoenix was a city of 48,000 souls living in a state that counted its population as a mere 435,000. And such a national backwater it might have remained had not Mark and others waged the legal and political battles described in this book to get Arizona the water that would turn it from "harsh and arid" into a destination of choice, and Phoenix from, quite literally, a cow town into the fifth largest city in America. Of course, Mark's achievement in wresting for Arizona the water needed to accommodate growth is not the only reason for our growth: the development of air conditioning helped. But it was Mark, and later the electric utility organized by Frank Snell, who made it possible for us to conquer nature.

The magnitude of Mark's achievement during the long litigation over the allocation of available water cannot be overestimated, and is brilliantly told here. The difficulty Mark faced can best be understood from Mark's own appraisal, cited by Dr. August. When he finally agreed, at Governor McFarland's urging, to take over the case, Mark described it as being in "a hell of a mess." As any reader of this book will come to agree, that was a serious understatement.

What is not well known is the challenging personal context in which Mark accepted this assignment. Not only were Mark and Frank Snell building and leading what had become the state's preeminent law firm, but Mark, widely considered the Dean of Arizona trial lawyers, was certainly not short of major litigation that required his attention.

Parachuting into such a difficult situation as the water case had become, with so much at stake for our community and state, took both extraordinary commitment and courage. As detailed by Dr. August, Mark devoted countless hours to becoming completely familiar with the substantial legal and factual background and the evidence already presented to the Master. Then, although Arizona had finished putting on its case in chief, and while California was presenting its case, Mark "pulled the plug" with only the hope—and certainly no assurance—that the Master would even consider the entirely different approach Mark believed Arizona had to take. Both Arizona's future and Mark's reputation were very much at risk.

As was evident in the case at hand, Mark had the ability to work easily with many types of lawyers, all able, all strong willed, all entitled to the courtesy and respect that Mark accorded all his colleagues, from his adversaries to his co-counsel, from the most senior partner to the youngest associate. He was unassuming and gracious, not only a very skilled and effective advocate, but a wonderful parent and a friend.

Although Mark will be best remembered for watering our thirsty agriculture, making it possible for the area to attract and hold a population sufficient to support our industries and our world-famous real estate market, many of us will remember a different legacy.

Mark understood that those of us who practice law have been given a license by the community that enables us to do work that is both exciting and remunerative. That, he reminded us, places upon us a special obligation to serve the community—to succor its needy, to represent its unrepresented, to see that the law is applied equally to rich and poor, and to support projects that turn a city into a community.

Somewhere along the line in his wandering from Wisconsin through Texas and on to Arizona, Mark came to believe that unto whomsoever much is given, of him shall be much required; and to whom men have committed much, of him they will ask even more. Mark's ability to communicate that to his successor generations at Snell & Wilmer may well be for many of us an even more important legacy than the growth of our state to one with the resources to sustain the over six million people who now inhabit it—and the additional millions who surely will follow.

John Bouma
Chairman
Snell & Wilmer

✴ ACKNOWLEDGMENTS

For years I dreamed about finding the time and resources to write about Phoenix attorney Mark Wilmer and his preeminent place in the history of the American West. Then, in March 2003, while visiting friends in Tucson, I received a call from Patty Johnson, Director of Public Relations at the Phoenix-based law firm of Snell & Wilmer. She said my name had come up in discussions about the legendary Arizona attorney who argued the *Arizona v California* Supreme Court case that shaped the region's future and altered the lives of millions of people. The firm, she said, was interested in discussing with me a Wilmer biography, and could I schedule a time to meet with Snell & Wilmer chairman, John Bouma, and partner David Rauch? "Yes," I said, scarcely disguising my excitement about the prospect.

Bouma and Rauch were smart, serious, and carefully analyzed my responses to their questions. Somehow, I passed the test and commenced working on one of the most important and enjoyable scholarly journeys of my career. Access to records and people, office space, financial assistance, and, most importantly, intellectual and emotional support, were forthcoming and critical to the resulting manuscript. The attorneys and staff at Snell & Wilmer were unfailingly gracious during the years of research and writing, and for the opportunity to work with people of this caliber and grace, I am thankful.

The legal communities in Arizona and California familiar with the significance of the case and knowledgeable of the numerous lawyers and judges involved in *Arizona v California,* have my undying gratitude. In addition to Snell & Wilmer's Bouma and Rauch, I want to gratefully acknowledge attorneys Grady Gammage, Jr., Edward "Bud" Jacobson, Jack Pfister, Robert Begam, Tom McCarthy, Tom Galbraith, Judge C. Kimball Rose, and James D. Kitchel, among others too numerous to name, who read all or parts of the manuscript and offered invaluable suggestions for revision and clarification. All of the attorneys noted above are scholars of the first rank who critiqued, cajoled, and directed me through uncharted waters.

The Board of Directors of the Arizona Historical Foundation (AHF) at Arizona State University, my employer, allowed time, travel, and tolerated the mood swings and erratic behaviors that attend such projects. Archivists and librarians at Stanford University, Arizona State University, University of Arizona, University of California at Los Angeles, and the Arizona Department of Archives, Manuscripts and Public Records, assisted me at every turn. My staff at AHF, Susan Irwin, Linda Whitaker, Judy Eisenhower, Jared Jackson, Elizabeth Scott, Erica Johnson, and Rebekah Tabah supported me throughout the research phase and successive manuscript drafts. The encouragement of Jon Talton, a distinguished journalist and novelist of the first order, enabled me to persevere to the end. Robert Nelson, columnist for *The Omaha World Herald*, helped immensely in offering suggestions to improve the manuscript. Former Arizona Senator Dennis DeConcini and Arizona State University Foundation Vice-President for Community Partnerships, Diane McCarthy, a former four-term state legislator and Arizona Corporation Commissioner, always responded to my requests for help and assistance.

Finally, Mark Wilmer's family and descendants opened their homes and hearts to me during this process. Mark Bernard Wilmer, Charles Mark Wilmer, Elizabeth Wilmer Sexson, and Genevieve Wilmer Hendricks, talked candidly about their father, assisted in my discoveries and brought me into their respective families in ways I never expected. Without their openness and cooperation, this book would not have been possible, and my dream about writing on one of the most important people in the history of the twentieth century American West came true.

✳ INTRODUCTION

On October 9, 1986, I sat in my rental car at the Albuquerque, New Mexico, airport, looking for a self-described "slight, bespectacled, eighty-five-year-old retired judge" and lawyer named Simon Rifkind. One week earlier, the then-legendary special master of the *Arizona v California* Supreme Court case had somehow found my home phone number in Tucson, Arizona, where I was serving as assistant director of the Southwest Center at the University of Arizona. Rifkind called to ask if he could hitch a ride to the Inn of the Mountain Gods on the Mescalero Apache Indian Reservation in Ruidoso, New Mexico. In a scheduling incongruity of unprecedented scale, we were the two guest lecturers at the annual meeting of the New Mexico Bar Association. I learned later that one of my former professors had tipped off Judge Rifkind to my ongoing research on former Arizona Senator Carl Hayden and the long, convoluted history of Colorado River development.

I had intended to sit in on Judge Rifkind's plenary address in Ruidoso, but I never conceived that he would call and ask for a ride to the conference. As he told me his flight number and estimated time of arrival in Albuquerque, I regrouped: "Judge Rifkind," I stuttered, "do you mind if I have a tape recorder on for the four-hour ride between the airport in Albuquerque and Ruidoso?"

"Not at all," he replied, "I know what you are doing, young man, and I want to talk about Carl Hayden and Mark Wilmer."[1]

I was stunned and excited. At this stage of my research I had learned that Hayden's writings and utterances in Congress had influenced Rifkind's thinking in his various analyses of the legal issues concerning the interstate conflict over the Colorado River system, and I knew that Wilmer was one of the Arizona attorneys who had argued the case, but at the time, I was focused on Hayden's political role in the broader issues surrounding the Colorado River rather than Wilmer's legal contributions to the case. I had seen perfunctory correspondence between Wilmer and Hayden's administrative assistant, Roy Elson, but at this time Wilmer was little more than a name that I knew was a part of the legal team in *Arizona v California*.

For an octogenarian, Rifkind was energetic, precise, and funny. As we headed down I-25 toward Ruidoso, we discussed Senator Hayden at length and he allowed that the Arizona senator's arguments in the debates surrounding the 1928 Boulder Canyon Project Act, and Wilmer's focus on that legislation, played a major role in the findings of his *Special Master's Report* of December 5, 1960, a celebrated legal rumination that framed the ultimate outcome of *Arizona v California*.[2] Then he turned his attention to Mark Wilmer. As we approached our destination in Ruidoso, he pivoted in his seat, looked directly at me, and said, "That attorney from Arizona, Mark Wilmer, is the guy who...changed the course of the history of the American West....He deserves some attention.

"That earlier group [Arizona's legal team]," he continued, "was playing right into the hands of California, but Wilmer changed Arizona's approach to the case, and he was masterful in oral arguments in San Francisco."[3]

The not-so-subtle message remained with me and I filed this information away, thinking that, some day, when I completed my manuscript on Carl Hayden, I might have time to take a look at Wilmer and the legal history that surrounded the water resource development in the American Southwest. Maybe, I thought, I would write an article and submit it to the *Western Historical Quarterly* or *Pacific Historical Review.* I later realized that "I got the cart before the horse"; a book on Wilmer was actually a prequel to my earlier effort, *Vision in the Desert: Carl Hayden and Hydropolitics in the American Southwest* (Fort Worth: TCU Press, 1999). And, with the assistance of Snell & Wilmer, which Mark Wilmer founded with Frank Snell in 1938, I have been able to place the role of the monumental Supreme Court case *Arizona v California* into its proper historical context. I never conceived in 1986 that one of Arizona's foremost litigators and distinguished members of the bar, Mark Wilmer, would shape the economic, legal, and political future of the American West.

For most of the twentieth century, Mark Wilmer and the Colorado River lived parallel but separate lives and, in retrospect, seemed unlikely partners in shaping the American West of the twenty-first century. But Wilmer's life and career were destined to place him at the center of one of the most influential Supreme Court cases of the twentieth century; his entrance into it was preceded by a half-century of roiling political and legal controversy. Indeed, many court cases could be considered "The Case of the Century," starting with Fatty Arbuckle's murder trial early in the 1920s and extending through the Scopes Monkey Trial, the Sacco and Vanzetti case, *Brown v the Board of Education,* and subsequent televised high-profile murder trials. These cases pale in comparison to *Arizona v California,* the Herculean legal and political battle that stretched back over a century for an equitable share of the Colorado River. To this day *Arizona v California* is being argued and deliberated.

By the time Wilmer settled in the Salt River valley in the early 1930s, he realized that four basic commodities made possible civilization in the arid West: land, air, sunshine, and water. Only one of those commodities, water, was easily captured and transportable.[4] Water has sometimes been regarded as a private use good. When it is beneath our land we can pump it and use it. Also, it has been regarded as something closer to a common use good, as, for example, when it is in a free-flowing river available for capture and use at no cost, but not readily subject to alienation. When unlimited amounts of water exist, this distinction does not matter much; it might not even be noticed. But when it is scarce, as it is in the arid regions of the American West, institutions, laws, and societies are organized around its management.

Indeed, Senator Jon Kyl of Arizona emphasized the essential nature of water to Arizona when he issued a press release entitled, "Lifeblood of the West," and announced, "The story of Arizona is in many ways the story of our effort to secure adequate water for our future."[5] The unique qualities of water as a commodity have been played out in Arizona's history of shaping a harsh and arid environment to make it habitable for large numbers of people. The early part of that history is about agriculture. Since the middle of the twentieth century the "hydropolitics" of Arizona have turned toward accommodating the increasingly urban nature of the state. These unique qualities of water framed Wilmer's role in the history of the arid Southwest and defined his towering professional career.

For Arizona, the seminal water case, *Arizona v California,* the longest Supreme Court case in American history (1952–1963), constituted an important step in the construction of the Central Arizona Project (CAP), a plan crucial for the development of Arizona's economic livelihood.[6] According to Senator Kyl, one of the nation's leading legal and political authorities on water issues, Wilmer's leadership in introducing a crucial change in legal strategy "helped secure for Arizona a substantial water supply thereby removing the only obstacle to growth and prosperity in Arizona."[7] Wilmer's change in the strategy of the case occurred in 1957 over a year after the trial portion of the case began in San Francisco and over five years after Arizona had brought suit against California.

In 1952 the State of Arizona invoked the original jurisdiction of the U.S. Supreme Court by filing a complaint against the State of California and seven of its public agencies.[8] Later, Nevada, New Mexico, Utah, and the United States were added as parties either voluntarily or on motion. The basic controversy in the case was over how much water each state had a legal right to use out of the Colorado River and its tributaries. After preliminary pleadings the Court referred the case to George I. Haight, and, upon his unexpected death in 1955, to Simon Rifkind, as special master to take evidence, find facts, state conclusions of law, and recommend a decree subject to consideration, revision, or approval by the Court. The master conducted a trial lasting from June 14, 1956, to August 28, 1958, during which 340 witnesses were heard orally or by deposition, thousands of exhibits were received, and 25,000 pages of transcript were filled. Following numerous motions, arguments, and briefs, the master, in a 433-page volume reported his findings, conclusions, and recommended decree, which were received by the Court on January 16, 1961. The case was extensively briefed, argued orally twice, the first time for sixteen hours and the second, over six hours. Generally, as the Supreme Court saw the case—after eleven years of consideration and hearings that took place from San Francisco, to Phoenix, to New York, to Washington, D.C.—it turned on the meaning and the scope of the Boulder Canyon Project Act of 1928, a legal theory introduced when Mark Wilmer took over the case for Arizona in 1957.

Wilmer's legal theory can be best understood when the Boulder Canyon Project Act is placed in historical context. The enormity of the Southwest's water challenges, the inability of local organizations or individual states to agree on how to conserve, divide, or distribute waters, and the ultimate action by Congress at the request of the states creating a great plumbing system of dams and public works controlled and operated for the purpose of conserving and distributing the waters of the Colorado River system all played into the Supreme Court's deliberations on the case.

Robert G. Begam, one of the seven staff attorneys who worked on the legal team with Wilmer on *Arizona v California* and the last living Arizona participant in the case, recalled the profound sense of "urgency and importance" surrounding the historic legal process. As he put it in November 2006, "If we did not win this case, Arizona would be nothing more than a home for Gila Monsters....We had to round up the resources to win it and we had to work very hard at it." He added that "if we did not win this case we would not acquire title to enough water to justify the multi-billion dollar project which Carl Hayden would get for us [Central Arizona Project]....If we did not win, the future of Arizona was dismal."[9]

Arizona's ultimate victory was a direct result of this changed legal strategy, though the outcome remained uncertain until the very end of the case. For example, after sixteen hours of initial oral argument in the Supreme Court and during the unusual six hours of re-argument noted above, as Wilmer wrote shortly after the conclusion of the case, "concern was felt that the case was lost" because the Court seemed to be focusing its questions on issues relevant mainly to matters that Wilmer had discarded earlier as "unsound and not supported in the law"—legal theories of equitable apportionment and prior appropriation.[10]

The Court, however, sided with Arizona's position, authored by Wilmer, which was a legal argument based on a congressional apportionment scheme of Colorado River water found in the congressional consideration and passage of the Boulder Canyon Project Act of 1928.[11] In short, Wilmer's position was grounded in the statutes and congressional action, and though Arizona's previous legal team overlooked what seemed obvious to Wilmer after long contemplation and study, the challenge facing him when he took over the case—especially the "change in strategy"—was formidable. With the legal victory over California in 1963, Wilmer's life and status changed dramatically; he was the man who "won" the Colorado River for Arizona.

When Arizona's victory was announced on June 4, 1963, public reaction flowed forth, and Wilmer received literally hundreds of letters, telegrams, phone calls, praising him for his leadership and his victory. Laura and George Danieli, in a congratulatory note to Wilmer, reflected the sentiments of most residents living in the Grand Canyon State. Their comments, correctly, focused on the future: "We thank you, our children thank you, and our children's children thank you....You are certainly the 'Hero' of the Future for Arizona.... May our small voice be heard amongst all the shouting."[12]

Chapter One

MIDWEST TO
SOUTHWEST

Today, like a century ago, rolling green fields of corn, hay, dairy cows, and grain frame the small town of East Troy, Wisconsin, tucked sixty miles inland from Lake Michigan near the southeastern corner of the state. With a population approaching 4,000, East Troy and its environs form a pastoral community where its largely German and Irish pioneers have left a cultural imprint that residents embrace and protect. The past and present mix easily; median income, housing values, and education statistics stand far above state and national averages. Crime is virtually non-existent, and locals consider their quality of life idyllic. "East Troy," says one lifelong resident, is a town of "integrity, patriotism, and industriousness." In a place where winters last forever and summers can be sultry, wildlife and humans have achieved an enviable balance with nature. With little pretentiousness or effort, East Troy, Wisconsin, recalls a pre-industrial society that reflects, in many ways, the American agrarian ideal.[1]

On July 18, 1903, Mark Bernard Wilmer, whose professional career would shape the arid American Southwest and its legal, political, and economic history, was—somewhat paradoxically—born into this verdant community of farmers, dairymen, and small town merchants. In 1904, his parents, John Bernard Wilmer and Elizabeth Johnston Wilmer, purchased the "Stetson Place," that served both as a dairy and a farm, seven miles east of East Troy, in the hamlet of Honey Creek, which, Mark recalled in later years, "had a population of just over 300 souls."[2] Thus, his earliest years were spent on the family farm, "one of the better dairy farms in Honey Creek," where his father grew corn, hay, grain, and a variety of other crops as well as maintaining a good-sized dairy of between forty and fifty cows. "It was mostly a farming operation," he remembered, "with my father growing as much of the feed as he could for the animals," which included pigs and sheep along with the dairy cows. The enterprise produced a good living for John Wilmer's family.

Young Mark, the sixth of seven children, attended Honey Creek public schools—actually a two-room school—until third grade. Then his Catholic family, under the prodding of their parish priest, required that Mark attend parochial school.[3] They went to church in Waterford, about six miles northeast of Honey Creek, and Mark was supposed to attend school there. The family traveled to church each Sunday by horse and buggy, which, once a week, posed no problems for the family; in fact, the Sunday outings became a welcome respite from the daily drudgery of the farm. But for Mark to attend parochial school in Waterford every day, his father would have to hitch up a horse and drive him to Waterford, which was not practical. They had to find another way.

About seven miles southeast of Honey Creek, in Burlington, was another Catholic church and school. The priest at Waterford said that Mark could be

One-year-old infant Mark
Bernard Wilmer. Wilmer
Family Photo Collection.

Wilmer Family Home in Honey Creek, Wisconsin. Courtesy Wilmer Family Photo Collection.

excused from attending school there if he went to the parochial school in Burlington, which sat midway on a train route that passed within a half-mile of the Wilmer farm. The daily run between Waukesha to Chicago held the key to Mark's early parochial education. The "milk train," carrying dairy products to Chicago from Wisconsin's farms, left Waukesha in the morning and stopped a short walk from the farm at 7:30 A.M. It returned in the late afternoon around 4:30 P.M. Besides dairy products, it carried passengers, and an eight-minute ride to the Catholic school in Burlington would only cost 10 cents. For two years Mark woke up in the morning, walked to the tracks, caught the train and returned home at night. He thought Burlington was a "good-sized" town; the education he received there held him in good stead. With his two-year stint at Catholic school complete, Mark's family reenrolled him in the public schools in Honey Creek.[4]

Though he liked school Mark was an average student. He admired and respected his father and his work ethic, but he knew at an early age that he preferred something other than life on the farm. As he progressed through grammar school, Mark combined book learning with a daily routine of dairy and farm duties—taking care of livestock, milking dairy cows, and stacking hay. He enjoyed fishing the many streams and lakes and took this boyhood

Mark (standing) and brother
Bernard in Honey Creek,
Wisconsin (1910). Wilmer
Family Photo Collection.

passion for the outdoors into his adult years. Also, according to his daughter, Elizabeth Wilmer Sexson, he read constantly; "He would hide in the barn so he could read."[5] He attended public high school in Burlington, riding the same trains he did when he was in parochial school. He graduated in 1922, describing himself as "not an outstanding student,"[6] and knew other vocations beckoned. Upon graduation he left home, choosing not to work on the farm. He searched for employment beyond the confines of Honey Creek and, not surprisingly, the years of daily trips to Burlington exposed him to a more fast-paced, comparatively urban lifestyle. The distinguishing characteristics of a new America could be foreseen—urbanized, centralized, industrialized, and secularized. The teenaged Wilmer adapted to this changing civilization in seamless fashion. He found work close to home, in Burlington, driving a truck for an ice cream company. After a year there he moved to the emerging metropolis of Milwaukee, where he continued working, first for another ice cream company and then for a tool manufacturer.

Twelve-year-old Mark Wilmer, riding his bicycle on the Honey Creek farm. Wilmer Family Photo Collection.

Throughout his childhood and teen years, Mark's parents, especially his father, emphasized the benefits of formal education beyond high school.[7] And while working in Milwaukee, he visited the campus of Marquette University, a Jesuit school founded in 1881 that seemed a natural extension of Mark's earlier parochial education.[8] In the fall of 1924 he began course work, where his less-than-stellar academic performance suggested that he might pursue goals outside the realm of academia or the professions. At Marquette, however, Mark grew interested in law, though the reasons for this interest remained murky throughout his life. As he put it in 1994, shortly before his death, "I had a brother who was a little older who went to law school. While I was at Marquette I decided to become a lawyer. Why? I don't know. I'm quite sure though that I did evidence some considerable interest in law and that sort of thing for some reason. I don't know what it was." The influence of an older brother or the fact that he was inescapably drawn to the law, Wilmer, by age twenty, appeared to have decided upon a career path.

He began with a pre-law curriculum: history, philosophy, and as comparatively new field, political science. At Marquette he first learned to appreciate the classics, poetry, and mystery novels.[9] After two years of effort the academic

Burlington High School
graduation portrait (1922).
Wilmer Family Photo
Collection.

horizon looked less than promising. "I was not an outstanding student in those days," the way he used to describe himself earlier in life, and at the end of his second year at Marquette he, like other students, submitted to an academic review conducted by the dean, Father Fox. Fox asked Wilmer what he was going to do. "I'm going on to law school," Mark replied. Fox responded, "I wouldn't recommend that." He continued that he thought Mark should continue in liberal arts and study Greek, Latin, and trigonometry. The dean pronounced that Mark should take "something that you will have to study to learn because up to the present time you've been getting by on nothing but bluff."[10] Wilmer, who had his sights set on Marquette's law school, demonstrated a large degree of restraint, said, "Fine, Father," and left the interview. Wilmer ignored the priest's admonition and applied to Georgetown College of Law in Washington, D.C., where he was accepted.[11] At the time Georgetown was looking for students rather than the reverse.

Between 1926 and 1929 Wilmer attended Georgetown law school. Tuition and books amounted to about $300 per semester, so in order to help pay for his legal education Mark returned to Honey Creek in the summers to work with his father on what had become a very successful dairy farm. Also, the family provided further financial assistance. At Georgetown, Mark sharpened his analytical skills and learned to study. He performed at a high level of proficiency in his course work and impressed his professors with his breadth of knowledge, resolve, and writing abilities. As he approached graduation, Mark had no fixed agenda; he seemed preoccupied with the task at hand and that was course work. As he recalled, "I don't think I had any real plans as to what I was going to do. I didn't look that far ahead."[12]

He became well-acquainted with a night school law student from Massachusetts, James Farrell, who lived in the same fraternity house and who had graduated from Georgetown a year earlier. They discussed practicing law together, and, musing about the future, they kept returning to the suggestions of an elderly Department of Justice lawyer from Texas who urged them to head west. They focused their attentions on San Angelo, Texas, and Phoenix, Arizona. Their senior acquaintance said, "They're both coming cities but Phoenix is hotter than hell." He added, "The thing with Phoenix is that it's a

l-r, Wilmer on the steps at Marquette University with Jimmy Wilson (1924). Wilmer Family Photo Collection.

Wilmer, top row, second from left, posing with basketball champion team mates (1925). Wilmer Family Photo Collection.

place where you have a choice between there and hell, and you'll probably pick hell instead of Phoenix." In spite of that drawback, he told the two newly minted attorneys, "You know that's [Phoenix is] the place for a young man." Nevertheless they decided to head to Texas first, and shortly after law school graduation ceremonies on June 9, 1929, Farrell and Wilmer, in a "seventeenth-hand used Buick," set forth across the country on roads that challenged the hardiest traveler. Ultimately, they made it to Texas.

Meanwhile, the two intrepid young attorneys had filed with the Texas Secretary of State copies of their diplomas from Georgetown along with three letters of recommendation from faculty and lawyers. At the time Texas had a diploma privilege for Georgetown graduates, and Wilmer and Farrell, after signing documents before a notary public, received their certificates of admission to the Texas State Bar.

In the overstuffed Buick, they visited Harlingen, Corpus Christi, and San Antonio, places that had entered into their discussions concerning establishing a law practice. After considering these three cities, they headed to the Texas Panhandle. Still not satisfied, they turned southwest. After weeks of driving, surveying, polite introductions, and speculation, they decided, in October 1929, to establish a practice in the heart of west Texas, in San Angelo, the seat of Tom Green County. In a few weeks the stock market crash and the subsequent economic depression that settled upon the country for a decade or more set the tone for what turned out to be a challenging period for the short-lived partnership of Wilmer and Farrell.

While the two struggled to gain a foothold in the San Angelo market in the context of a sharply declining economy, a lawyer from Fort Stockton—located 150 miles to the southwest—happened into their office. Noticing that the practice was less than brisk, the visiting attorney suggested, "Why don't one of you guys go to Iraan," an oil boomtown southeast of Fort Stockton. "There will be some business there," with all of the people seeking work moving to the area which, at the time of its discovery, was considered the world's largest shallow oil field. Based upon this advice, Wilmer, in the spring of 1930, opened up a satellite office in Iraan, Texas.[13]

l-r, Squeaky Williams, Al Bruckner, and Wilmer at Georgetown Law School (1926). Wilmer Family Photo Collection.

The Iraan experience not only proved a critical juncture in Wilmer's fledgling career, but also, inadvertently, led him to Phoenix, Arizona. He began practice in modest and deliberate fashion. He recalled "getting his meals from divorces and things like that," and, in serendipitous fashion, he met the manager of the boarding house run for the Illinois Pipe Line employees, a Mrs. O'Brien. Her son, Austin, whom Wilmer had befriended at Georgetown, had recently graduated and established a law practice in Phoenix. Wilmer enjoyed receiving a free home-cooked meal from Mrs. O'Brien from time to time, and he learned that another law school classmate, James A. "Jim" Walsh, who graduated a year before in the class of 1928, had also headed to Phoenix with Austin O'Brien. Wilmer held O'Brien and Walsh in high regard and hoped to visit them in the near future.

In January 1931, Mrs. O'Brien called Mark and said that she wanted to travel to Phoenix to visit Austin and her new daughter-in-law, Sarah. She had a dependable car and asked if Mark could ride along. Not overly busy in Iraan, Mark took her up on the offer. Perhaps, he thought, Phoenix was a new horizon.

The Southwest's desert metropolis shows its best side in the winter, and to the twenty-seven-year-old attorney the weather and striking vistas con-trasted sharply with what he had known in Wisconsin, Washington, D.C., or central Texas. As he stated in 1994, "I liked the place and I stayed." Actually, he visited Walsh, who practiced in a Mesa-based firm headed by Michael Joseph Grattan Dougherty, an established lawyer with a sterling reputation. Mark heard from Walsh that Dougherty had just learned that one of his clients, the Roosevelt Water Conservation District, was having bond problems and friction with the Salt River Project. Walsh told him that Dougherty might need to hire another lawyer. Mark, enjoying his first few days in Arizona, listened with rapt attention.

Wilmer took the initiative. He scheduled an appointment with Dougherty and learned that he too hailed from Wisconsin. The two established a speedy rapport—Wilmer left the office with the promise of a job as long as he passed the bar exam. Before he departed Arizona he registered with the Arizona State Bar, established a residence with Austin O'Brien, and prepared for the move. He headed back to Texas, closed the office in Iraan, told Jim Farrell goodbye, and returned to Arizona. He took and passed the Arizona bar exam in May of 1931.[14]

Even before the results of the bar exam were announced, Wilmer began working for Dougherty. He and Walsh served as associates, with Mark's salary at $25 per month. As Wilmer worked on Roosevelt Water Conservation District legal issues in 1931, he could scarcely know that water, his first professional legal charge in Arizona, would become a defining element in his legal career. Moreover, these first hours of work—on bonds for water resource development infrastructure and relations with the Salt River Project—were a small part of a much larger complex of regional water rights issues that, twenty-five years hence, would consume him for several years and place him at the center of the legal, political, and environmental history of the twentieth-century American West.

At the outset of his legal career in his adopted state, Wilmer heard of Arizona's already long and tempestuous relationship with California and other Colorado River basin states over the use and distribution of Colorado River water. He also maintained a work ethic that would serve him well: he read everything and knew, as one of his longtime colleagues, Edward "Bud" Jacobson recounted much later, "the front, back, and middle of everything." He was neither impetuous nor impulsive in how he conducted his work, but rather studious, thorough, and systematic. His work day extended into the evening hours, when he would read law, history, and anything else that added to his intellectual warehousing.[15]

Just prior to his arrival at Dougherty's firm, the State of Arizona, on October 13, 1930, instituted an action—the first of many—against the secretary of interior and the States of California, Colorado, Nevada, New Mexico, Utah, and Wyoming to enjoin construction of Hoover Dam and the All-American Canal as well as to enjoin performance of contracts for the delivery of stored water at the dam. In effect, Arizona attempted to stand in the way of the construction of what became Hoover Dam and the All American Canal that diverted water from the Colorado River to the Imperial Valley.

In addition, this bill of complaint sought to have the Boulder Canyon Project Act of 1928 and the Colorado River Compact of 1922 declared unconstitutional. The case and the public policy issues surrounding it were rooted in the colonization and settlement of the arid Southwest. Moreover, at first blush, recent history suggested that California was unified in its approach to Colorado River development while Arizona was confused, misguided, and embroiled in an internecine struggle marked by no small amount of political posturing and intrigue.[16]

At issue was Arizona's desire and contention to put its fair share of Colorado River mainstream water, and the waters of its tributaries within the state, to beneficial use. The Colorado River held the key to sustaining the economy, life, and civilization in the region. California, from the advent of federal reclamation law in 1902, moreover, had been an assertive and active participant in water resource development along the lower Colorado—much more active than Arizona—thereby advancing its legal rights to mainstream water.

AN ARIZONA CONTEXT

In his move to depression-era Arizona, Wilmer entered a world shaped by water (or the lack of it), culture, and tradition unlike anything in his previous experience. He learned quickly, however, and, though his early legal career centered on issues other than water or natural resources development, he gained familiarity with some of the pertinent factors that forged Arizona's intimate and problematic relationship with its most precious natural resource.

Indeed Wilmer's early legal career in Arizona in the 1930s was not far removed from territorial and early statehood developments that would later inform his arguments before the Supreme Court a quarter century later. For example, soon after the outbreak of war between the United States and Mexico in 1846, Colonel Stephen Watts Kearny and his Army of the West encountered the Pima Indians farming along the Gila River. The invading Americans, en route to their military destination in California, marveled at the agricultural abundance and the extensive irrigation works. They realized immediately, as the Spaniards and Mexicans had before them, that irrigation along the river predated the Pimas.[17] By the time Spanish explorers of the seventeenth century discovered prehistoric ruins in central Arizona, their builders, the Hohokam, had been gone for more than two hundred years. Archeologists continue to debate the nature and extent of their more than 350 miles of canals along the Salt River in the Phoenix area and the additional canals in southern Arizona.[18] It was the most extensive prehistoric irrigation system in North America, and the Hohokam, according to recent scholarship, irrigated approximately 100,000 acres of land in the Salt River valley alone. One authority has noted that while the Hohokam are recognized as the premier desert irrigation specialists of the prehistoric era, they actually used many methods to control and use water. Besides an extensive canal system, they developed terracing, check dams, rock piles, and linear and grid borders. Additionally, like other prehistoric cultures in Arizona, Hohokam water resource development fell into two categories: irrigation methods (canals and ditches) and indirect methods, reflected in soil moisture conservation. These methods provided palpable technological precedents for the region's European successors.[19]

The irrigation works built by the Hohokam evidenced the earliest impact of water management on Arizona's traditions. While the popular conception linking the American West with rugged individualism remains an ideal image, the reality of pre–twentieth century civilization in what is now Arizona differs sharply from it. Life in this environment—inimical to human settlement—required cooperation and a shared plumbing system. In fact, the earliest forms of government in the world may have arisen in the Middle East over the need to construct and share water distribution facilities.[20] In the Southwest, the irrigation works of the Hohokam present similar early evidence of the necessary cooperative endeavor that leads to an institutionalized civilization.

As Spaniards colonized the Southwest in the sixteenth and seventeenth centuries, they consciously adopted American Indian settlement patterns, often displacing existing towns and villages where water could easily be conveyed for irrigation. Beyond these impacts, Spaniards introduced and reconfigured agriculture in the region. They brought a myriad of new crops and introduced livestock and domesticated animals. The Spanish also created a new language of water use.[21] The Spanish word *acequia,* or canal, is still used today; water users in Arizona continue to refer to the *zanjero,* or ditch tender. The acequia districts of northern New Mexico are the oldest extant governmental units of European settlement in North America.

The Spanish influenced Arizona and the Southwest most significantly in the area of law. The Spanish maintained a near obsessive interest in water regulation, reflected in volumes of land grant documents and government officials' diaries about interminable water rights disputes. The single most important Spanish water legacy is reflected in the Latin phrase, "qui prior est in tempore, potior est in jure," meaning, first in time, first in right. This legal doctrine of "prior appropriation" became the cornerstone of water law, not only in Arizona, but also throughout the trans-Mississippi West.[22] Notably, the doctrine of prior appropriation remained in place during the Mexican period (1821–1848) and formed the legal framework regarding the use and distribution of water when Colonel Kearny promulgated his legendary code of 1846. That code resulted in continuing the Hispanic traditions of water and land use until the creation of Arizona Territory in 1863.

One of the first actions of the Territorial Legislature was to enact a comprehensive legal code. Known as the Howell Code for its author, Judge William T. Howell, the document contained several provisions that addressed water resources in the nascent Arizona territory. Howell was from the mining state of Michigan, and, in an inspired notion, he attempted to reconcile local conditions with the emerging nation. The legal code retained the Spanish and Mexican customs of prior appropriation. Concerning the regulation of acequias, Howell asserted that water should be held appurtenant to the land.[23] Mining law under the Howell Code also followed the theory of prior appropriation, giving the rights to the first person to discover minerals. As the pace of American settlement in Arizona Territory quickened, the Howell Code and its implications loomed large for those who competed for land and water.

As settlement in the arid region of Arizona grew, the suitability of portions of the region for growing crops became clearer. Flat land and sunshine were available in abundance in a mild year-round climate. But to expand the irrigation works that supported widespread agriculture required something more significant than simply getting along with your immediate neighbors: outside capital and expertise. The distant government of the United States of America would be the source of that money and expertise.

The post–Civil War population influx into Phoenix and the Salt River valley depended upon the importation of American cultural, legal, and political institutions. Realizing that utilizing the still-evident Hohokam canal system could save time and money, entrepreneurs and schemers like Jack Swilling commenced the essential activity of water resource development. By 1870, Phoenix maintained a community of 240 residents with roughly 1,500 acres under cultivation, relying on the Salt River and a web of irrigation ditches or wells to address growing community demands.[24]

The decade of the 1880s saw increasing government domination of development. Although imaginative individuals continued to pursue private initiatives, the advent of the National Irrigation Association, headed by reclamation pioneers William Ellsworth Smythe and George Maxwell, marked this shift. Maxwell, in particular, epitomized the noisy booster for a federal solution to the aridity of the West. With the passage of the Newlands Reclamation Act of 1902, Maxwell and his followers claimed victory, and the federal government became the dominant force involved in all aspects of western irrigation and reclamation.

In many ways, however, the 1890s were a disaster for Arizona Territory. During mid-February 1891, "the biggest flood of the Salt River that had ever been known," erased years of human effort and toil. The flood reached the valley on February 20 and for several months thereafter residents remained isolated from the outside world. After the floodwaters receded and settlers reclaimed what remained, they clamored louder than ever for river storage, regulation, and federal aid. Not surprisingly, they also wholeheartedly supported the efforts of Smythe and Maxwell. And, in what became a cruel irony, a decade-long drought followed the flood of 1891.[25]

Intermittent floods and drought led, inevitably, to legal fights. In 1892, on the heels of the flood and an ensuing monsoon that dumped only about half of the average expected amount of rain, Judge Joseph H. Kibbey, the chief justice of the territorial supreme court, tried to resolve a number of water rights and canal company disputes that punctuated the increasingly chaotic community of water users. Kibbey's landmark decision in *Wormser v Salt River Valley Land Company* (1892) reaffirmed the doctrine of prior appropriation. A significant aspect of the ruling held that water belonged to the land and not to any particular canal company and that it could not be sold as a separate commodity. The "Kibbey decision," which linked water to land would serve as a model for water law and subsequent legislation throughout the West.

Eighteen years later, on March 1, 1910, Judge Edward Kent essentially affirmed the Kibbey decision in *Hurley v Abbott* (1910). The Kent Decree determined the prior rights of all acreage in the Salt River valley to Salt River water, and even adjudicated when each parcel had first been cultivated. The Kent Decree, in its determined complexity, took into consideration elements of the federal Newlands Reclamation Act, and enabled Arizona to undergo a seamless transition into statehood in 1912, especially as it concerned water law administration. The decree stands as one of the great early monuments to Arizona's maturing legal system.

Meanwhile, Salt River valley residents organized and successfully lobbied the Theodore Roosevelt administration to obtain the first great federal
reclamation project for the new state. When a dam was constructed at the
confluence of Tonto Creek and the Salt River, it was the largest dam built in the
world up to that time. Roosevelt himself came to dedicate the dam bearing his
name, and noted that with a new water supply and flood protection he could
foresee a day when the Phoenix Valley might hold 150,000 people.[26] As the
Kent Decree unfolded, Roosevelt Dam was nearly complete, and a new relationship developed between local water users and the federal government.
While the bulk of these users were farmers, on October 1, 1910, City of
Phoenix officials executed a water contract with the Reclamation Service for
the delivery of water.[27] Judge Kent, to his enduring credit, had recognized the
urban dimension of portions of the Salt River Valley in the Kent Decree, and
this was reflected in the map designating urban areas that accompanied his
legal rendering in the *Hurley v Abbott* (1910) case.[28] Ultimately, the annual
renewal of water delivery contracts with the Department of Interior's
Reclamation Service became routine until 1917, when the Salt River Valley
Water Users Association took control of the project. On March 20, 1919, the
City of Phoenix executed its first water contract with the SRVWUA. Public
ownership and government stewardship characterized this Progressive Era
evolution in water policy.

Thus Wilmer settled into a world where the SRVWUA, which would
ultimately become the Salt River Project and emerge as one of the most
important institutions in Arizona, shaped water policy within the fastest-
developing area in the state.[29] Like other valley residents he appreciated this
unique institution and doubtlessly knew that it was one of the most effective
special purpose governments in the United States.[30] In effect, Wilmer's
adopted state appeared well-prepared institutionally to address its water use
and distribution challenges within its borders. But that intrastate solution was
not the entire story. California's explosive population growth during the
1920s and the increasing amounts of water required to fuel this growth
threatened Arizona's longstanding water rights claims to the Colorado River,
which cut across northwestern Arizona, carved the Grand Canyon, and
formed Arizona's western boundary with the Golden State. George W. P. Hunt,
seven-time governor who was serving his last two-year term in office when
Wilmer moved to Arizona, had staked the bulk of his mercurial political

career on "saving" the Colorado for Arizona and at the same time vilifying California for its water greed and imperial designs on this contested resource. Indeed by the time of the two states' first visit to the Supreme Court in 1930, they were already well-engaged in the battle of the century. Little did Wilmer know he would be drawn into the struggle over twenty-five years later.

Chapter Two

THE FIRM
AND THE RIVER

Depression-era Arizona offered little for newly minted lawyers and, like everyone else, Wilmer adapted to the culture of scarcity and sacrifice. Bunking with fellow law associate Jim Walsh in their humble Mesa, Arizona, bungalow, Wilmer embarked on his Arizona career with a sense of hope and optimism. Almost immediately, however, his confidence in Michael Dougherty began to slip—particularly regarding his business practices and approach to the law. Dougherty, for example, hesitated in cutting paychecks and seemed unable to work efficiently with clients. Wilmer later described the situation: "Jim was then getting $50 a week and I was getting $25 weekly, but we didn't know that Dougherty spelled it W-E-A-K-L-Y because many times we didn't get paid on time. And I was living with Jim... and we were sort of living out of the same pocketbook. And I guess we decided it would be just as easy to starve on our own as with him." So, the two young attorneys looked elsewhere to further their careers.[1]

By mid-1932 Wilmer and Walsh left Dougherty. Wilmer later described this early transition in his Arizona work environment: "We met Frank Beer at the time. He was associated with a lawyer in Chandler named Arthur Price who was an old-time lawyer there—not very active." Thus Wilmer began his partnership with the short-lived firm, Beer, Walsh, and Wilmer. Beer maintained an office in Chandler, and Walsh and Wilmer remained in Mesa. Notably, during the summer of 1932, Wilmer transferred his activities to the Chandler office because Beer went to Florida in a successful effort to convince his then-girlfriend to marry him and move to Arizona. During that period, Wilmer became acquainted with the people in Chandler and made such an impression that he was elected town attorney, a position that brought in the handsome sum of $25 per month. Later, this retainer increased to $40 per month.[2] Beer, however, never really commenced practice with his new partners.

He was appointed to the state legislature, moved to Phoenix, and took no time to say goodbye. In early 1933 Beer, Walsh, and Wilmer downsized to Walsh and Wilmer.[3] As Wilmer put it later, "His future was brighter in Phoenix without us." Wilmer left the Chandler office and returned to Mesa, though he remained the Chandler town attorney until 1939.

The new partnership struggled in the depths of the depression and Wilmer said that in 1934 "things were pretty tight, particularly when the banks closed." "It's kind of a shock," he recalled, "not being able to cash your check."[4] They were not doing too well, but they were eating and existing mostly on notary fees. During the summer of 1934, Walsh secured work from the Homeowners Loan Corporation, which was, at that time, foreclosing on home loans in Phoenix. So, Wilmer remained in Mesa, in his multipurpose practice, and Walsh worked in Phoenix, driving back and forth between the Homeowners Corporation and Mesa.[5]

It was during this period in Mesa that Wilmer met and married Genevieve Tibshraeny, a lovely young woman from a prominent East Valley Lebanese family. She was the love of his life. A legendary cook with a great sense of humor, Genevieve was the perfect compliment to the rising legal icon. Accounts about their relationship vary little: Wilmer was devoted to his wife for the remainder of his life as they raised four children together. Mark Bernard, commonly known as "Bernie," was born on September 1, 1937, in Mesa, Arizona. A second boy, Charles Mark, known as "Mark" in the family, was born on December 31, 1938. Shortly thereafter, on June 8, 1940, Elizabeth, "Liz," entered the world on June 8, 1940. Finally, Genevieve, or "Gen," was born on November 19, 1943. Their reminiscences confirm the fact that their parents loved and admired one another and that they led an almost idyllic childhood in north central Phoenix, attending St. Francis grammar school and ultimately residing at 2202 East Colter Street, near present-day Biltmore Fashion Park. Like many Catholic children in Phoenix, Liz and Gen advanced to Xavier High School, and Bernie and Mark attended both Brophy Prep and St. Mary's Catholic High School where they completed their high school education.[6] All attended and graduated from college; Mark continued his education receiving his law degree from the University of Arizona. Today he maintains a robust legal practice in Phoenix.

Meanwhile, as Wilmer began family life in Mesa, several professional opportunities altered the nature and direction of his legal career. In December

1934 newly elected officials assumed office. Harry Johnson, who won election as Maricopa County attorney, offered Wilmer, who had already developed a sterling reputation as a litigator in the local courts, a job as deputy county attorney. He accepted the position, which paid $2,500 per year, and, in January 1935, went to work in Phoenix; Walsh returned to Mesa full time.[7]

For the next two years Wilmer prosecuted various transgressors of the law. As he put it, "I did a lot of prosecuting... and I became the chief prosecutor and tried quite a few murder cases, abortion cases, just a lot of cases." He achieved a high conviction rate and further burnished his reputation as a first-rate trial attorney. His courtroom savvy drew the attention of Arizona attorney general Joseph Conway. In January 1937, he lured Wilmer away from Maricopa County and into the state attorney general's office. His stint as an assistant attorney general was short-lived, however, as Maricopa County officials convinced him to return to the county as special council in charge of prosecuting a gambling ring that included Sheriff Roy Merrill and a host of other public officials. Indeed, the culture of corruption, payoffs, and

Newlyweds Mark and Genevieve Wilmer (1934). Wilmer Family Photo Collection.

Family Portrait (1944). L-R, Genevieve, Elizabeth, Mark Bernard, and Charles Mark. Wilmer Family Photo Collection.

gambling bothered Wilmer. He said, "In those days [mid-1930s] the county was full of slot machines, and of course the two hot races were for county attorney and sheriff... I was disgusted, really, that gamblers could come into the county attorney's office." He elaborated, "Maricopa County and the whole state were infested with slot machines. You couldn't go in a service station and not see a couple of slot machines sitting there, and then after a time I noticed that some of the people I recognized as gamblers, or what have you of that ilk, would come into the county attorney's office, shut the door, and pretty soon it became very clear that there was monkey business afoot. In other words there was protection..."

In fact the corruption in the county attorney's office and the sheriff's department was the main reason Wilmer accepted the offer to move to the attorney general's office. But, the sense of obligation to his community weighed heavily on him, and, for the better part of 1937, he prosecuted many gamblers and government officials, some of whom, like Sheriff Merrill and County Attorney Johnson, were former friends and colleagues. In the end, a series of convictions, hung juries, acquittals, and legal persuasion eliminated, for the most part, the political and social corruption reflected in illegal gambling and payoffs in Maricopa County. By this time, the thirty-four-year-old prosecutor was seen as a legal and political reformer. Outside of the lingering effects of the depression on the regional economy and his personal fortunes, his future seemed bright.[8] In a time when other Arizona attorneys struggled to survive, Wilmer virtually flourished in a whirlwind of legal activity and public service. Importantly, during this period, Wilmer spent an enormous amount of time before the two trial judges in Maricopa County Superior Court, where he had gained enormous respect as a trial lawyer. He was busy and in demand, and as the gambling scandal and related prosecutions came to a close in 1938, Wilmer surveyed his options.

Meanwhile, Frank L. Snell, a well-known and established attorney based in downtown Phoenix, who migrated to Arizona in the mid-1920s after graduating from the University of Kansas School of Law in 1924, became "snowed under" with work and began to search for some much-needed help.[9] Prior to establishing his law practice in Phoenix, Snell, instead of accepting a comfortable job with Hartford Insurance Company at the then-attractive salary of $200 per month upon graduation, headed west to Arizona and began his career in the copper mining boom town of Miami in Gila County. There much

Fishing at San Carlos Lake (1939) . Wilmer Family Photo Collection.

of his work centered on business transactions and civil and criminal trials. Moreover, in Miami he met and married Elizabeth Berlin. Mining town litigation and its business implications, in time, led Snell to focus almost exclusively on business representation; in 1927 he moved to Phoenix to practice with Fred Elliott, forming the law firm Elliott and Snell.[10] By 1935, the aging Elliott, sought to reduce his workload and, making a dignified transition into retirement, on December 23 turned the practice over to Snell, who soon joined Riney F. Salmon and Charles L. Strouss, forming the law office of Snell, Strouss, and Salmon.[11]

As Wilmer "got through with that mess at the county attorney's office," in 1938, Snell, Strouss, and Salmon experienced internal discord and "differences in philosophy." Riney Salmon left the firm. Needing a replacement, Snell sought the counsel of the members of the Maricopa County Superior Court. He asked, "Who is the best trial attorney in the state?" Each judge first mentioned Wilmer, a lawyer whom Snell had never met. Wilmer recalled, "I got a call from Frank Snell asking me to come see him. I knew who Frank was. I knew he had a very good practice, so I went up and visited with him; he told me he needed a trial lawyer and he understood I could try some lawsuits. So I became an associate of Frank Snell." On August 1, 1938, Snell, Strouss, and Wilmer signed the memorandum of agreement affirming their partnership.[12] Accounts vary as to where the two first met—it appears that Wilmer visited Snell's office—but both agreed that their first conversation was lengthy and focused on legal philosophy and the practice of the law. The conversation went well, according to both parties, and they decided to become partners without at first bothering to work out the financial terms. In fact, during Snell & Wilmer's fiftieth anniversary celebration in 1988, Wilmer recalled that he never exchanged a harsh word with Snell during their half-century plus together.[13]

The first meeting between Snell & Wilmer also contained an ironic twist. Wilmer recalled some very specific and definitive comments that Snell believed were essential to the practice of law: "When I talked to Frank the first time, and I've kidded him about this many times because he had a good... corporate practice and that sort of thing, but he said, well, I think you ought to know I don't believe in big law firms, and he said, I recall in the Depression some of those big law firms couldn't pay their help. He said, I don't believe in that, I don't believe in politics. He said, I think you should not mix law with politics.

He said, I don't believe in cocktail parties, I don't think that's the thing of a lawyer. He said I just think that you ought to understand that I don't envision any big law firm, I don't envision any political influence or anything like that." Fifty years later, Wilmer chuckled as he reminisced and offered his opinion on these matters: "I said, well, Frank, it doesn't really make any difference to me because I have very much the same ideas. Frank somehow… won't admit that he really told me those things."[14] In sharp contrast to his pronouncements in 1938, the Snell & Wilmer law firm, especially during the second half of the twentieth century, grew into one of the largest full-service law firms in the western U.S. with more than 400 attorneys in six offices located in Arizona, California, Nevada, Colorado and Utah. Moreover, Frank Snell led a coterie of Snell & Wilmer partners and associates in taking leadership roles in shaping the political and business cultures in their respective communities.[15]

From the outset of his partnership with Snell, Wilmer's "fundamental responsibility" was trying lawsuits. He tried personal injury suits for plaintiffs—one or two per month—and defended insurance companies. Cases rarely ran over four or five days. Discovery and interrogatories differed vastly from today; they were less thoroughgoing and lacked modern formalities. He rarely involved himself in criminal work because he did not care to practice in that area though he defended friends who were accused of driving under the influence. There was probate work, labor litigation, an occasional lawsuit involving a will and some Internal Revenue fraud cases. Beyond what he called "routine litigation," Wilmer took on some probate work and collections. By the end of the 1930s he was earning $10,000 annually; a handsome sum in the still-challenging depression years preceding World War II.[16]

THE COLORADO RIVER: A BRIEF INSTITUTIONAL HISTORY

As Wilmer solidified a preeminent place among Arizona's trial lawyers in the 1930s, the Colorado River continued to insinuate itself into the political and economic life of Arizona and the first Supreme Court defeat at the hands of California in 1931 prefigured three decades of Arizona frustrations. The river's natural and institutional history provided a perspective on the first *Arizona v California* (1931) case. From its source in the Rocky Mountains, the Colorado River drained some of the most stunning, hostile, and arid topography in the United States. Its 244,000 square miles of drainage area flowed nearly 1,400 miles in a southwesterly direction through deserts, canyons, and lush valleys. Within the United States the river drained watersheds in Wyoming, Colorado, Utah, New Mexico, Nevada, Arizona, and California. Before emptying into the Gulf of California, the Colorado crossed the international border near Yuma and flowed its last hundred miles through Mexico. Despite its large tributary system, which included the Gila and Salt Rivers (Wilmer's earliest legal work in Arizona, as noted earlier, dealt with the Salt River) the Colorado was not a truly major river or heavy flowing stream. In fact, it ranked only sixth in volume among the country's rivers. Average precipitation in the basin amounted to only fifteen inches and evaporation reduced runoff by ninety percent. Based on records kept since 1922, the remaining 10 percent of runoff amounted to only 15.5 million acre-feet annually, or one-twelfth the volume of the Columbia River. As a result of the demands placed upon the flow by the seven states and Mexico, the Colorado, according to its most distinguished historian, Norris Hundley, Jr., had been the most litigated, regulated, politicized, and argued-about river in the world.[17]

Arizona objected to two federal actions as they related to the river: the Colorado River Compact (1922) that divided the waters between basins and the Colorado River Basin Project Act (1928) that, among other things, provided for the construction of a dam at Boulder Canyon and an All-American Canal in California. The two federal actions were tied together— mutually reinforcing laws—and, from the outset, Arizona leaders had problems with both.

The origins of these two federal acts cannot be precisely traced, but nineteenth century visionaries and dreamers contributed significantly to developments that affected Wilmer's analyses and his later arguments in behalf of Arizona in *Arizona v California*. John Wesley Powell, for example, stimulated the imaginations of millions in the late 1870s and early 1880s when he argued for a more rational approach to the problems posed by the arid West, particularly as it pertained to the organization and settlement of these lands. Powell, in his "Report of the Arid Lands of the United States," predicted accurately that that the construction of reservoirs would enable Americans to divert water to California's fertile lowlands. Though he failed to envisage the precise location of what became known as Hoover Dam, his ideas, nevertheless, struck a responsive chord among his contemporaries.[18]

Others acted on the notion that the river was a source of potential livelihood. Significantly, their actions predated those of government agents, drafting reports about the Colorado River system and its tributaries. In 1849 Dr. Oliver Wozencraft, on his way to the California gold fields, conceived a plan to irrigate the Imperial Valley. Though he spent a frustrated life in a vain attempt to fulfill this dream, his inspiration laid the groundwork for later generations. In 1879, no less a promoter than John C. Fremont—then serving as territorial governor of Arizona—endorsed a scheme to flood the Salton Sink with Colorado River water. The plan outraged his Arizona constituents on the east side of the river thus prefiguring future animosities over the dispensation and use of Colorado River water. It took another nineteenth-century pioneer to take Wozencraft's dream to fruition. In 1892, Charles Rockwood, while investigating possibilities of irrigated agriculture along the Mexican border, realized that the Imperial Valley, as Wozencraft had observed, could be a vast year-round garden if water could be diverted to the land. After years of false starts, setbacks, and financial maneuvers, Rockwood, in 1896, created the Colorado Development Company.[19] With the aid of internationally acclaimed engineer George Chaffey, Rockwood succeeded in delivering water to the Imperial Valley on June 21, 1901. This beneficial use, Wilmer reasoned correctly, gave those California users a distinct advantage in a system of law that recognized prior appropriation; first in use, first in right.[20]

The water delivery system traversed Mexican territory for fifty miles, and Mexico sought to exact a high toll in water, money, and other concessions for the use of her land.[21] Moreover, revolutionary activity on the border threatened the quantity and quality of Imperial Valley's water supply. Wealthy Americans created further consternation: a group of Los Angeles businessmen, led by *Los Angeles Times* publisher Harry Chandler, were revealed to be the largest landholders in the Mexican delta. By 1905 Chandler and his syndicate owned nearly 850,000 acres, most of which they leased to Mexican, Chinese, and Japanese tenants. These sets of circumstances prompted the movement for an "All-American" canal, which, Arizonans noted, stood to benefit Imperial Valley water users.[22]

In the early twentieth century, a natural disaster affected relationships among the Colorado River basin states and further stimulated the movement for an All-American Canal. In February 1905 the winter snowpack in the

Mountain West began an early melt; flood waters in the Colorado River system began rising, and, within a matter of a few weeks, the geographic feature known as the Salton Sink became the Salton Sea. The flood, among other things, ruined Rockwood and forced his company into bankruptcy. He surrendered control of his company to the one private sector entity that could help him—the Southern Pacific Railroad. In exchange, its money and manpower helped Rockwood control the river. By 1907 Southern Pacific workmen had the river back within its banks.

The consequences of the flood, however, left Imperial Valley residents with two masters over their water supply; the Southern Pacific Railroad and a Mexican corporation, Sociedad de Irrigacion y Terrenos de la Baja California, which controlled the water supply south of the border. Imperial Valley residents began to look for alternative institutional management for answers to their problems. In their efforts to free themselves from two creditors and wrest their water supply from Mexican control, they saw the need to establish public control over the irrigation works.

Out of this natural disaster and fractured administrative structure came the Imperial Irrigation District, later one of Mark Wilmer's most potent legal adversaries within the State of California. In 1911 Imperial Valley lawyer Phil Swing and businessman and promoter Mark Rose led residents in a new direction with the creation of IID, which remains today one of the most powerful public agencies in California and the West. This new agency gave valley residents the ability to elect directors, issue bonds, levy assessments, condemn property, and, perhaps most importantly, purchase and operate the Imperial Valley's irrigation system. The effort took five years and the settlement of numerous legal conflicts; however, in 1916, the Southern Pacific, anxious to get out of the irrigation business, sold the assets of the Colorado Development Company for $3 million, and IID focused its energies on Congress and lobbied continuously for a water delivery system for IID wholly within the United States.[23]

If the great flood of 1905–1907 contributed in part to the creation of IID and the movement for an all-American canal, it also served notice of a pressing need for flood control and storage along the lower reaches of the river. Arthur Powell Davis—nephew of John Wesley Powell and at the time an engineer in the newly created U.S. Reclamation Service—emerged as the chief spokesman and most influential advocate of federally sponsored flood control and water storage on the Colorado.[24] With this proactive approach, the federal government became a major player in Colorado River law and politics during the first decade of the twentieth century and represented another formidable set of interests with which Arizona had to contend.

Much later, as Wilmer studied this period in the river's legal and institutional history, he saw Davis not only as the earliest champion for flood control, but also as its first staunch advocate for comprehensive development. In fact, in 1902 Davis had devised a plan for the "gradual comprehensive development of the Colorado River by a series of storage reservoirs." Davis had the ear of President Theodore Roosevelt. Roosevelt, soon after the devastating floods, called upon Congress "to enter into a broad comprehensive scheme of development for all irrigable land" along the river. Later, as he survived a change in administrations, Davis took this information to President Woodrow Wilson's secretary of interior, Franklin K. Lane. He, in turn, earmarked funds to launch an extensive investigation of the Colorado River. In 1914, Davis ascended to the head of the Reclamation Service and directed this survey. Southern Californians, and especially Imperial Valley residents, were delighted because they foresaw development of comprehensive irrigation and flood control works as the result of the study. Even more, IID lawyers, like Phil Swing, who parlayed his considerable influence into a congressional seat several years later, saw their district gaining a firm hold on their prior rights to increasing amounts of mainstream water. And, private businesses joined with local governments to form organizations like the League of the Southwest to promote development of the Colorado River for the benefit of humanity.[25]

Meanwhile, in November 1917 the IID convinced Interior Secretary Lane to conduct a survey determining the feasibility of the proposed All-American Canal connecting the Imperial Valley with Laguna Dam, a diversion structure that supplied irrigation water to the Yuma Project on the Arizona side of the river. The valley thereby could link up with an established federal reclamation project. In effect, the federal government had joined forces in the dedication of even more water, infrastructure, and legal rights to California. As it turned out, Secretary Lane assented to the All-American Canal feasibility study, but IID had to pay two-thirds of the cost. IID agreed to the terms. A committee of three engineers, called the All-American Canal Board, completed its study toward the end of 1918. In December it issued a preliminary report that called for the construction of a sixty-mile-long canal at an estimated cost of $30 million. Over the vigorous protests of Harry Chandler and the so-called "Los Angeles Syndicate" who opposed the canal because it would compromise their Mexican land investments, Imperial Valley residents, in a January 1919 referendum, overwhelmingly endorsed the project. Armed with the report and electoral mandate, IID attorney Phil Swing increased the political pressure for congressional support of a federally funded All-American Canal.[26]

California continued to pursue its resource goals in aggressive fashion. Five months after the IID plebiscite, California congressman William Kettner submitted the first of several bills in 1919 and 1920 calling for the construction of an all-American canal and various other flood control and irrigation structures on the river. One of Kettner's bills, H.R. 6044, submitted on June 17, 1919, called for the construction of an all-American canal without a storage dam farther upstream. The House Committee on the Irrigation of Arid Lands held extensive hearings on the bill.

Arizona's congressional delegation and the Wilson administration opposed these early efforts: they reasoned that the Californians, in their zealousness to put Colorado River water to beneficial use in the Imperial Valley and elsewhere, were trying to put the cart before the horse. A flood control and storage dam should precede the construction of an all-American canal for Imperial Valley. If additional land were put under cultivation, Reclamation Director Davis suggested, "it will threaten the water supply of the whole valley." Furthermore, premature construction of an all-American canal would increase the danger of flood.

Arizona congressman Carl Hayden elaborated on this point, for uppermost in his mind was the safety of Arizona's Yuma Reclamation Project. "There must be reservoir construction, and in addition the Imperial Valley should pay some equitable part of the cost of water storage." Hayden, in discussing the Kettner bills, broadened the issue at hand and told the Californians: "You are now coming to Congress asking an extraordinary thing be done by the passage of this legislation and Congress must look to the development not only of the Imperial Valley, but the Colorado River valley as a whole, and that can only be fully developed by storage." In effect Hayden served notice that he opposed California gaining prior right to the Colorado River with the aid of the federal government.[27]

In seeking to protect Arizona interests, Hayden proposed legislation of his own, HR 9421, "a distinct improvement over the Kettner bill," according to Interior Secretary Lane, which provided for a storage reservoir, an all-American canal, and preferential treatment for returning World War I veterans.[28] Discussion of these earliest bills exposed sharp differences on how to approach Colorado River development, yet also revealed broad areas of agreement.

Arizona too wanted to conserve and develop the river's resources. Arizonans, since the territorial period (1863–1912), had clamored for some form of Colorado River diversion project. In the mid-1880s, territorial governor Nathan Oakes Murphy, a Republican appointee in a Democratic-leaning territory, proposed a rudimentary version of today's Central Arizona Project when he called for damming the river near Grand Canyon to irrigate the land south to Phoenix. The governor suffered much editorial abuse for what one newspaper editor called his "chimerical schemes." Even so, one of the governor's most outspoken critics, Anson Smith, editor of Kingman's *Mohave County Miner* and a prominent territorial legislator, quickly became a staunch proponent of Colorado River development. Smith editorialized that storage could provide electricity for mines and water for agriculture, thus turning central Arizona into a "Garden of Eden."[29] In fact, Wilmer's research into this footnote of history concluded with the notion that the Kingman newspaperman, like so many other Arizonans at the end of the nineteenth century, spent a considerable portion of his time campaigning for multiple use of the river.

The international dimension of the river became a topic of discussion in these early congressional debates. Secretary of State Robert Lansing, for example, objected to any Colorado River development bill because, he mused, an all-American canal should be built only after a treaty had been negotiated with Mexico. "Equity and comity" entitled Mexico to some of the river's flow, Lansing asserted, citing a treaty drafted in 1906 that awarded Mexico 60,000 acre-feet annually from the Rio Grande. By January 1920, Congress realized that Colorado River development posed problems of enormous legal, engineering, political, diplomatic, and economic complexity. Reclamation Director Davis emphasized the need for further scientific studies rather than hastily crafted and ill-conceived legislation. "The most feasible point for storage," he allowed, "is in Boulder Canyon" in Arizona, but the

Reclamation Service required more investigations. "We have made surveys there for a high dam," he added, but high water and the exhaustion of funds curtailed these studies. So, in May 1920, a compromise was struck. Congress tabled Kettner's bill, heeded Davis's advice, and approved the Kincaid Act— named after Moses Kincaid, House committee chairman—which authorized the secretary of interior to complete ongoing surveys, with special attention to the needs of the fast-developing Imperial Valley. As Wilmer saw it, by 1920 California had made huge strides in achieving its goals, while the other basin states, including Arizona, were just awakening to the implications of these forceful legislative initiatives to the federal government.[30]

Chapter Three

A QUESTION
OF RELEVANCE

Wilmer's later reading of the record also revealed that the informal, not always agreeable, but powerful alliance between IID and the Reclamation Service had alarmed not only Arizona's congressional delegation but also the representatives of the other Colorado River basin states. Beyond this, upper basin leaders had begun expressing what could best be described as a visceral fear that the lower basin states would develop more rapidly and then lay claim by prescription and prior appropriation to an inordinate amount of Colorado River water. In addition to these growing concerns, the City of Los Angeles made known its desire to secure power and water for its rapidly expanding population. So, like Arizona, the upper basin states—Wyoming, Utah, Colorado, and New Mexico—viewed Southern California urban and agricultural water users as a threat to their future development, since California projects would put a large share of the river's flow to prior use. Certainly, by the 1920s, basin-wide sentiment toward California could be summed up as in the *Tombstone Epitaph:* "California was in the game to hog it all."[1]

At a portentous League of the Southwest meeting in Denver in August 1920, Governor Oliver Shoup of Colorado, after issuing some provocative and candid statements to attendees about California's water greed, introduced his legal adviser, Delphus E. "Delph" Carpenter.[2] Carpenter offered a recommendation to assuage upper basin fears; his proposal led ultimately to the creation of the Colorado River Commission and the Colorado River Compact negotiations, one of the most significant developments not only of the legal and political history of the river, but also the history of the American West.

At the time of the league meeting in Denver, Carpenter was serving as a member of the defense counsel in the eight-year-old *Wyoming v Colorado* (1922) Supreme Court case. The suit centered on the rights to the waters of the Laramie River, which rose in Colorado and flowed northward into Wyoming. Hoping to spare the seven states that shared the Colorado River the cost, turmoil, and often unsatisfactory results of a Supreme Court decision, Carpenter put forward ideas he had first outlined eight years earlier. Carpenter feared that the population growth and rapid agricultural development in states sharing the same river basins would rob Colorado, and perhaps other states, of their right to a fair share of water. To avoid that troubling scenario, he advocated action under little-used Article Six of the U.S. Constitution, which enabled states, once receiving permission from Congress, to negotiate treaties among themselves. Specifically, he sought to invoke the compact clause of the Constitution—a clause previously used to settle boundary disputes—and apply it to interstate water rights. The result was a mechanism by which complex issues involving interstate water rights could be settled through negotiation without litigating them before the U.S. Supreme Court.[3]

Arizona's congressional delegation appreciated the legal theory underlying Carpenter's 1920 proposal. Such an interstate compact would assure slower-developing states that they would receive protection, while at the same time the Colorado River could be put to beneficial use. Carpenter also believed that an agreement among the states could incorporate both a lower basin dam and a provision for upper basin protection. At this historically significant League of the Southwest meeting, delegates adopted a resolution affirming Carpenter's legal concept, calling for a compact to determine present and future rights of the states who claimed interest in the Colorado River. Further, the resolution suggested that the seven states authorize the appointment of commissioners for the purpose of entering into an agreement and for the subsequent ratification by the state legislatures and Congress.[4]

THE COLORADO RIVER COMPACT OF 1922

By spring 1921 all state legislatures had taken a formal first step toward the goal of forming a Colorado River Commission with the intent of arriving at some kind of interstate agreement. On May 10, 1921, Arizona governor Thomas Campbell joined the six other basin state governors in Denver to issue a request of President Warren Harding to publicly support Colorado River Compact negotiations even though Arizona, at the time, harbored strong state's rights views concerning the river within its borders. Just three months after the governors' call for action, President Harding, on August 19, 1921, signed the Mondell bill, sponsored by Republican House majority leader Franklin Mondell (R-Wyoming), who introduced legislation calling for a Colorado River Commission comprised of representatives of each of the states as well as a federal representative.

Harding took another action that further surprised stakeholders in the river, naming Secretary of Commerce Herbert Hoover as the appointee to represent the federal government in negotiations. Although Hoover's appointment astonished some, none questioned his honesty, integrity, or international reputation. In the end, he served as chairman of the commission.[5]

Meanwhile, the engineering study conducted under the aegis of the Kincaid Act was approaching completion. The so-called Fall-Davis Report, named after Interior Secretary Albert Fall and Reclamation Commissioner Arthur Power Davis, contained no surprises. It recommended construction of an all-American canal and a high dam capable of generating power at or near Boulder Canyon. On December 8–9, 1921, Davis held a public hearing in San Diego and told his listeners: "In the northwestern corner of Arizona there is a profound and very deep narrow canyon, where it would be feasible to build a dam 700 feet high."[6]

In addition to acquiring scientific knowledge and engineering insights, a major influence that not only paved the way for the seven-state agreement, but also the two basin concept, was the *Wyoming v Colorado* Supreme Court decision rendered January 5, 1922. The Court reaffirmed the rule of priority over streams shared by states that adhered to the rule of prior appropriation. Thus water users in California, who had a head start on their upstream neighbors, were gaining the first right to the water in the Colorado. In deciding *Wyoming v Colorado*, the Supreme Court allowed the application of the priority rule on interstate streams, even if the water was transferred out of the basin for use. The decision favored fast-growing California and placed that state in a strong legal position to gain prior rights to Colorado River water. Therefore, upper basin representatives, especially, felt "badly exposed." They believed that they had to come away from forthcoming negotiations with a compact.[7]

On January 26, 1922, the Colorado River Commission began hearings in Washington, D.C. After intermittent meetings throughout the West during that year, the commission concluded its negotiations with the signing of the compact on November 24, 1922, at Bishop's Lodge in Santa Fe, New Mexico. This so-called "Law of the River," would serve as the legal touchstone—the starting place—from which Mark Wilmer would argue for Arizona's allotment for Colorado River system water.[8]

The Colorado River Compact's provisions have been widely discussed and analyzed elsewhere. Its chief innovation, the brainchild of Colorado's commissioner Delph Carpenter, divided the Colorado River watershed into two basins, with the division point at Lee's Ferry, in the rugged canyon lands of northern Arizona near the Utah border. The commissioners, in forging an accord, allotted the upper basin—Wyoming, Colorado, Utah, and New Mexico—7.5 million acre-feet of water annually. The lower basin, comprised of Nevada, Arizona, and California, received 7.5 million acre-feet of mainstream water per year, plus an additional 1 million acre-feet under the vaguely worded and controversial Article III (b): "In addition to the apportionment... the Lower Basin is hereby given the right to increase its beneficial consumptive use of such waters by one million acre-feet per annum."[9] How Wilmer interpreted this article and argued it before the special master thirty five years later, and how California's legal team arrived at different conclusions and conflicting interpretations, would profoundly impact the outcome of *Arizona v California* and the shape of the economy, culture, and demographics of the American Southwest.

Article III (b) reflected Arizona's interests in the beneficial consumptive use of the waters of the Gila River, the Colorado River tributary whose watershed lay almost entirely within Arizona. According to one distinguished student of the Colorado River Compact, Arizona's representative, William S. Norviel, "played a major role in shaping the treaty that was eventually drafted." Norviel may have compromised significantly on the figure of one million acre-feet because Arizona's tributaries, primarily the Salt and Gila systems, according to contemporary accounts, produced between two and three million acre-feet of annual surface runoff. Norviel explained to Arizona officials that "it was understood though not expressed, that the one million acre-feet from the Gila would practically take care of or offset all the water produced" in Arizona. Since the commission apportioned water to basins rather than states, such an understanding, implied or otherwise, could not be expressly written into the pact. Chairman Hoover lent unofficial credence to Norviel's claim when, after signing the compact, he gave an autographed picture of himself to the Arizona commissioner that carried the inscription: "To the best fighter on the commission. Arizona should erect a monument to you and entitle it one million acre-feet!"[10]

Article IV of the compact addressed the hydroelectric power issue. Agriculture and water for domestic use took precedence over water for power generation. The compact maintained no provision for a storage dam; the upper states had scuttled California's attempt to include it in the agreement. As a result of this omission, flood protection on the lower reaches of the river had to await congressional action. Many foresaw litigation in the future as they digested the significance of Article VII. That article, in curious fashion, addressed American Indian rights to the Colorado River. Dubiously referred to as "Hoover's Wild Indian Article," it was, in reality, a non-article. "Nothing in this Compact," it stated, "shall be construed as affecting the obligations of the United States of America to Indian tribes." Indeed, future generations wrestled with this costly omission. Likewise, Wilmer concluded, the commissioners virtually ignored Mexican rights on the river. If the United States recognized the rights of Mexico in the river, Article III (b) stipulated that both basins must share the obligation in equal proportion.[11]

Despite its limitations, omissions, and ambiguities, it was soon heralded as the "Law of the River." The label carried the erroneous implication that the agreement would somehow keep the river out of the courts. Ottamar Hamale, solicitor for the Reclamation Service, Hoover's legal advisor, and a leading voice for federal control of western waters, wrote: "This settlement was reached within a year, while settlement in the court of the *Wyoming v Colorado* case required about eleven years and is unsatisfactory to both sides involved. The compact was not intended to be a complete settlement but a big step in the right direction and as big a one as can be made at this time."[12]

THE STATUTORY KEY: THE BOULDER CANYON PROJECT ACT OF 1928

While Arizonans prepared to debate the pros and cons of the Colorado River Compact in their state legislature, no one knew that it would take Arizona twenty-two years to ratify it, an unusual and frustrating chapter in Arizona's water history. As Arizonans indulged themselves in a debate of state's rights versus federal control over the river, California marshaled her forces, and her actions in Congress during the course of compact negotiations raised concerns.

The first of several Swing-Johnson bills—named after California congressman Phil Swing and his upper house colleague, Senator Hiram Johnson—signaled California's ultimate intentions. H.R. 11449, introduced in the House of Representatives on April 25, 1922, contained provisions for storage, power production, and an all-American canal.

Arizona's lone congressman, Carl Hayden, opposed the bill and used his senior position on the House Committee on the Irrigation of Arid Lands, to derail the objectionable legislation for the remainder of the session. In fact, Hayden informed the chairman of the committee: "I intend to use any and every legitimate means to prevent action on the bill." Through a variety of maneuvers, Arizona's representative and senators kept the Swing-Johnson bill, in its various forms, from reaching the floor of the House or Senate for nearly five years after its initial introduction.[13]

Yet what ultimately became the Boulder Canyon Project Act of 1928, and the congressional debates that led to this legislation, in large part, led to the sum and substance of the *Arizona v California* Supreme Court decision. A quarter of a century later, Mark Wilmer, as he pored over the subcommittee hearings, committee markups, floor debates, and related discussions, as well as the eleven volumes of Supreme Court testimony, knew this bill held the key not only to Arizona's rights but also to what Congress intended as it pertained to Colorado River system water rights. He became one of the most astute students of the Boulder Canyon Project Act of 1928.

As Arizona's congressional delegation fought off California's attempts to pass the Swing-Johnson bill, the state moved into an even more intransigent position as it related to ratification of the compact. Without a seven-state agreement, there could be no legislative action and therefore no development on the river.[14] Ultimately, the other states and the federal government engineered a solution to the political logjam created by Arizona. Shortly after Arizona's Sixth Legislature failed to ratify the compact in 1923, Delph Carpenter, who originally proposed the idea, suggested to Herbert Hoover and other federal officials that the agreement be allowed to become effective after six states had agreed to its provisions. Despite protests from Arizonans, by mid-1925 the legislatures of the upper states and Nevada had approved the six-state formula. California threw a political wrinkle into the plan when it made its ratification contingent upon federal approval of "a storage dam" at or below Boulder Canyon. Upper basin leaders balked at this concept, and

Representative Swing and Senator Johnson devised another way to secure a Boulder Canyon dam. When they reintroduced their bill for the third time on February 26, 1926, it included a provision making the Colorado River Compact effective with six-state ratification. While Arizona temporarily derailed this legislative maneuver, it could not halt the unalterable power of California, the upper states, and the federal government.[15]

From 1926 to the end of 1928, while Mark Wilmer studied torts, contracts, and administrative law at Georgetown, Arizona's leaders fought to delay what they considered a "force bill," which sought to compel them to conform to the will of the other states, particularly California. Meanwhile, in the elections of 1926, Congressman Carl Hayden, who had been Arizona's lone representative in the House since statehood, ran against incumbent Senator Ralph Cameron, won the election easily, and advanced to the U.S. Senate, where he joined Senator Henry Fountain Ashurst and would remain until his retirement in 1969. He assumed his new position knowing that passage of the Swing-Johnson bill was inevitable. On January 21, 1927, as he transitioned to the Senate and after he had submitted a "Minority Report" on the legislation to the House, he pled publicly for three hours before the House Rules Committee. While the Swing-Johnson bill provided not a dollar for reclamation in Arizona, he claimed, it gave California $31 million for a water delivery system (All-American Canal) and provided a federally subsidized hydroelectric power plant to generate cheap electricity to stimulate growth in Southern California. The requirements of Los Angeles and other California cities did not justify passage of such legislation at the expense of Arizona. The Swing-Johnson bill, Hayden told his colleagues, was "purely and selfishly a California measure."[16]

Wilmer read Hayden's statements with interest, and they informed much of what took place in the Supreme Court over forty years later. Wilmer noted that Hayden touched upon several potent legal issues: Mexican rights to mainstream water, state's rights, the six-state compact, power royalties, and an equal division of mainstream water between Arizona and California. Enactment of the Swing-Johnson bill, Hayden prophesied, "could only result in protracted interstate litigation over Colorado River rights." "Arizona," he warned, "would be compelled to file suit in the U.S. Supreme Court to restrain construction of Boulder or Black Canyon Dam until the rights of Arizona in and to the Colorado River are determined."[17]

Ultimately, after a filibuster, threats of fistfights, and an executive session that "deprived the Senate gallery of one of the wildest scenes since war days," the Seventieth Congress began its second session on December 5, 1928, with the express purpose of passing the fourth version of the Swing-Johnson bill. Despite Hayden's and Ashurst's vigorous opposition in the Senate, on December 16 it passed the Boulder Canyon Project Act by a vote of 64–11. The House approved the Senate version two days later by a vote of 167–122. President Calvin Coolidge signed the legislation into law three days later, ending one phase of the controversy and signaling the beginning of another.[18]

Few measures have had a greater impact in the region than the congressional action that authorized Hoover Dam and the All-American Canal. It was a move that in 1944 spurred a controversial water treaty between the U.S. and Mexico and precipitated a series of Arizona-generated actions in the Supreme Court that culminated in *Arizona v California*. In addition to these implications, the legislation repealed the law of prior appropriation as it applied between the upper and lower basins. Much to the chagrin of Arizonans, the terms of the Colorado River Compact of 1922 became effective with passage of the Boulder Canyon Project Act of 1928. Most pundits thought that the legislation gave California everything and Arizona nothing.

Later, Wilmer appreciated the efforts of Arizona's senators and congressmen. California, he discerned, in winning support for passage agreed to limit itself to a specific amount of the 7.5 million acre-feet allocated to the lower basin in Article III (a) of the compact. The act also contained the Pittman Amendment, named for the Nevada senator, Key Pittman, who introduced a compromise that outlined the Arizona-supported concept of a lower basin, tri-state agreement. This amendment would loom large in the later Supreme Court case as Wilmer convinced the special master, Simon Rifkind, of its significance. Under the Pittman Amendment's terms, Nevada received 300,000 acre-feet of water annually; California, 4.4 million; and Arizona, 2.8 million, plus "exclusive rights to the Gila River." Finally, under the terms of the Pittman proposal, Arizona and California divided equally any surplus mainstream water.[19]

Wilmer, on his first reading of the law, saw that other Arizona contentions were included in the legislation. The construction, repayment, and maintenance of the All-American Canal were separated from the dam and the power plant. Arizona's congressional delegation suggested the arrangement in 1922 during hearings on the first Swing-Johnson bill and had consistently pressed for its separate financial status. Moreover, the bill recognized the principle of a power royalty, or tax. Arizona and Nevada were to receive 18.75 percent of surplus profits of power revenues. Though Arizona appeared to have lost several battles in the war with California, the Golden State's victory was far from complete.[20]

In fact, this portion of the bill, in subsequent years, became most controversial. Wilmer's interpretation and skillful presentation before the special master in the late 1950s gained Arizona a huge victory within the larger Supreme Court decision. It later prompted one of California's leading authorities on Colorado River issues to write testily: "Thirty-five years later the U.S. Supreme Court would misconstrue this action and decide that the Boulder Canyon Act provided a statutory apportionment of the waters of the lower Colorado." He sniffed that Congress was "merely suggesting a way in which the lower states might settle their problems themselves."[21]

Thus as Wilmer established himself as a top-flight trial attorney in Arizona and entered into an enduring agreement with Frank Snell during the 1930s, the Colorado River, conversely, frustrated Arizona's political and business leaders as they attempted to assert claims to its considerable water and power potential. Arizona leaders were unable to muster the political will and consensus within the state to form a definite public policy about the Colorado River. Most agreed that the Colorado River Compact of 1922 and the Boulder Canyon Project Act of 1928 represented a federal government–California partnership devoted to denying Arizona its rightful share of Colorado River resources. Meanwhile, California's leaders, unified and focused—reflected in a resolute and effective congressional delegation—marshaled its forces to put the Colorado to beneficial use within its borders. They were working within judicial and congressional guidelines, and they doubtlessly smiled inwardly as Arizona's leadership fulminated against them.

Chapter Four

ARIZONA
ADRIFT

Just three weeks after President Coolidge signed the Boulder Canyon Project Act bill into law, on January 15, 1929, Arizona's Colorado River Commission authorized Attorney General K. Berry Peterson to file suit in the U.S. Supreme Court. On October 30, 1930, the State of Arizona formally submitted its petition. As noted earlier, Arizona contended that the Colorado River Compact, the Boulder Canyon Project Act, and the water and power contracts were unconstitutional. Strangely, Arizona looked outside the state for legal expertise and hired Idaho attorney John Pinkham Gray, reputedly "one of the outstanding lawyers in the West," to assist its stable of attorneys. Attorney Gray avowed, "California and the federal government were not going to override roughshod Arizona sovereign rights." The state's rights approach proved legally anemic: on May 13, 1931, the Court rejected Arizona's suit 8–1 without prejudice, asserting that the Boulder Canyon Project Act "represented a valid exercise of congressional power." The Court, per Justice Louis Brandeis, held, *inter alia,* that the compact and the project act were constitutional, that the river was a navigable stream and that the secretary could construct the dam authorized by Section 1 of the project act.[1] One month later, physical proof of that power became evident as workers began excavating diversion tunnels for the dam at Black Canyon, which, after much congressional wrangling, would be called "Hoover Dam."[2]

As suggested at the outset, for the first three decades of the twentieth century, Mark Wilmer and the Colorado River controversy in the American Southwest lived parallel, yet separate, lives. Inexorably, at mid-course, they would find each other. Wilmer's arrival in the Grand Canyon State in the spring of 1931 coincided precisely with the end of the first chapter of the titanic struggle among seven states and Mexico for rights to the lifeblood of the region. Later, as Wilmer familiarized himself with the legal issues surrounding Arizona's first Supreme Court filing, particularly the interpretation of the Colorado River Compact of 1922 and the Boulder Canyon Project Act of 1928, he realized that little had changed over the next twenty-one years, when, in 1952, the Supreme Court commenced its final disposition of the case. As Wilmer read the ruling of *Arizona v California* (1931) he realized that Arizona had no consistent statewide water policy, its political leadership was divided, and that California, in its inherent complexity, had nevertheless proceeded in a unified fashion concerning her claims to the river. Prior to his arrival in the Grand Canyon State the two-decade controversy between Arizona and California had heated to feverish intensity. The national press covered the struggle for the Colorado on a regular basis and, though new to Arizona, he undoubtedly followed the story with interest.

For the next stage of his legal career in Arizona, Wilmer developed his skills as a competent, even outstanding, litigator, which would, by mid-career, stand him first among his peers in the courtroom. What confounded him and countless other Arizona citizens over the next phase of the controversy was how state leaders fumbled away a host of opportunities to enter the Colorado River sweepstakes in a meaningful way while California, with laser-like focus, continued to gain prior rights to Colorado River resources and put water to beneficial use in the state.

A host of unresolved problems frustrated the state's leaders, and the confusion and factionalism that characterized Arizona water policy during the 1920s continued through the 1930s and New Deal era. Several powerful political and agricultural organizations continued to excoriate California's water and power greed while at the same time reaffirming their commitment to state-owned-and-operated reclamation programs. Similarly, states' rights Democrats, for the most part, dominated Arizona's political affairs during the period, promising to "save" the Colorado for Arizona, yet offering little new or progressive in water resource development policy. Democratic governors, including the aging George W. P. Hunt, who served his last term between 1930 and 1932, and his successors in the thirties—Dr. Benjamin B. Moeur (1932–1936), Rawleigh C. Stanford (1936–1938), and Robert T. Jones (1938–1940)—maintained proprietary views concerning the Colorado and opposed Arizona's entering into the Colorado River Compact. In effect, Arizona experienced the expansion and benefits of federal reclamation during the New Deal in theory, not in practice.[3]

During these years California began enjoying the benefits of the Boulder Canyon Project Act. Although slowed by the Great Depression, construction of Hoover Dam was completed in 1935. The following year hydroelectric power reached the Southern California coastal plain. Beginning in 1939, the Metropolitan Water District of Southern California, much to the alarm of Arizonans, commenced delivery of Colorado River water to its customers. Imperial Valley residents, in 1942, saw water delivered by the All-American Canal. As a result of these developments, Southern California and the Imperial Valley prospered, attracting millions of newcomers in subsequent decades. Not surprisingly, Arizonans looked warily to their west and vented their frustrations in a variety of futile ways.[4] This included another interstate suit pertaining to the Colorado River.

On February 14, 1934, in Arizona's second petition to the U.S. Supreme Court, Governor Benjamin Baker "B. B." Moeur and his administration asked to perpetuate testimony intended for use in future legal action. In this unusual legal maneuver, the Arizonans, once again, hoped to gain what they had lost in their opposition to the Colorado River Compact and the Boulder Canyon Project Act. State officials wanted a specific amount of mainstream water for future use and exclusive rights to Gila River water. Ironically, Arizona based its longstanding claims on testimony given during negotiations surrounding the drafting of the compact. Arizona's junior senator, Carl Hayden, predicted accurately the outcome of the suit; because Arizona had not ratified the Colorado River Compact, it could not base its claims on that document. Indeed, in a unanimous ruling on May 21, 1934, the U.S. Supreme Court rejected Arizona's claim, ruling that the introduction of the proposed testimony was not relevant because, among other things, Arizona had refused to ratify the compact.[5]

As the Supreme Court considered its second *Arizona v California* case, Arizona leaders took dramatic steps to express their extreme displeasure with California and the federal government. In 1932, the Department of Interior announced that it intended to contract with the Metropolitan Water District of Southern California for the construction of a water storage and power dam near Parker, Arizona. When news reached Arizona, Governor Moeur informed federal officials that he opposed further development on the river until Arizona's rights were clearly defined. He based his opposition on three fundamental issues: though Arizona was not a signatory to the Colorado

River Compact he wanted to protect Arizona's water rights promulgated in the document; he had been advised earlier that construction of Parker Dam would not commence until a satisfactory resolution to Arizona's water claims was resolved; and he believed that construction of Parker Dam was illegal. In February 1933 Moeur wrote Ray Lyman Wilbur, outgoing secretary of interior, stating flatly that the proposed diversion dam could not be placed on the river without Arizona's consent and advising Wilbur that the state would take action in opposition to construction.[6]

Despite this warning and others, the Interior Department entered into a contract with MWD for the construction of Parker Dam. Late in the fall of 1934, as MWD employees began construction of a bridge between Arizona and California, Governor Moeur acted on his threat "to repel any invasion or threatened invasion of the sovereignty of the State of Arizona." On November 10, 1934, Moeur declared martial law on the construction site and ordered a unit of the National Guard to occupy the area. In addition to the 101 men sent to Parker, an "Arizona Navy," comprised of the riverboats *Julia B* and *Nellie Jo,* joined the guardsmen in the "war" with California. Offering to diffuse the highly charged situation, an unhappy secretary of interior, Harold Ickes, ordered work suspended until the dispute had been resolved. After months of fruitless negotiation, the federal government, on June 14, 1935, filed suit in the Supreme Court to enjoin Arizona from interfering with the construction of Parker Dam. The Court, however, ruled against the federal government and held that the consent of Congress was necessary before the dam could be constructed. In effect, the Court asserted that the U.S. government had failed to show that construction had been authorized and therefore no grounds existed for granting the injunction.[7] Arizona leaders, however, had little time to rejoice. The Seventy-fourth Congress, shortly after the ruling, by Act of August 30, 1935, authorized construction of Parker Dam.[8]

In November 1935, Arizona filed another bill of complaint against California, Colorado, Nevada, New Mexico, Utah, and Wyoming, asking for a judicial apportionment of the unappropriated water of the Colorado River.[9] The Court, per Justice Harlan Stone, denied the petition on the ground that the United States was an indispensable party. Specifically left undecided was the question whether an equitable division of the unappropriated water of the Colorado River could be decreed in a suit in which the United States was a party.[10]

Between 1930 and 1936 Arizona had been a party in three Supreme Court cases as they pertained to the Colorado River. Also, Arizona's congressional delegation found itself at odds with state leaders. They questioned a dogmatic adherence to a "state's rights" water policy and disavowed Governor Moeur's histrionics concerning the calling out of the National Guard. Such tactics, though colorful, helped Arizona congressmen little in gaining favorable federal compromises. Moreover, in the context of the nation's economic crisis, it seemed foolhardy to expend state funds for the purpose of halting construction of Parker Dam.[11] While the celebrated miniature war with California made exciting press, sold newspapers, and focused attention on the perceived aggressors, the days of "saving" the Colorado for Arizona were over. The state needed to explore alternative approaches.[12]

With the election of Sidney P. Osborn in 1940, Arizona underwent a water policy revolution at the state level. Once a state's rights advocate and ardent opponent of the regionalism inherent in the Colorado River Compact, Osborn informed the electorate that he now favored the interstate agreement. He told Arizona lawmakers that with the passage of the Boulder Canyon Project Act of 1928, the era of philosophizing and theorizing about the river had ended: "Whatever our previous opinions about the best place or plan, we can only recognize that decisions have been made and the dam constructed."

Moreover, the series of legal calamities in the 1930s combined with a massive drought in the 1940s created a water- and power-shortage crisis in the state. In addition, a pending water treaty with Mexico and California's announced plans to increase annual use of mainstream water by 2 million acre-feet, posed serious and immediate threats to future Arizona water supplies. Thus, in a special session called specifically to deal with the Colorado River, the legislature, on February 9, 1944, first passed a bill authorizing a water delivery contract with the secretary of interior providing the annual delivery of 2.8 million acre feet of mainstream water, plus one-half of "any excess or surplus ... to the extent for use in Arizona ... under the compact." Soon thereafter, on February 24, 1944, Osborn signed the bill that ratified the compact, thereby ending over two decades of controversy within Arizona. These actions, importantly, enabled Arizona to fight its reclamation battles within rather than outside the evolving legal and political framework.[13]

Other forces drove Arizona leaders to reevaluate their positions. An unprecedented population influx taxed water supplies and forced officials to take a more scientific approach to the limitations of an arid environment. In the two decades preceding 1940, Arizona's population had grown 67 percent to approximately 500,000. By 1945, 200,000 more people had moved to the state. Significantly, most of this growth was concentrated in and around Phoenix and Tucson, prefiguring the urban nature of Arizona's growth in subsequent decades.[14]

A final—yet major—factor convinced Arizonans that they must chart an alternative course. The issue of Mexican rights to the Colorado River had been one that Arizona leaders hoped they could address after they resolved their differences with neighboring states. On February 3, 1944, however, State Department officials completed arduous, complex negotiations with their Mexican counterparts culminating in an agreement that promised delivery to Mexico of 1.5 million acre-feet of water annually from the Colorado River. For once, it seemed Arizona and California agreed on an issue: both states believed the amount excessive. Nevertheless, U.S. negotiators, motivated by the Good Neighbor Policy and the recent close cooperation between the two countries in the global conflict, favored the generous allocation. The Roosevelt administration, in view of the pressing international situation, hesitated to force Mexico to accept a lesser amount of water.[15]

The implications of the Mexican Treaty were abundantly clear. Unless Arizona took steps to put mainstream water to beneficial use within the state, California and Mexico could claim a prior right to Arizona's claimed share. Bureau of Reclamation engineers, during hearings on the Mexican treaty, underscored that point when they reported that water supply figures were significantly less than previously believed.[16]

With all these factors in mind, in October 1943, Arizona's senior senator, Carl Hayden, in typically discreet fashion, secured congressional appropriations for the U.S. Bureau of Reclamation to conduct an inventory of irrigation and multiple-use projects in the lower Colorado River basin that could be made ready for construction when servicemen returned home at the end of World War II. Capitol Hill observers, preoccupied with winning the war, hardly noticed the apparently innocuous legislation. After all, Hayden had spent his long career in Washington supporting the bureau's affairs. Few lawmakers questioned his judgment in reclamation matters.[17]

To close observers, however, Arizona's tacit cooperation with the bureau in conducting a survey punctuated the dramatic shift in the state's stance on the Colorado River. Beyond signaling Arizona's apparent rapprochement with the federal government and the other basin states who had signed the Colorado River Compact of 1922, the inventory held profound significance for the development of the Southwest during the second half of the twentieth century and the early years of the twenty-first. This marked the first meaningful step in Arizona's already decades-long quest actually to divert its claimed share of Colorado River water to the burgeoning heart of the state.

No wonder Senator Hayden felt a great sense of accomplishment in 1944 when Bureau of Reclamation officials announced the results of their inventory. Paradise Valley, north of Phoenix, and the Gila River valley, east of Yuma, were likely candidates for postwar projects. Bureau engineers also recommended building a water storage and power dam at Bridge Canyon, above Boulder Dam and near the southern boundary of Grand Canyon National Park. Viewed as the key structure in the bureau's plans for Arizona, the proposed Bridge Canyon Dam would regulate silt buildup and provide 75,000 kilowatts of additional electric power. Although cast in the most general terms, this "working paper" (as reclamation officials called it), gave hope to those who dreamed of putting water to beneficial use in central Arizona.[18]

Hayden quickly took advantage of the new political climate, convincing the Senate Irrigation and Reclamation Committee to make a complete study of the need for irrigation and electric power development in his home state. On July 31, 1944, a subcommittee convened five days of hearings in Arizona to discuss the bureau's recently completed preliminary reports on importing Colorado River water and to survey the state's various irrigation needs. As Arizona's junior senator, Ernest McFarland, put it, "The information gained . . . will be the basis for legislation for future development in Arizona."[19]

In Arizona, meanwhile, Governor Osborn continued his efforts at water policy reform and institutional reorganization. He created two new agencies of government: the Arizona Power Authority and the Arizona Interstate Stream Commission. The APA became the agency with the authority to bargain for, take, and receive electric power from the waters of the mainstream of the Colorado River. The governor, with advice and consent of the state Senate, appointed its five members. Similarly, with the ratification of the Colorado River Compact, the Arizona Colorado River Commission passed out of existence. In its place, Osborn formed AISC to protect the state's interest and prosecute its claims to Colorado River water before Congress and the courts. Again, with advice and consent of the Senate, the governor appointed its seven members, like those of the APA. Significantly, from the date of its formation, AISC focused its energies at gaining approval of CAP.

In the context of the effort to secure CAP authorization, local business leaders formed a private, nonprofit association, the Central Arizona Project Association, to support the efforts of the state's congressmen. Organized on July 1, 1946, CAPA was comprised of agricultural, business, professional,

Formal Portrait (1944). Wilmer Family Photo Collection.

and industrial people who saw diversion of Colorado River water as fundamental to the future of Arizona's economy. The association raised money, provided research and legal assistance, lobbied for, and publicized the project. Moreover, CAPA worked closely with AISC, lending its services and personnel. Finally, CAPA provided links among federal government, state government, and private sector individuals involved in issues related to CAP.[20]

PLANS, POLITICS, AND THE SUPREME COURT

During the first set of Senate hearings on the CAP concept, E. B. Debler, the Bureau of Reclamation's director of planning, presented various proposals for what he called the "Central Arizona Diversion." Debler explained that the investigations commissioned by Senator Hayden's committee on postwar planning had located three possible routes for the proposed diversion of approximately 2 million acre-feet of water. The Marble Gorge Plan, the most expensive and technically complex project, would require seven years to construct at an estimated cost of $487 million. The Bridge Canyon Dam Plan, the most widely discussed proposal, would take six years to construct at a cost of $325 million. The Parker Pump Plan, the least expensive of the three alternatives, could be completed in three years at a comparatively modest cost of $134 million.[21]

A noteworthy feature of the hearings was the introduction of Tucson and Pima County into the emerging CAP concept. During the third day of testimony, Tucson city manager Phil Martin announced that the city and county were interested in obtaining a share of Arizona's allotment of Colorado River water. He presented the senators with petitions from the City of Tucson and Cortaro Farms Company requesting an allocation of 70,000 acre-feet annually for domestic and agricultural uses.[22]

Shortly after the conclusion of the Arizona hearings, Hayden directed funds to the Bureau of Reclamation for the purpose of commencing full-scale feasibility studies for a central Arizona water delivery system. In the context of postwar planning and reconversion to a peacetime economy, he quietly funneled funds to the bureau for what its engineers now were calling "The Central Arizona Project."

The earliest CAP planning studies focused on selecting the proper diversion route. With surprisingly little controversy, federal and state officials by February 1947 arrived at a general agreement on the Parker Pump Plan for diverting Colorado River water to central Arizona. Secretary of Interior J. A. Krug signed the final feasibility report on February 8, 1948, and justified construction of CAP because it was essentially a rescue project designed to avert serious disruptions in Arizona's predominantly agricultural economy. Beyond that, Tucson, which obtained its water from an overdeveloped and rapidly shrinking groundwater basin, desperately needed additional supplies of surface water so that it could survive and develop. Moreover, Krug cited the unprecedented postwar migration of people to the Southwest, which imposed an urgent need for additional hydroelectric power in Arizona and the southern sections of California, Utah, and Nevada. CAP would transform the Colorado River into a truly multipurpose natural resource that would replace depleted groundwater, create hydroelectric power for a developing region, provide supplemental water to lands currently in production but not adequately irrigated, and increase Tucson's domestic water supply. Citing the varied and pressing need for additional water in Arizona, Secretary Krug recommended that "the Central Arizona Project be authorized for construction, operation, and maintenance by the Secretary of Interior under the general plan set forth herein."[23]

Three issues needed resolution before further action took place. First of all, the lingering water allocation question between Arizona and California required a final answer. California contended that the annual flow of the Gila River, estimated at one million acre-feet, should be included in Arizona's allotment of Colorado River water. Arizona, of course, countered that the Gila, including water put to beneficial use under the San Carlos Reclamation Project and Coolidge Dam, was exempt from allocation formulas. As proof Arizona cited the Colorado River Compact and the Boulder Project Canyon Act of 1928, neither of which deducted the Gila River flow. Krug noted that if the controversy were resolved in favor of Arizona, the Interior Department could move quickly to implement CAP plans. At the same time he hinted that in the event that California prevailed, there might not be enough water allocated to Arizona to justify construction of CAP.[24]

Arizona also needed to adopt a groundwater control law that effectively limited the average annual withdrawal from groundwater basins within and reasonably tributary to the areas served by CAP. Finally, the state had to organize an improvement district to help repay construction costs and oversee local management of the project.[25]

Meanwhile, Hayden and his junior colleague, Senator Ernest McFarland, initiated congressional action on CAP. On June 18, 1946, McFarland introduced S 2346—the Bridge Canyon Project Bill—to the Seventy-ninth Congress. Because McFarland's legislation had been drafted and introduced prior to completion of the comprehensive feasibility study, Congress refused to take action on the early version of a CAP bill, citing the lack of sufficient technical data to conduct hearings. Hayden and McFarland introduced an identical bill (S 433) at the opening of the Eightieth Congress on January 19, 1947. It met the same fate as its predecessor. Despite their failure, these early drafts of CAP bills signaled Arizona's legislative intentions.[26]

Hearings, votes, political maneuverings, public relations campaigns, and struggle against an obstinate and formidable California commenced anew. No small number of parliamentary maneuvers could override California's superiority in numbers, especially in the House of Representatives. Arizona senators Hayden and McFarland campaigned within Arizona for CAP. They declared that the project was "the future of Arizona," and that California was the obstacle to the enactment of desired legislation. In a 1950 radio address Senator Hayden discounted California's repeated claims that CAP was not economically feasible, asserting, "By compact and by contract there is sufficient water in the Colorado River belonging to Arizona to provide an adequate supply for Arizona's agricultural and domestic needs." Also, this phase of the controversy differed in distinct ways from the earlier debates over the Swing-Johnson bills and the Boulder Canyon Project Act of 1928. During the earlier confrontation, the people of Arizona were divided and expended much energy fighting each other; the CAP effort saw the state united.[27]

Local and state politicians, business leaders, and the general public actively supported the legislation. Arizona governor Dan Garvey proclaimed a "CAP Week" while the CAPA and AISC churned out press releases and literature geared to educating the public. And, on June 2, 1949, the Senate Interior and Insular Affairs Committee reported on S 75, yet another CAP bill, with a "Do Pass" recommendation. While Arizona's senators had to wait for the second session of the Eighty-first Congress to convene, this bill held promise. After much more astute political maneuvering in the Senate Rules and Appropriations Committees, Hayden and McFarland watched confidently as the Senate passed S 75 on February 21, 1950, by a vote of 55–28.[28]

l-r, Arizona Senator Ernest McFarland, Senate Sergeant at Arms, Joseph Duke, and Arizona Senator Carl Hayden discuss passage of the first Central Arizona Project bill in the U.S. Senate on February 21, 1950. Author's files.

The political battle shifted to the House of Representatives, and California prepared to respond to the Arizona victory in the Senate. Their congressmen trained their sights on John Murdock, the able Arizona congressman and former history professor at the Arizona State Teachers College (later renamed Arizona State University), who ranked second in seniority on the Public Lands Committee. California banked on the strategy of delaying action on the bill for several years—when the House delegation from California would increase. Preliminary reapportionment figures indicated that in the 1952 federal elections California's representations in the House would grow from twenty-three to thirty members. It would then have exactly as many representatives as all other reclamation states combined, prompting California representatives Claire Engle and Norris Poulson, a former mayor of Los Angeles, the two most outspoken critics of CAP, to suggest that California could then exercise veto power in important water matters.[29]

Murdock knew he faced an uphill battle in the House. He was chairman of the Subcommittee on Irrigation and Reclamation of the Public Lands Committee, but three Californians—Poulson, Engle, and Richard Welch—sat on the subcommittee and were all outspoken opponents of CAP. The *Phoenix Gazette* lamented "with no Hayden in the House to steer the project, and a solid block of California representatives to stop it, the CAP had practically no chance of success."[30] During the Eighty-first Congress, California introduced twenty-three separate Colorado River bills and referring the entire question of water rights to the Judiciary Committee, thus outflanking the Arizona delegation of Murdock and Harold "Porky" Patten.

Close observers knew the delay tactic was masterminded by Northcutt "Mike" Ely, the determined California lawyer who had spent virtually his entire legal career on issues related to water law. Ironically, Ely's father, Sims Ely, was a former editor and publisher of the *Arizona Republic* and wrote a widely read book on Arizona's colorful past, *The Lost Dutchman Mine*.[31] The younger Ely, who was born in Phoenix on September 14, 1903, was in every sense a contemporary of Wilmer. He attended Stanford University and Stanford Law School, graduating from the latter in 1926. He practiced law 1926–1929 in New York. When fellow Stanford graduate Herbert Hoover assumed the presidency of the United States in 1929, Ely was appointed executive assistant to Secretary of Interior Dr. Ray Lyman Wilbur, whose remarkable overlapping careers also included that of physician, dean of the Stanford Medical School, president of the American Medical Association, and president of Stanford University.[32] During his four-year stint at the Interior Department, Ely became intimately involved in reclamation policy, negotiating Hoover Dam water and power contracts, maintaining a ringside seat during the all-important debates surrounding the Boulder Canyon Project legislation. During the 1930s and 1940s Ely became one of the nation's most prominent experts on water issues and mineral rights and, significantly, the chief legal advisor and litigator for California in Colorado River matters.[33] Officially, he served as special counsel to the Colorado River Board of California, that state's counterpart to AISC, from 1946 to 1976. Additionally, during that same period he was special assistant to the California attorney general. In effect, he personified Arizona's legal opposition in the growing legal and political controversy.

Despite Murdock's efforts, the House counterpart to S 75 never emerged from the Public Lands Committee. As the second session of the Eighty-first Congress adjourned in December 1950, CAP legislation had passed the Senate, languished in the Public Lands Committee of the House of

Representatives, and brought forth again the unresolved question of rights to the Colorado River.[34]

In January 1951, the Eighty-second Congress convened and Arizona's congressional delegation reintroduced CAP bills in both houses of Congress. Naturally, the focus of attention was on the House legislation introduced by Representatives Murdock and Patten, H.R. 1500 and H.R. 1501, identical CAP bills, and indeed close observers voiced mild optimism because Murdock, due to the outcome of the 1950 congressional elections, had risen to chairman of the House Interior and Insular Affairs Committee. That apparent advantage notwithstanding, California and its supporters still outnumbered Murdock and his allies on the committee. On February 21, 1951, Murdock called to order the first of twenty-three sessions on CAP legislation. The committee rehashed previous testimony, introduced new reasons to support their respective positions, but made little progress. Always, the issue of water rights remained. Finally, California's representatives moved to break the stalemate and in mid-April, Representatives Sam Yorty, Claire Engle, and Norris Poulson asked fellow member John Saylor of Pennsylvania to offer a preferential motion to postpone further consideration of the bill until the water rights issue had been adjudicated in the Supreme Court or the ever-elusive agreement among the lower basin states had been made.[35]

On the morning of April 18, 1951, Chairman Murdock, sensing he was losing control of his committee, reluctantly recognized Congressman Saylor. The Pennsylvanian said: "I move you, Mr. Chairman, that H.R. 1500 and H.R. 1501 be postponed until such time as the use of the water of the lower Colorado River Basin is either adjudicated, or a binding mutual agreement as to the use of the water is reached by the states of the lower Colorado River Basin." The motion was quickly seconded, and, by a vote of 16–8, the committee shelved the bill. A stunned Howard Pyle, Arizona governor who was waiting in an ante room preparing to address the committee in behalf of CAP, nevertheless requested to make a statement. His brief, impromptu fulmination reflected the sentiments of CAP supporters. "I think this is one of the most depressing moments of my life," he said, and "a delaying action on the part of California has been the thing they have aspired to most of all."[36]

Representative Engle of California termed the developments "a signal victory for California," yet Arizona senators Hayden and McFarland refused to abandon their cause in the Eighty-second Congress. They reintroduced S 75 in the Senate in a last-ditch effort, though this version, significantly, carried an article that provided for the adjudication of the water rights issue in the Supreme Court. On May 29, 1951, the Senate, for the second time within a year, held a floor debate on a CAP bill. On that day, Senator Hayden delivered one of the longest addresses of his career. He explained and interpreted for the Senate the recent events that transpired in the House of Representatives and questioned California's "unjustified objection" to what was due water-poor Arizona. He reminded California's two senators, William F. Knowland and Richard Nixon, how he had helped in securing funding for their state's Central Valley Project. This exceedingly rare floor speech from the so-called "Silent Senator" prefigured future developments because he devoted much time to the unresolved question of water rights.

Section 12 of the 1951 CAP Senate bill contained a provision for a Supreme Court determination of water rights. Senators Joseph C. O'Mahoney of Wyoming and Eugene Milliken of Colorado, distinguished lawyers and upper basin supporters of the bill drafted that section. Echoing Governor Pyle's lament, Hayden told the Senate that California wanted "delay, and more delay; delay for many years to come in hope that in the meantime more people will go to southern California and thereby a greater need for the water will be built up." Section 12 of S 75, therefore, addressed directly the intent of the Saylor motion in the House of Representatives, for it had the effect of withholding any appropriation for the construction of irrigation works intended to bring Colorado River water into central Arizona until the Supreme Court decided that enough water existed for CAP. If California succeeded in killing CAP, Hayden warned, it could conceivably apply the same tactics to hinder development in the upper states. On June 5, 1951, the Senate, despite persuasive opposition arguments presented by senators Nixon and Knowland, voted 50–28 to authorize the $788,000,000 CAP. This gave the bill new life in the House where six weeks earlier it had been left for dead.[37] Unfortunately for Arizona and Congressman Murdock, whose political career hung in the balance, hopes that the House would reconsider the legislation never materialized. The House adjourned without further deliberation and again, Arizona appeared to have lost another major legislative battle with California over Colorado River water.

Twice then, in 1950 and 1951, Arizona secured passage of a CAP bill in the Senate only to see it derailed in the House. California Congressman

Norris Poulson aptly described his state's perspective on this politically charged phase of the fight over the Colorado: "The only sure way to be reelected in California is to oppose the Central Arizona Project."[38] Indeed Arizona had lost the overall congressional battle, but Section 12 of S 75, which called for a new effort in the Supreme Court, held promise for Arizona as political leaders calculated their next move. Ultimately, the legislative battles over CAP provided a catalyst for addressing the sharp and longstanding differences between Arizona and California. Unable to effect a compromise acceptable to both parties, in 1952 Arizona leaders surprised many when they took assertive action and put forward the mosaic of contested issues to the Supreme Court. As several students of *Arizona v California* (1963) have noted, the case was one of the most complex and fiercely contested in the history of the high court.

Chapter Five

ARIZONA V CALIFORNIA

Arizona governor Howard Pyle—a war correspondent during World War II and owner of KFAD Radio (later KTAR) in Phoenix—knew how to utilize the print and electronic media to full advantage. On Wednesday, August 13, 1952, he displayed his flair for the dramatic and his considerable political communications skills. On that day Arizona filed suit against California and asked the Supreme Court to take jurisdiction in the battle over use of Colorado River water. Pyle marked the action as "a new chapter in a fight for life by the whole state." J. H. "Hub" Moeur, son of the former Arizona governor and chief counsel for the Arizona Interstate Stream Commission, filed a fifty-four-page motion and complaint with the high tribunal charging that failure to settle the longstanding dispute threatened the state's economy with destruction. The action, prepared by Moeur; Perry M. Ling, special counsel to AISC; Burr Sutter, special counsel to AISC; Alexander B. Baker, chief assistant attorney general; and Fred O. Wilson, Arizona attorney general set in motion *Arizona v California*.[1]

Further, the filing declared Arizona's groundwater supply could no longer support its 725,000 irrigated and ranch lands; unless additional water was obtained, over thirty percent of that cultivated acreage would be lost. The complaint stated that the only source of water to prevent such a catastrophe was the mainstream of the Colorado River. It asked that (1) the Supreme Court take jurisdiction in the dispute; (2) the Court hold that Arizona was entitled to 2.8 million acre-feet of mainstream Colorado River water annually as set forth in the Boulder Canyon Project Act of 1928; and (3) that California was limited in perpetuity to 4.4 million acre-feet of water annually as provided in the California Limitation Act of 1929.[2]

In Washington, where the filing took place at 2:50 P.M. that day, Senator Hayden welcomed a small group of somber-faced Arizonans to his office.

After a brief exchange of pleasantries he stuck a battered white straw hat on his bald head, strode to the door and beckoned, "Come on boys, let's get this done." The group walked to the U.S. Supreme Court building, and Moeur filed the bill of complaint against California. After witnessing the filing, the then-seventy-four-year-old Hayden issued a short statement to the press. "I believe this action," he told those gathered at the steps of the Supreme Court, "will make possible the settlement of a most serious controversy which is delaying the development of the Colorado River basin." "If the Californians are sincere in their oft-repeated demands for court action," he added, "then they will welcome the opportunity to present their side of the case." With that, Arizona launched the monumental *Arizona v California* Supreme Court case.[3]

California's response to what newspapers described as a "surprise action," was immediate and negative. Their representatives in Washington, unable to secure a copy of Arizona's motion before the close of the clerk's office on that Wednesday, nevertheless blasted the suit. John Terrell, lobbyist for the Colorado River Board of California, called the filing "part of a plot to get Senator Ernest McFarland and Representative John R. Murdock reelected to Congress." He stated further, "I think . . . it was part of a program designed by Interior Secretary Oscar Chapman. . . . McFarland and Murdock are both in serious political trouble in Arizona. The administration is making a serious effort to rescue them." Though Terrell's political instincts regarding the fate of McFarland and Murdock were on the mark—both would lose their reelection bids to Barry M. Goldwater and John J. Rhodes, respectively—his analysis of the motivation for the suit was not correct.[4] He added that California welcomed a judicial settlement to the thirty-year-old dispute and opined that California would not oppose the leave to file the Arizona suit.[5]

The comments and actions of Arizona's junior senator, Ernest McFarland, an attorney, former county judge, and longtime friend of Wilmer's, accurately framed the suit filing and infuriated California.[6] Indeed California's water leaders had singled out McFarland as the nefarious broker from a God-forsaken state who had worked a deal with the Truman administration in furthering Arizona's interest. A *Los Angeles Times* editorial of August 3, 1952, stated that the purported court filing was "cooked up . . . in a backroom of the Democratic National Convention. It was designed to aid the reelection of Senator McFarland of Arizona. It was put into execution by

Secretary of the Interior Oscar Chapman with all the finesse of a butcher boy pole axing a steer in the Chicago stock yards, the aroma of which it appropriately bears."[7]

McFarland, the Democratic Senate majority leader, was indeed in a pitched political battle for survival with former department store scion and Phoenix city councilman Barry Goldwater, the Republican nominee for the Senate. Senator McFarland took advantage of the situation to deliver his message. "This was not the first time California interests have made charges against me," McFarland allowed, "but I want the people of Arizona to know that this action was carefully planned months in advance—not in Chicago but in my office with Senator Hayden, Congressmen Murdock and [Harold] Patten, and representatives of the Arizona Interstate Stream Commission." "I went over our complaint with our attorneys. It is carefully drawn and in my judgment states a cause of action. This is the reason Representatives Engle and Poulson are protesting so vigorously."

And, in a prophetic afterthought, he added, "There is no question but what California, from their statements made now and earlier, will fight our securing funds for the Central Arizona Project, even after our rights are adjudicated. Even Senator [Richard] Nixon has said in the past that he would make an all out fight to defeat what he calls our 'steal' of Colorado River water. This suit is just one step: we will have to take other action in Congress to build this project."[8]

Arizona's contentions had changed little since the 1920s. The state asserted that California had made contracts for delivery of over 5.3 million acre-feet of water annually despite laws limiting it to 4.4 million acre-feet. That limitation notwithstanding, Arizona's attorneys argued that California's construction of reclamation works capable of diverting 8 million acre-feet of water annually posed a threat to Arizona and other basin states. According to Arizona's attorneys, for the state to sustain its existing economy it required 3.8 million acre-feet of Colorado River system water per year. Furthermore, Arizona relied on and asserted its rights to water under a variety of federal and state actions including the Colorado River Compact, the Boulder Canyon Project Act, and the California Limitation Act of 1929; additionally, the state had entered into a water delivery contract with the federal government.[9]

California registered no objection to Arizona's motion. A substantial team of attorneys, led by the brilliant and indefatigable Northcutt Ely, agreed

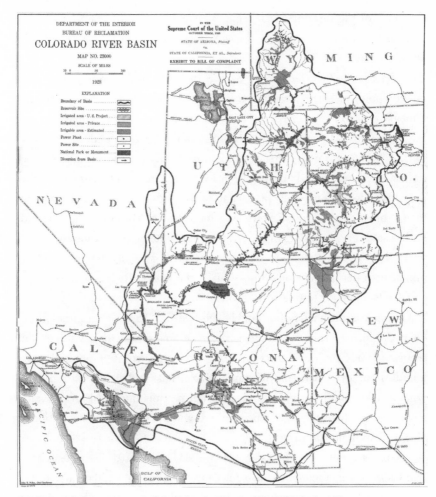

U.S. Bureau of Reclamation map of the Colorado River Basin in 1928. Author's files.

with the U.S. solicitor general, Archibald Cox, who advised the Supreme Court that the U.S. government had an interest in the case and would move to intervene if Arizona's motion were granted. On January 19, 1953, the Court granted Arizona's original motion, and the bill of complaint was filed.[10]

On May 20, 1953, California responded to Arizona's bill of complaint. In nearly 500 pages of narrative and supporting documentation California's attorneys contended that their state had a right to the beneficial consumptive use of 5.362 million acre-feet of Colorado River system water per year under the terms of the Boulder Canyon Project Act and contracts with the secretary of interior. Moreover, California claimed prior appropriative rights to the use of that amount of water and that these rights were senior to Arizona's and therefore superior. Finally, California argued that Arizona, by failing to ratify the Colorado River Compact within the specified six months (when the other six states had done so in 1923), as well as her subsequent attempts to have the agreement declared invalid and the Boulder Canyon Act declared unconstitutional, precluded her right from interpreting these statutes.[11]

As California lawmakers had done in Congress, California attorneys commenced a campaign of judicial delay. A blizzard of motions and filings postponed the start of the proceedings, while the number and complexity of the issues raised prompted the Court to appoint a special master to hear arguments. On January 1, 1954, George I. Haight, of Chicago, Illinois, was officially named as special master. The Court directed Haight to find the facts specially and state separately his conclusions of law and submit them to the Court together with a draft of the recommended decree. But after ruling on several preliminary motions, he died suddenly before formal hearings began. On October 10, 1955, Simon Rifkind, a sharp-witted federal jurist from the Southern District of New York, replaced Haight. Rifkind's instructions ordered him to proceed under the original order of reference.[12]

After the first few years of judicial jousting, but prior to formal hearings, the case entered an important preliminary phase where California desired to have the four upper basin states, New Mexico, Utah, Wyoming, and Colorado, joined in the suit, reasoning that these states, too, had a pertinent interest in the outcome. As Arizonans knew by this time, this procedure could threaten to extend the case by many years. California could continue drawing water from the mainstream while Arizona could not move forward on CAP.[13]

Prior to his passing, Judge Haight held hearings on the issue in February 1955 in Phoenix and recommended against California's request to join the upper basin states. Rifkind continued consideration of the issue and held that California's objection must be heard and ruled upon by the full U.S. Supreme Court. Meanwhile, Arizona's legal team underwent the first of several reorganizations during the eleven-year course of the suit. Quietly, Chief Counsel Moeur, acknowledging his limitations as a litigator, looked for assistance and advised AISC to hire New York attorney Theodore Kiendl, who, it was hoped, would provide direction and leadership for the Arizona team. Also, a recent arrival to Phoenix, John P. Frank, joined the team in 1954 and was appointed chief litigator. Frank, who had attended the University of Wisconsin Law School and graduated in 1940, also received a J.S.D. from Yale Law School in 1947. Adding to these impressive academic credentials, he had served as a law clerk to Justice Hugo L. Black during the October 1942 term of the U.S. Supreme Court. He was also assistant professor of law at Indiana University 1946–1949 and associate professor of law at Yale University 1949–1954. During his tenure at Yale he was associated with the Anti-trust Division of the U.S. Department of Justice. He joined the firm of Lewis and Roca in 1954 and almost immediately AISC tapped the thirty-four-year-old, with a reputation as a headstrong and opinionated legal practitioner, to argue Arizona's various motions before the special master.[14]

At this stage, incredibly, the sitting governor of Arizona officially entered the proceedings. Those opposed to the joinder motion prevailed upon Governor Ernest McFarland to become involved in the pending hearings because of his "position, prestige, and experience." Former Senator McFarland, who two years after his upset loss to Barry Goldwater had revitalized his political career with a gubernatorial election victory over incumbent Howard Pyle in 1954, needed little persuasion to become directly involved in the lawsuit. Earlier, representatives from the upper basin states and Arizona held a strategy session at the old Hay-Adams Hotel in Washington, where they determined that McFarland should make a final summary and a "personal" plea to the Supreme Court.[15]

McFarland traveled to Washington with Ben Avery, then a reporter for the *Phoenix Gazette*; the two had struck up a cordial relationship and often caravanned together. In fact, the governor would customarily request permission from publisher Eugene Pulliam to have Avery accompany him on trips. Pulliam, the inveterate Republican promoter, doubtlessly obtained inside "Democratic" information from Avery, who, it turns out, was a longtime "conservative" Democrat.[16]

Avery related McFarland's careful preparation for his appearance before the Supreme Court. He stayed up until 4:00 A.M. pacing the room the night before, meticulously organizing, checking, and rechecking his thoughts before committing them to paper and then to memory, and much to the horror of future archivists and historians, casting crumpled pages in the wastebasket. McFarland felt it was important to appear without notes or brief. Meanwhile, on December 8, 1955, Arizona's youthful chief litigator, Frank, began these proceedings arguing against the California motion to add the upper basin states to the suit. He focused his discussion on the Colorado River Compact of 1922, which, he correctly reiterated, separated the two basins. Frank gave way to Hatfield Chilson of Loveland, Colorado, who argued the upper basin's collective resistance to being California's straw men, stating, "If we had a real stake in this lawsuit, we would not have to be forced to get in—we would be clamoring to get in."[17]

Governor McFarland took the remaining time for his final plea and summary. In his argument he noted that three years had already been spent on this issue and predicted that another fifteen would be added if the four additional states became involved, during which time "the economy of Arizona would be ruined." He then related the legislative history of CAP, highlighting California's litany of delaying tactics, and suggested that this "was more of the same."[18]

The hearing was held on a Thursday, and all expressed great surprise with the speed of the Supreme Court's decision. The following Monday, December 12, 1955, the Court ruled in a 5–3 decision (Earl Warren abstaining) in favor of Arizona. "The motion of California to join States of Colorado and Wyoming as parties to this cause is denied," the decision read in part, and "the motion to join Utah and New Mexico as parties is granted only to the extent of their interest in Lower Basin waters." This unprecedented appearance by a sitting governor and the victory suggested to some a turning point as well as a newly configured political and legal approach to the case. California's governor, Goodwin Knight, expressed great bitterness and uttered ominously that the "tea leaves had turned" though much more lay ahead.[19]

Soon, McFarland, whose intellectual and political engagement in *Arizona v California* proved critical, made some executive decisions that charted a new course for his state. His direct role in the Colorado River controversy, first as a U.S. senator (1941–1953), then, as governor (1955–1959)—who also happened to serve directly as a litigator in the case—focused his attention on the legal team and the facts and theories it put before the special master. Rifkind allowed thirty years later: "McFarland did a hell of a good job when he argued that motion back in December of 1955."[20] What was more important, perhaps, McFarland and others close to the case realized that Arizona had charged out of the gates and stumbled badly; they began to realize that they needed to sharpen their legal theory, modify their legal team, or both; or else they would lose the case.[21]

On June 14, 1956, formal hearings on *Arizona v California* began in the
U.S. Courthouse in San Francisco, California.[22] During that fateful summer,
and into the fall, Arizona presented its case in full. Essentially, Arizona's position
was that, as a matter of fairness, it should have water to sustain its economy.
"The prosperity and welfare of a large and important area of our Union is

U.S. Supreme Court Special Master, Simon Rifkind, who presided over the *Arizona v California*
Supreme Court case beginning in 1955. Simon H. Rifkind Center for Arts and the Humanities.

involved," Arizona's John P. Frank proclaimed at the outset of the proceedings in San Francisco. In fact, Frank's statements mirrored the operative, yet inchoate legal argument set forth five years earlier by Moeur and the rest of Arizona's attorneys. Frank sought to clear title to Arizona's use of water from the Colorado River based on untenable principles of equitable apportionment. In effect, Arizona contended, "an argument for the proof of a need for water in Arizona should determine the right to water."

Due to Arizona's "equitable apportionment" legal theory and growing personality conflicts within the Arizona legal team, by the end of 1956 Arizona's case had become mired in squabbling about the economic feasibility of CAP itself—about supply, use, and even comparative economic value of land. In effect, Arizona had not developed a coherent legal strategy. The tangential nature of the "equitable apportionment" argument threatened the foundation of Arizona's case. As the complainant's witnesses sought to affirm the need for water to sustain Arizona's fragile water-based agricultural and ranching economy, hope for victory appeared increasingly remote. Fate intervened on February 17, 1957, when Special Master Rifkind suffered a heart attack.[23]

Ray Killian, at the time executive secretary of AISC, stated simply, "The whole situation was chaotic." Chief litigator Frank's approach and attitude alienated his fellow attorneys, and Arizona officials monitoring the trial in San Francisco could not discern a cogent legal theory that framed Frank's reasoning in the case. For the lawyers who had gone to San Francisco to prove Arizona's right to Colorado River water, it was the worst of times. "The morale of the whole group was pretty low," Killian remarked. Wayne Akin, AISC chairman, complained of a lack of leadership and management strategy. He lamented, "The commission had hired a famous New York lawyer [Theodore Kiendl], but he had failed to provide leadership."[24]

Sidney Kartus, a longtime water lobbyist, political provocateur, and ardent supporter of Arizona's cause in the case, was the official observer of the proceedings for the Arizona Legislative Council, a committee comprised of leaders of the Arizona state Senate and House. On February 23, 1957, he issued a report to the council that, in many ways, captured the spirit of the hearings.[25] In fact, over the course of the trial, Kartus submitted several reports that described the nature and direction of the case. In the cover letter to his February 1957 report, he advised, "As such observer I attended the sessions of the trial held in San Francisco, California from February 11 to

February 18, 1957, when they were temporarily suspended due to illness of the master. Resumption of the trial is scheduled for May of this year." He added, "This report is a continuation of that previously submitted by me on October 3, 1956, to the Speaker of the House of Representatives as a member of a special committee of the House appointed to observe the court sessions during that year, and covering the period June 14 to August 27, 1956. I have attended and reported on every day and practically every moment of the entire trial up to the present time." Thus the Kartus reports provide an ongoing Arizona perspective on the trial that parallels the recorded and transcribed testimony. At the time that Rifkind's medical emergency interrupted the trial, it was obvious to Kartus and AISC officials observing the testimony that change was needed.[26]

According to the report dated February 23, 1957, "Arizona had presented its case in chief, and the States of California and New Mexico had submitted opening statements." An order of the master required the California defendants to present their cases next. In accordance therewith, the Imperial Valley Irrigation District of California began its case on the first day, February 11, 1957. Counsel for the district made an opening statement, and then placed upon the stand its first witness, who had been district superintendent and engineer for many years. This witness recited the history of the initiation of earliest efforts looking to development of Imperial Valley for irrigation purposes beginning with its inception shortly before the Civil War. Arizona's legal team knew that they were in for a long series of witnesses supporting California's argument for prior appropriation rights to the Colorado River.

Notably, the first Imperial Valley witness began to testify about recent history and began to provide testimony that related to notices of appropriation (water filings) on Colorado River water for the valley beginning in the 1890s, and the Imperial Irrigation District's counsel offered evidence and exhibits consisting of documents, maps, survey reports, and other data that could form links in the chain of title in California deriving from such notices or filings on the Colorado. Arizona counsel Frank objected on the ground that appropriations were irrelevant. In fact, the number and frequency of Arizona objections to the witness's testimony prompted Master Rifkind to determine, on February 13, two days into this set of hearings, that the issue of relevancy must be addressed. He then heard arguments on this point from counsel of all parties on that day and on the following day, February 14, 1957.

In addition, Chief Counsel Ely of California, on February 11, 1957, filed a sixty-two-page brief in support of its allegation that appropriative rights "are relevant and material to the issues of litigation." Ely asserted that the state law of prior appropriation and beneficial use governed water rights in the Colorado River under the laws of all states in the river basin, and that this law was recognized and confirmed by acts of Congress. Ely argued that appropriative rights were recognized and protected by the Colorado River Compact, Boulder Canyon Project Act, and contracts based on those acts. Moreover, he suggested, "the unbroken line of [court] decisions upholding priority of appropriations as the controlling principle in interstate water litigation makes any extended argument in justification of that principle unnecessary." Two more points rounded out California's position. Ely told the Court that appropriative principles were being extended in the American West and were increasingly supplanting riparian law in eastern states. He concluded that Congress, the courts, and history had made prior appropriation the dominant and most effective water law in the land.

Arizona filed no reply brief but instead relied on oral argument. Frank sought to convince the Court that appropriation law, which was, in fact, Arizona law, would be absurd, time-consuming, obsolete, and ineffective in the adjudication of interstate water cases like the one before the Supreme Court. He sought to persuade Special Master Rifkind that he should not rule on the basis of law but rather ignore the law and make the secretary of interior the sole arbiter of water rights. Contracts made by the secretary, according to Frank's reasoning, would prevail over appropriative rights under the Arizona contention. There were no precedents for such a position and many precedents to the contrary.[27]

Further, Frank referenced the transcript of a special master's proceedings in a previous interstate water case in the Supreme Court where appropriative rights were placed in evidence. He sought to ridicule the length and time spent by the master in establishing water title, for example, to a small area of land. Frank omitted the fact that the equal protection of the law must extend to all—big or small—and the courts will take as much time as necessary for a proper adjudication and an equitable decision. In fact, Frank appeared to forget that Arizona was a small state in comparison to California, and as a minority state compared with the other six states of the Colorado River basin it must rely on this principle for the protection of its rights in the river. Frank sought to criticize other aspects of prior appropriation that had long been accepted in the reclamation states of the American West. He attacked various local customs and practices that had been incorporated into the law; Master Rifkind admonished him that "Arizona counsel would not find it easy to breach such rights."

Indeed, while California commenced its case on a solid note, and Arizona's chief litigator, Frank, began immediately pestering California witnesses with countless objections, courtroom observers, like Kartus, knew that Arizona's case had not gone well; in fact it had gone poorly.

At one merciful point Arizona secured some minor successes. For example, Frank's repeated objections to a particular aspect of California's testimony, and Rifkind's rulings to sustain his objections, a welcome moment of levity swept the federal courtroom. After ten exchanges of "objection, sustained" between Frank and the special master, Arizona's counsel allowed California's attorneys to proceed with a question to the witness. Rifkind looked quizzically at Frank and queried, "Objection?" Frank, without missing a beat, shot back, "Sustained." The brief amusing interlude notwithstanding, California's response to Arizona's case in full, consistent and based on laws—like prior appropriation—and contracts with the federal government, at this time, seemed unassailable. Ely and his team stated with confidence that under various laws, agreements, and contracts, it had the right to 5.3 million acre-feet of water per year, that the 1 million acre-feet Arizona got from the Gila should be deducted from its mainstream claim of Colorado River water, and that it was foolhardy to grant Arizona water for its farms and ranches at the expense of California's growing urban civilization. Thus at the time of Rifkind's heart attack some of the legal team thought the case against California was already lost.[28]

Back in Arizona, Governor McFarland huddled with his advisors, AISC officials, and state bar leaders to assess the situation. Arizona had presented its case in full, and most agreed that, by the spring of 1957, it was in a "hell of a mess."[29] State leaders were frantic: the dream of CAP seemed to be slipping away, much like the Supreme Court case. A flurry of dire meetings in late February and early March 1957 brought together the governor, AISC, Salt River Project, and state legislators.

On March 4, 1957, at one of several hastily organized strategy sessions in Phoenix, Wayne Akin, AISC chairman, noted that "personalities" among the lawyers, in addition to the overall deficiency in the presentation of Arizona's case, played a significant role in the downward trend of the case. One week later, at a session of the Arizona Joint Conference of the House-Senate Appropriations Committee—the committee that held the purse strings for AISC funding and therefore the lawsuit—Chairman Akin signaled the beginning of an important modification in the execution of Arizona's case: "There has been a change in strategy management," he told the committee, "from [John P.] Frank to [Charles] Reed," the respected, well-organized water rights lawyer from Coolidge. "Mr. Reed has been appointed unequivocally as the strategy manager of the suit," he added, "and he has accepted. . . . This is a radical change and will take time to organize, so it would be impossible to state what changes will be made at this time."[30]

Nielson Brown, Arizona state senator, then asked whether Frank would be kept on the team in a subordinate position. Those familiar with Frank knew the answer, but Akin responded that it depended entirely on whether Frank respected Reed's leadership and management directives. "There is no contract with him," Akin told Brown, "he is on a month to month basis . . . whether or not he stays on is entirely in the hands of the commission, and if Reed doesn't feel he would be useful and needed, they would let him go." Senator W. B. Mattice questioned Akin, wondering if AISC was unanimous in their feeling regarding the change. Akin responded, "Yes," and that there had never been any adverse debate about it. "They are definitely unanimous on this. . . . There is no equivocation about the unanimity of the commission in this matter."[31]

"When you are fighting the kind of suit we are fighting you must have the best legal talent that can be employed or you will lose the suit," Akin explained to the committee. Arizona's attorneys, he inveighed, were up against the finest talent in the United States, and they needed excellent talent to meet it. He continued, our team of five or six attorneys "are facing thirty lawyers and we can't match California dollar for dollar." (In fact, Akin estimated that California was spending $10 for every $1 that Arizona spent.) Even more, everyone in the case was under tremendous strain. Besides Master Rifkind's recent heart attack, "twenty-one people had died or become incapacitated since the trial started; lawyers have collapsed in the courtroom." In reality, Akin was arguing not only for more state funds to secure the best legal talent but also for a winning combination of people and ideas.

Chapter Six

ENTER
MARK WILMER

With Reed in place and Frank ostensibly removed from the case, Governor McFarland, AISC, and others that comprised the Arizona brain trust agreed that further changes were needed to upgrade the legal team. McFarland wanted "the best litigator available in the State of Arizona." He asked Mark Wilmer to meet him at the Capitol on March 18, 1957. Joining the governor and Wilmer at this momentous meeting were Victor Corbell, president of the Salt River Project; Superior Court Judge Charles Bernstein; AISC chairman Wayne Akin; Charles Reed, the newly installed chief counsel; and Frank Snell, Wilmer's partner.[1] "I don't remember there being any extended discussion," Wilmer recalled in 1989. "I had talked with Charlie Reed a little bit about it" and knew the case was in disarray. Wilmer said that it was "sort of a delicate situation.... Charlie [Reed] and I had talked about it quite a bit ... I had previously employed him in cases and we had worked together before. They explained to me what a problem they had ... the problem with John P. Frank and the problem with everything. So, I had a general knowledge of where the thing was, but I wasn't particularly up on it.... Anyway, McFarland simply said that it had reached a point where they were going to make a change and, 'We're advised by the local Bar that they recommend you.' We didn't have a hell of a lot to talk about ... because I knew generally what it was all about and I knew it was in a hell of a mess and I guess I felt I had no choice."[2]

The evening prior to this fateful meeting, Governor McFarland had called Wilmer at his home, told him that the Arizona Bar Association, and virtually everyone else in the legal community, recommended that he take over the *Arizona v California* case. After hanging up the phone and inform-ing his wife and four children that he was visiting Governor McFarland the next day, he added that he might be doing "the biggest thing in history, or else I might get run out of town."[3]

Much was at stake for Wilmer and his increasingly prominent law firm. During the 1940s and 1950s, Snell & Wilmer had become much more than an institutional legal giant; in many ways it now shaped the state's civil, economic, and political agenda. Significantly, Joseph T. Melczer, Jr., and James Walsh, Wilmer's former housemate and legal partner in the 1930s, joined the firm shortly after World War II and it became known as Snell, Wilmer, Walsh, and Melczer. Then, Edwin Beauchamp arrived, and his name was added to the letterhead. Recognizing the unwieldy nature of the firm's name, Walsh, the lawyer to whom everyone went with tough problems, in 1950 suggested that the firm name be shortened to Snell & Wilmer.[4] All agreed.

In the 1950s, as the firm grew in attorney numbers and prestige, it located its offices in the Heard Building in downtown Phoenix. More importantly, the firm's regional prominence and contributions to the bar and the community were increasingly noteworthy. Wilmer, as evidenced by his appointment to try the *Arizona v California* case, had established his position as the preeminent trial lawyer in Arizona. Snell, on the other hand, had emerged as a visionary who helped Phoenix and Arizona capitalize on post–World War II economic and cultural opportunities. For example, he was instrumental in the merger of the state's two largest utilities into Arizona Public Service and also helped find a constructive use for an abandoned World War II flight training facility in Glendale. The American Graduate School of International Management— the Thunderbird School—continues to play a key role in training graduate students in the complex area of international and global economic issues. His efforts at reforming the corrupt city government with fellow community leaders Walter Bimson, Sherman Hazeltine, and Eugene Pulliam, among others, laid the groundwork for a more efficient local and state government that needed to address the needs of thousands of returning veterans and their families after World War II. And, during the 1950s, as *Arizona v California* wound its way from San Francisco to Washington, D.C., Snell and other members of the firm worked quietly yet diligently to end segregation in Arizona.[5]

Just prior to the announcement that Wilmer would join the state's legal team in *Arizona v California,* John P. Frank called a press conference and announced that he was resigning from the case. The tone and timing of the public pronouncement upset Wilmer and a lot of other people, including Governor McFarland. Frank said that he must now move on to greater

challenges; Arizona's case in chief had been presented, the heavy lifting had
been done, and now the second team of lawyers needed to follow through
with the foundation he had laid. One prominent attorney commented,
"Wilmer never forgave him for that."[6]

On April 3, 1957, the change to Arizona's legal team became public. On
that day, the *Arizona Republic's* editorial page announced under the headline,
"Water Case Shift," "Wayne Akin, Chairman of the Interstate Stream
Commission, has announced a major shakeup in the legal staff representing
Arizona's water suit against California." The editorial outlined the reason for
the change: "The conduct of the entire Arizona case seems to have been
marked more by intramural bickering than by the presentation of a factual,
hard-hitting case which would impress the Court.... But you don't have to
be a Sherlock Holmes to deduce that Arizona finds itself in a less than satisfactory situation at present." "Otherwise," the editorial offered, "there
wouldn't have been a switch in command ... and we trust that the reorganization will have a salutary effect on the entire legal staff and will result in a
sharper, more effective presentation of the state's case." Thus, during Rifkind's
two-month-long recovery period, Governor McFarland, the legislature, and
AISC officials took dramatic and decisive action and named "Charles H.
Reed, Coolidge lawyer," as "chief counsel for Arizona when Supreme Court
hearings resume in California next month." "He replaces J. H. Moeur, of
Phoenix," the editorial continued, "who remains general counsel for the
Interstate Stream Commission (an official Arizona body) but who will hence-
forth have nothing to do with the Supreme Court case." Moeur's health had
deteriorated; the *Republic* allowed, "Mr. Reed is a younger, more vigorous
man who has been counsel for the San Carlos Water District for many years."

Almost as an afterthought the *Republic* reported, "Mark Wilmer,
Phoenix attorney, will join the Arizona staff in the position of lead trial
counsel. He is regarded as one of Arizona's most competent trial lawyers and
shall be of immense value when the trial reopens before Judge Rifkind, the
Supreme Court Master in the case." Fifty-four years old and at the height of
a highly successful legal career, Wilmer took on the case of his lifetime.[7] His
life, and the State of Arizona, would never be the same.

Wilmer and Reed shared a mutual respect and admired each other's
professional abilities. Wilmer later described Reed as "an exceptionally
hard-working man ... a good lawyer. He understood what law was all

about .... Charlie was just a hell of a good lawyer." Additionally, Wilmer liked the challenge he faced, although Reed, when he began talks with Wilmer about the new legal team, had told him, "You've got a loser at this point." And then, they addressed their respective roles in administering the case. "I don't remember how this discussion came about," Wilmer reflected, but early on we discussed Charlie's "position in the case." Because Wilmer held him in very high regard, he said, "'Well, Charlie, look. Why don't we do this, you be the Chief Counsel and I'll try the damned lawsuit.' Because I wasn't going to have anyone else try the lawsuit. I can't do that." After the two agreed to the division of labor and responsibility, Wilmer said, "Go tell Wayne Akin it's all right with me.' And, he did." So Reed was listed as chief counsel with the understanding that Wilmer was running the lawsuit. Put another way, Wilmer wanted unfettered right to try the case as he saw it and immediately worked out an agreement whereby his role and the role of Charlie Reed were clearly defined in the newly constituted legal team.[8] In short, Wilmer would try the case and Reed would manage the Arizona legal team.

Regarding the state of the case when he accepted the offer from Governor McFarland and AISC, Wilmer stated, "When John P. Frank had been sort of calling the shots with this guy from New York, Ted Kiendl ... he got the lawsuit in a sorry mess, to speak frankly about it, and Charlie had been there as the lawyer from the San Carlos District. And there was Jack [John E.] Madden, and there was Cal [Calvin H.] Udall, and Burr Sutter, and I don't remember the others. When Arizona's case had been completed and California had started to put their case on, one of the early California witnesses was on with respect to the prior appropriative rights of Imperial Valley and California, of which, of course, they had a jillion. John Frank had been telling the local boys, Madden and Cal and Reed, 'don't worry about it. I've got it under control.' Wilmer advised that things were not under control because, really at that point, it "was life or death." The Master took Frank's relevancy objection under advisement and "then he'd denied our objection," to California's prior appropriation evidence. The Californians would continue to hook their legal star to prior appropriations: first in use, first in right.

Wilmer knew the fundamental problem was that Arizona lacked a legal theory, like prior appropriation, to support its case. In April and May 1957, Wilmer and the staff searched for a legal theory to frame their case; they "twisted and turned and looked and looked." "You know," he said, "ultimately you got to get something that you feel in your head is sound, is honest, is realistic." In the context of his researching the case he came across the debates in the *Congressional Record* about the bills introduced by California that led to the passage of the Boulder Canyon Project Act of 1928. The project act, according to Wilmer's reading, besides providing for the construction of Hoover Dam also arguably allocated the waters of the lower Colorado River basin. California got 4.4 million acre-feet per year; Arizona, 2.8 million acre-feet; and Nevada, 300,000. He read with great interest another provision that required California to pass a law limiting itself to the 4.4 million-acre feet annually from the Colorado as stated in the project act. The more he studied the project act and the events that led to it, the more he realized that the "only sound basis we had was the fact that Arizona was intended by Congress to receive the 2.8 million-acre feet per year. The more we studied that the more we became satisfied that not only was that a feasible, but that it was a controlling, consideration."

In effect, Congress' intent to award Arizona 2.8 million acre-feet was the way to overcome California's claim to appropriative rights exceeding 4.4 million acre-feet. Also, Wilmer, who grew up in Wisconsin, recalled an early Supreme Court case from his native state where "someone had built a dam." He continued, "The question was, who got the water? The Supreme Court said the party who stores the water has the right to distribute it, and here was the United States, who had stored water in the Boulder Canyon reservoir and Congress had the right to say how this water was to be distributed."[9]

In terms of refitting and redeploying Arizona's legal resources in the spring of 1957, Wilmer and Reed made critical moves: "We decided, first of all, that we didn't want John Frank on board" and "secondly that we would get rid of Ted Kiendl, but maybe it shouldn't be too quickly." Kiendl was one of the top trial lawyers with one of the major New York law firms. Another well-known New York lawyer, Arthur Dean, had first been engaged to represent Arizona, but his firm's California clients "raised hell," causing Dean to conclude that he had a conflict of interest. Dean had recommended Kiendl, who was also very well known, but, according to Wilmer, was too old. Reed and Wilmer decided to keep Kiendl on the team because, unlike Frank, "he was too well-liked." They carried him along for their first session with the special master, after he had reconvened the case; at the end of the first set of hearings with Wilmer now arguing the case, Kiendl knew he had done nothing and he said, "Let me go." So, according to Wilmer, "that left Charlie and me running the case."[10] Later, when asked if at this time he was lead counsel in the case, Wilmer responded, "Well, I was lead counsel in the sense that I took Ted Kiendl's and John Frank's place."[11]

In brief, in 1957–58, three important changes took place that reshaped regional history: Governor McFarland and state leaders, wisely, reconfigured Arizona's legal team, replacing John P. Frank and Theodore Kiendl with Charles Reed and Mark Wilmer. Wilmer, in turn, filed a courageous "Amended and Supplemental Statement of Position" in the summer of 1957, and, finally, one year later, on August 13, 1958, Arizona filed its amended pleading, which formed the sum and substance of the arguments that resulted in the favorable *Special Master's Report* in 1960 and the victory in the Supreme Court in 1963.[12]

WILMER'S GAMBIT

Perhaps the single most significant legal ploy that took place in the long history of the struggle for Arizona's rights to Colorado River system water occurred on August 5, 1957, when Wilmer filed the strongly worded "Amended and Supplemental Statement of Position by Complainant, State of Arizona" in which it argued that its prior position was no longer operative, was unsound and not based in the law. As Wilmer expressed it in the amended statement of position: "Arizona considers its Statement of Position heretofore filed herein and certain legal conclusions and arguments set forth in its various pleadings filed herein unsound and not supported in the law in relation to the proper interpretation of Sections 4(a), 5, and 8 of the project act and Articles 3 and VIII of the Compact."[13] The audacity of the document cannot be overstated. Wilmer had commenced what became a remarkable turnabout in the case: "We jumped off a cliff," he said.[14]

Wilmer said he used "rather strong language" because if he did not "we might be shut out and never go to the window to collect the bet." Some of his advisors, however, expressed skepticism about this approach; for that reason they asked Governor McFarland to review the amended petition prior to submission to the Court. "He did. Spent nearly a full day" on it, Wilmer said. Then, voluntarily, McFarland issued a statement approving of the action and endorsed it. Thus if Wilmer and the legal team "went down the river, he went with us." "McFarland," Wilmer later reflected, "really endeared himself to me."[15]

The *Arizona Republic* announced on August 6, 1957, "Arizona Changes Claim in Colorado Water Suit: Gila Rights Held Separate," and proceeded to outline for its readers the profound change in strategy that had taken place between mid-February and early August. With Governor McFarland in attendance in the San Francisco courtroom to seal the significance of Wilmer's gambit, the *Republic* distilled the legal modification for its readers: "Arizona formally changed its position in the Colorado River water suit to claim 2.8 million acre-feet of water from the Colorado River in addition to the water it takes from the Gila River." "Attorney Mark Wilmer filed the change," it reported, "which amounted to a bill of 'divorcement' in that it claimed water rights to the Gila were acquired prior to and were separate from rights granted Arizona by the Colorado River Compact and the Boulder Canyon Project Act. In essence, the state now claimed that the Colorado River Compact protected perfected rights and that the Gila and tributary uses were perfected before the signing of the Compact."[16]

As noted above, this filing occurred shortly after a low point in the trial for Arizona when Judge Rifkind indicated that despite John P. Frank's prior arguments concerning the lack of relevance of appropriative rights, he would admit evidence with respect to California's claims of prior appropriation. As the case reached its nadir for Arizona in the summer of 1957, Arizona's legal team included Wilmer, Reed, Burr Sutter, John Geoffrey Will, Theodore Kiendl, Anthony O. Jones, Calvin Udall, and Robert Begam. All knew they faced a steep, uphill battle.[17]

For forty years prior to this bold filing, Arizona had adopted the position that the one million acre-feet referenced in Article 3 (b) of the Colorado River Compact of 1922 were Arizona's uses on the Gila River. Indeed Article 3 (a) and 3 (b) of this brief, four-page document had long played a crucial role for Arizona. Article 3 (a) sets forth the broad framework for dividing the waters: "There is hereby apportioned from the Colorado River System in perpetuity to the Upper Basin and the Lower Basin, respectively, the exclusive beneficial consumptive use of 7.5 million acre-feet of water per annum, which shall include all water necessary for the supply of any rights which may now exist." Article 3 (b) elaborates upon this basin system concept for apportionment: "In addition to the apportionment in paragraph A, the Lower Basin is hereby given the right to increase its beneficial consumptive use of such waters by one million acre-feet per annum." Unfortunately, during the course of

Wilmer with daughter, Elizabeth, in San Francisco during the hearings, July 1957. Wilmer Family Photo Collection.

Arizona's presentation of its case in chief, it became apparent that even under Arizona's definition of beneficial consumptive use it was using more than one million acre-feet of Gila River water. Therefore, if Gila River water were Article 3 (b) water, any excess over one-million acre-feet in the Gila would be surplus water which would have to be shared equally with Nevada and California.[18]

This meant that that this water was not subject to the California Limitation Act of 1929, which limited California to 4.4 million acre-feet of apportioned water under Article 3 (b) of the compact and one-half of the excess or surplus water "unapportioned." Thus, under the consistent position adopted by Arizona for forty years, every two acre-feet in excess of one million acre-feet utilized by Arizona on the Gila River would reduce by one foot the amount of water it could utilize from the mainstream. And, if the Court adopted California's definition of consumptive use, Arizona would be practically excluded from the utilization of mainstream waters.

In one gesture, Wilmer swept aside four decades of ill-advised argument concerning the meaning of Article 3 (b) by simple reference to Article 8 of the compact which provided that the compact should have no effect on "present perfected rights." Article 8, as it turned out, was a godsend to Arizona: "Present perfected rights to the beneficial use of waters of the Colorado River System are unimpaired by this compact. Whenever storage capacity of 5 million acre-feet shall have been provided on the main Colorado River within or for the benefit of the Lower Basin, then claims of such rights, if any, by appropriators or users of water in the Lower Basin against appropriators or users in the Upper Basin shall attach to and be satisfied from water that may be stored not in conflict with Article 3. All other rights to beneficial use of waters of the Colorado River System shall be satisfied solely from water apportioned to that Basin in which they situate."[19]

Wilmer's stroke of genius in this regard concerned a more careful reading and interpretation of the historical record. It was, as he reflected in an oral history interview with Zona Davis Lorig on September 8, 1994, the result of "thinking, thinking, thinking, thinking, and thinking." He read the eleven volumes of testimony up to the point that he entered the case and concluded, "this was bullshit, this was nonsense ... 3 (b) water had nothing to do with the case."[20]

His elaboration on this point provided a critical insight into his approach to a crucial issue. "Arizona had put on its case in full, spending most of it in proving how much water of the Gila River flow would have entered the Colorado," he told former Arizona congressman James McNulty in 1989, "but just almost nothing in the way of real hard-stuff argument. Although there was, I guess, many thousands of exhibits ... But as a matter of fact, when I took the case I had eleven volumes of crud, of the transcript. And I took it and I read every god-damned page of it." He also ventured that he was probably the only person who had read the entire transcript. He continued that prior to his taking over the case Arizona had taken the position that the Gila River was involved. But, he stated adamantly, "The Gila River was not involved." "When I went into the case, I was told that the Gila was a big object of controversy .... That the Santa Fe Compact was the big problem in that, there was this mysterious Article 3(a) and 3(b). I spent, I would say, three or four, or five months trying to figure out what in the hell the Compact had to do with it, before I finally decided, 'Well, this is just a lot of crap.' It had nothing to do with the case, really. And that's when we went from there. That's when we filed this thing with the Court that we think this case has been going in the wrong, wrong direction. We essentially confessed error as to the theory of the complaint and lawsuit, filed an amended complaint, and got the Master and the Supreme Court to go along with it."[21]

In the end, Rifkind agreed with Wilmer's interpretation that the Colorado River Compact played little, if any, role in the final disposition of the case.[22] And, the Supreme Court agreed with both. Justice Hugo Black, who delivered the opinion of the Court wrote, "We agree with the Master that apportionment of the Colorado River is not controlled by the doctrine of equitable apportionment or by the Colorado River Compact." "Nothing in that Compact purports to divide water among the Lower Basin States or in any way to affect or control any future apportionment among those States or any distribution of water within a State. That the commissioners were able to accomplish even a division of water between the basins is due to what is generally known as the 'Hoover Compromise.'"[23] The Boulder Canyon Project Act of 1928 did, in fact, reference the compact in several places and made the compact relevant to a very limited extent. The act specifically approved the compact and thereby fixed a division of waters between the basins, but it did not, as Wilmer pointed out, provide for an apportionment of water among the lower basin states.

Yet, where necessary, Wilmer used the Compact's limited relevance to his advantage. The new statement of legal position argued that Arizona's rights in the Gila River had been perfected as of 1922 upon the signing of the compact and therefore were present perfected rights under Article 8, which were not apportioned pursuant to Article 3 (b). This position, Wilmer reasoned, was further bolstered by the sound argument that the compact apportioned mainstream water between basins and not among the states of the respective basins.[24]

Furthermore, in the "Amended and Supplemental Statement of Position," Arizona claimed under Article 3 (b) that, to the extent there was any water left available in the Gila River, or any other tributary to the Colorado over and above its "present perfected" rights, it could increase its use of those tributaries up to one million additional acre-feet without participation from California because of the restrictions in the California Limitation Act of 1929. According to Wilmer, in the unlikely event that there was any surplus over these perfected rights in this additional one million acre-feet, California was entitled to a claim only up to 50 percent of this surplus.

"The Amended and Supplemental Statement of Position" was not an instance where a party's legal position was changed in the discovery stage of litigation. In this case Arizona had completed trial of its case in chief, which consumed thirty-seven court days and 5,000 pages of testimony and 200 exhibits comprising 10,000 additional pages. Also, at this time in the trial, California had nearly completed the presentation of evidence in support of its affirmative claims and in defense of Arizona's complaint.

California's chief counsel, Northcutt Ely, expressed his views on this profound change in course. He said that a portion of Arizona's statement "which indicates a disavowal of a previous legal position as 'unsound' was recognized by California as "candid and courageous" and "one not easy to make." The trouble was, he continued, that Arizona gave no indication of the extent to which it withdrew its "former allegations" and California now stood—after five years of proceedings—without precisely knowing where Arizona stood. California, Ely continued, had spent $1,034,000 in the case not counting the engineering work, the work of its Colorado River Board, and the expenditures of the co-defendant public agencies. He ended his response to Wilmer's amended filing by stating, "We cannot take lightly a complete pulling away of the underpinning of the suit on which we were hailed into court." As Wilmer recalled, "the Californians were flabbergasted."[25]

As noted earlier, an additional and more definitive modification that resulted from the amended filing was the shift from a case based on equity to a case based upon statutory apportionment. Arizona's original "Statement of Position," filed in 1952, lacked focus: it was not seeking equitable apportionment, but yet was seeking equity. In his opening statement, Ely responded for California, indicating whether Arizona admitted it or not, the case was one of equitable apportionment which California would meet on the question of equities. In the same statement, he said that California would rely heavily on the priority of appropriations in its case in chief.

Arizona's "Amended and Supplemental Statement of Position" took the battle to California on the issue of the so-called "Law of the River" as set forth in the compact, the project act, and the California Limitation Act. This was apparent in an exchange that occurred shortly after the filing of Arizona's amended position statement during a dispute over the admissibility of some California evidence.

Special Master Simon Rifkind stated, "This argument, in turn, raised the question as to whether Arizona had shifted its case from a plea based upon equity to a plea based on legal rights .... My understanding of the present position is—and I want Mr. Wilmer to listen carefully, because I want to be sure that I understand it—that Arizona bases her claim on certain legal rights arising out of the statutes, compact, and contracts." Wilmer responded, "That is correct, Your Honor."[26]

Rifkind continued, "And that it does not found its claim upon the circumstances that the birth rate in Arizona is higher than the birth rate in any other state or that the degree of migration to the State of Arizona is greater than the rate of migration to some other state. It says, 'You, Mr. California, are trespassing upon my legal rights. You have got your shoes on the metes and bounds of my land.' That is what I understand they say ... That may not be exactly the same as the theory upon which the case was originally presented. But I understand that that is the position into which Arizona has moved." Rifkind then asked if he had correctly interpreted and stated Arizona's position. Wilmer replied, "Your Honor, it is our position that under the Compact and the Project Act, Arizona has a definite right to a given quantity of water. We are asking this Court to determine that amount and to protect us in our use of it."

Wilmer continued the battle, moving it from the home ground of the Gila River to the mainstream of the Colorado for the remainder of the lawsuit. On August 13, 1958, Arizona filed an amended pleading in which it argued that the Colorado River Compact related only to the mainstream waters and not tributary waters.[27] Significantly, in this amended pleading Arizona took the position that the additional one million acre-feet of Article 3 (b) water referred to additional water flowing at Lee's Ferry to the lower basin and not to the lower basin tributary waters. Arizona asserted, therefore, that under the specific provisions of the Colorado River Basin Project Act of 1928, the water of the Gila River may only be used in Arizona and New Mexico. In effect, Wilmer recast Arizona's case as one involving principles of statutory construction and focused mainly on congressional authority and intent in the passage of the Boulder Canyon Project Act of 1928.

Put another way, Wilmer argued that Arizona had a definite statutory right to water under the terms of the project act, and that he was merely asking the Court to decide the specific amount of water and to protect Arizona's rights to that water. In sharp contrast to Arizona's previous approach, he now argued that how Arizona decided to use the water—whether for CAP or something else—was not relevant. Arizona, he asserted, needed a final determination of the statutory language creating a legal right to the water.

Opposing counsel Ely contended that language from the Colorado River Compact inhered in the project act and effectively apportioned to the lower basin states water from the entire Colorado River system rather than the mainstream only as Wilmer now contended. California argued that it could fill its 4.4 million acre-foot apportionment first out of the "system" which would include Arizona's tributaries and then turn to the mainstream as "surplus," a formula that would add a million acre-feet to California at Arizona's expense. Prior to Wilmer's arrival on the scene, Arizona countered meekly that equitable apportionment justified Arizona's dependence on and use of its tributaries.

Wilmer continued to hammer away through 1958 and sought proper statutory construction of the Boulder Canyon Project Act of 1928 to prove Arizona's rights to its own tributaries. The project act, he argued, dealt only with water in the mainstream of the Colorado River, allowing the respective states complete use of their tributaries within their borders. To prove this point, Wilmer cited the *Congressional Record* and detailed the legislative history to support his claims.

For example, in the debates surrounding the project act, the various senators, Wilmer claimed, consistently acknowledged that the tributaries—or at least the Gila—were excluded from the allocation they were making. Senator Hayden, in response to California senator Hiram Johnson, said that the California senator was correct in stating that the Senate had seen fit to give Arizona 2.8 million acre-feet in addition to all the water in the Gila.[28]

Further, Wilmer convinced the master and the Court to look even more carefully at the legislative history and debates to discern congressional intent. On May 28, 1928, the House of Representatives passed a Boulder Canyon

Project bill but did not provide for an allocation scheme. When the Senate took up the bill in December, pressure mounted quickly for amendments that would provide for apportioning the waters among the lower basin states and distributing to users within those states. Congress convened on December 3, 1928, and the Senate took up the bill two days later. Nine days later, in spite of the strong protests of Arizona senators Hayden and Ashurst, the bill, with a significant number of amendments, passed the Senate. Four days after that, on December 18, the House concurred, and on December 21, 1928, President Calvin Coolidge signed the bill.

Notably, when the bill first reached the floor of the Senate it contained a provision limiting California to 4.6 million acre-feet; Senator Hayden, on December 6, 1928, proposed reducing that amount to 4.2 million acre-feet. The next day Nevada senator Key Pittman argued forcefully that Congress should settle the matter immediately: "There is practically nothing involved except a dispute between the States of Arizona and California with regard to the division of the increased water that will be impounded behind the proposed dam; that is all .... Of the 7.5 million acre-feet of water let down that river they have gotten together within 400,000 acre-feet. They have got to get together, and if they do not get together Congress should bring them together." On December 8, New Mexico senator Sam Bratton, a lawyer and judge, suggested that the two states split the difference by limiting California to 4.4 million acre-feet. The next day the Senate adopted Bratton's amendment and on the following day, December 12, 1928, Senator Hayden asserted that the bill "settled" the dispute over the lower basin waters by giving 4.4 million acre-feet to California and 2.8 million acre-feet to Arizona. "One dispute," Hayden averred, "is how the seven and a half million acre-feet shall be divided in the lower basin. The Senate has settled that by a vote—that California may have 4.4 million acre-feet of that water. It follows logically that if the demand is to be conceded, as everybody agrees, the remainder is 2.8 million acre-feet for Arizona. That settles that part of the controversy."[29]

Clearly, Wilmer's approach to the case—rooted in history and congressional intent—convinced Judge Rifkind, in unequivocal fashion, to side with Arizona in the *Special Master's Report:* "Nothing in the words of the legislative history of Section 4(a) [of the project act] lends countenance to [California's] hypothesis. The second paragraph of Section 4(a) contemplates that Arizona could receive 2.8 million acre-feet of the 7.5 million acre-feet *in addition* to the exclusive use of the Gila within her boundaries."[30] Wilmer's reliance on the legislative history was so effective that it even overcame what one observer called "an unfortunate presumption against Arizona resulting from Justice Brandeis's 1934 Supreme Court opinion in a related water dispute between Arizona and California arising from language in the compact.[31] Later, in 1964, Wilmer wrote that "[h]ad Justice Brandeis had the benefit of this legislative history we have no doubt his opinion would have been otherwise."[32]

Special Master Rifkind's final report, issued December 5, 1960, and the decision of the Supreme Court of June 3, 1963, accepted Arizona's revised position, first promulgated on August 5, 1957. The mainstream flow of the Colorado River at Lee's Ferry was divided with 4.4 million acre-feet per year to California, 2.8 million acre-feet per year to Arizona, and 300,000 acre-feet per year to Nevada and 1.5 million acre-feet per year to the United States to satisfy its treaty obligation to Mexico.

Framing the issue as one of statutory construction rather than of various principles of water law proved remarkably effective. Upon reading the special master's *Draft Report* issued May 5, 1960, and the subsequent *Final Report and Recommended Decree,* issued December 5, 1960, Arizona took few substantive exceptions to Judge Rifkind's conclusions that affirmed Wilmer's theory.

The draft report of May 5, 1960, in fact, was the first palpable indication that Wilmer had profoundly transformed the case. Rifkind's narrative indicated that he had concluded that Arizona was entitled to 2.8 million acre-feet of water annually from the Colorado mainstream and that California could be forced to observe its self-imposed 4.4 million acre-feet limitation. Rifkind also held, at this time, that Arizona's use of Gila River water was apart from its Colorado River entitlement. As the *Arizona Republic* reported on May 10, 1960, "While the facts and the law both favored Arizona, full credit must go to attorney Mark Wilmer, who stepped into the case at a crucial point and did a remarkable job in representing Arizona."[33] Opposing counsel Ely acknowledged Wilmer's stewardship in reversing Arizona's position and on May 7, 1960, sent Arizona's litigator a letter that stated, in part: "I have the Special Master's draft report in *Arizona v California* before me, and I congratulate you upon your victory. We will do our best to upset it, of course, but you have won this round. You and your colleagues are to be congratulated on a very great accomplishment."[34]

Of course the case did not end with Rifkind's draft and final reports in 1960. There were briefs to be submitted and oral arguments before the U.S. Supreme Court. In January 1962 the Court heard sixteen hours of arguments. Ben Cole, the *Arizona Republic's* chief reporter covering the case at the time listened to the arguments and wrote, "The stars in the historic event were Arizona's Mark Wilmer, California's Northcutt Ely, and (U.S.) Solicitor General Archibald Cox. The duel between Wilmer and Ely was deeply dramatic." Cole informed his readers, "Ely is a compact man with crisp, thin hair and penetrating eyes. He opened and closed the four-day argument. Wilmer is a big man, more deliberate in speech and manner than his California opposite. When Wilmer began his argument, it was with the disadvantage a big man feels when he matches wits with a person of shorter stature. But the Phoenix lawyer quickly equalized the odds with capable handling of his argument relying wholly on the law and calmly blowing away California's case as only 10 percent material fact." The Supreme Court heard a second round of arguments, lasting six hours, on November 13 and 14, 1962; Cole wrote, "Wilmer's handling of Arizona's case was beautifully and competently presented."[35] Wilmer's daughter, Elizabeth Wilmer Sexson, then an eighteen-year-old, had attended many of the hearings with her mother and her fourteen-year-old sister, Genevieve, in San Francisco in 1958. Her memory of her father's courtroom deportment squares with Cole's. "I remember standing in that courtroom thinking about Dad, he's really good, he's *really* good, and he's good because I understand what he's talking about. He didn't talk down to people.... He was a farmer talking to his neighbor."[36]

Later, in 1963, the Supreme Court embraced the special master's findings and in its decision upheld Wilmer's core argument: "The Master concluded that, since the Lower Basin states had failed to make a compact to allocate the waters among themselves as authorized in Articles 4(a) and 8(b) [of the project act of 1928], the Secretary's [of the Interior] contracts with the States had within the statutory scheme of Articles 4(a), 5, and 8(b) effected an apportionment of the waters of the mainstream which, according to the Master, were the only waters apportioned under the Act."[37] When asked if the Supreme Court decision affirmed Rifkind's findings, Wilmer declared unequivocally, "It *did* affirm Rifkind's findings," and by implication Wilmer's arguments.[38]

Significantly, Wilmer's reliance on the debates recorded in the *Congressional Record* that led to the Boulder Canyon Project Act of 1928 proved most persuasive to the Court. The Supreme Court, in their ninety-five-page decision, quoted generously from the project act's legislative history and stated explicitly why it affirmed the special master's findings, and thus Arizona's arguments: "Under the view of Arizona ... with which we agree, the tributaries are not included in the waters to be divided but remain for the exclusive use of each State." Moreover, "Statements made throughout the debates make it quite clear that Congress intended the 7.5 million acre-feet it was allocating, and out of which California was limited to 4.4 million acre-feet only." The Court affirmed Wilmer's fundamental premise: "We are persuaded by the legislative history as a whole that the Act was not intended to give California any claim to share in the tributary waters of the Lower Basin states."[39]

In analyzing this aspect of the decision, the Court agreed with the master, and therefore Wilmer, that apportionment of the lower basin waters was not controlled by the doctrine of equitable apportionment or by the compact. The Court had acknowledged that it had used the doctrine of equitable apportionment to decide river controversies between states in the past, but, in those cases, Congress had not made any statutory apportionment. In *Arizona v California,* however, the Court decided that Congress had provided its own method for allocating among the lower basin states the mainstream water that they were entitled under the compact. Significantly, the Court ruled, "Where Congress has exercised its constitutional power over waters courts have no power to substitute their own notions of 'equitable apportionment' for the apportionment chosen by Congress."

What did Congress intend concerning apportionment of mainstream water? Under California's view, which the Court rejected, the first 7.5 million acre-feet of lower basin water, of which California had agreed to use only 4.4 million acre-feet, was made up of both mainstream and tributary water—not just mainstream water. Wilmer, however, in a relatively short time, convinced the justices that the tributaries were not to be divided but remain for the exclusive uses of each state. Further, Wilmer's research and case arguments revealed that the negotiations among the states in the 1920s and the congressional debates leading to the passage of the project act showed clearly that the language used by Congress in the act was meant to refer to mainstream waters only. Justice Black punctuated this point in his written opinion: "Inclusion of the tributaries in the compact was natural in view of the upper states' strong feeling that the Lower Basin tributaries should be made to share the burden of any obligation to deliver water to Mexico which a future treaty might impose. But when it came to an apportionment among the Lower Basin States, the Gila, by far the most important Lower Basin tributary, would not logically be included, since Arizona alone of the states could effectively use that river. Therefore, with minor exceptions, the proposals and counterproposals over the years, culminating in the Project Act, consistently provided for division of mainstream only, reserving the tributaries to each State's exclusive use."

When the Supreme Court ruling was finally announced on June 3, 1963, Arizona's congressional delegation and the legal team who argued the case considered it a huge victory. Cal Udall marveled at what had transpired and later said, "Mark and Charlie were great litigation leaders; Mark was the consummate oral advocate. His calm and effective style (and his insistence that his younger trial helpers, like the late Jack Madden and me, behave similarly) could not be overcome by the offerings of California's Chief Counsel and his many assistants."[40] The *Arizona Republic* front page announced on June 4, 1963, "The end of the eleven-year legal battle with California will shape the future of Arizona for all time to come and ranks in importance with the state's admission to the union. It will open the way for the long sought Central Arizona Project to bring water from the river into the populous centers of the state. [Senator] Hayden has already prepared legislation to authorize construction of the $1 billion project and expects to introduce it very soon." Characteristically, Wilmer took the victory in stride, expressing gratification and accepting congratulations from all who knew him, yet remaining low key and with his family. The Court, Wilmer told those around him, reasoned correctly that Congress "intended to and did create its own comprehensive scheme for ... apportionment." In addition, Congress had authorized the secretary of interior to utilize his contract power to implement a lower basin agreement. In fact, the Court gave Arizona what it had wanted since 1922, and *Arizona Republic* reporter Cole called the decision, "a personal triumph for Carl Hayden because the decision referred back twenty-five years to the December 12, 1928, debate in which Hayden pointed out that the Boulder Canyon Dam bill and its allocation formula settled the dispute over the lower basin waters."

After reading the opinion and dissent, Senator Hayden issued a rare statement to the press: "Naturally, I am pleased that the Supreme Court has in general followed the Special Master's recommendations with reference to the division of waters of the Colorado River. This is especially gratifying because it makes possible at last for us to put our rightful share of the waters to use in the Colorado River basin."[41] Governor Paul Fannin, an uncommonly discreet and subtle politician, measured his obvious enthusiasm: "I know our citizens recognize the responsibility we now have to forget any internal differences and join in a coordinated effort to derive the maximum benefits from the results of the Supreme Court decision."[42]

On June 5, 1963, two days after the decision, the *Arizona Republic,* in understated fashion, paid homage to Wilmer. Page five featured a small photo of Wilmer with the bold caption, "Draws Praise." Two short sentences completed the story: "Mark Wilmer, quiet-spoken Phoenix attorney yesterday was being showered with congratulations from colleagues throughout the state for the part he played in the Colorado River lawsuit. Wilmer handled most of the courtroom work."[43] Arizona's other attorneys who fought the eleven-year battle were jubilant, though two who played roles in the early days of the suit, Charles Carson and J. H. "Hub" Moeur, had passed away and were unable to share in the afterglow of the legal victory.[44]

Theodore Kiendl, the deposed New York attorney who left after Wilmer took over the case in 1957, demonstrated a high degree of elegance in a congratulatory letter to Wilmer written June 4, 1963. "On my way to the office this morning," he wrote, "I was delighted to read that Arizona was upheld over California in the Supreme Court decision, with but one dissent and that from the unpredictable Mr. Justice Douglas." He continued, "I suppose you have been deluged with congratulatory messages but I do want you to know that I attribute the result obtained, both from the Special Master, Judge Rifkind, and the Supreme Court of the United States, was due in no small measure to the genius of your advocacy. No greater result could have been obtained, and for the rest of your professional career you will be nationally known and admired for your coming to the rescue of the State of Arizona in the emergency that confronted it." Kiendl praised the work of Bill Meagher in the preparation of the briefs before the Supreme Court and added a telling afterthought, "I am writing both Judge Rifkind and Bill Meagher today, and hope that you will tell others interested in the Arizona victory how pleased the states' chief counsel in the beginning of the litigation is with the result that he feared would not readily be obtained."[45]

California, stung by the outcome, reacted with apprehension. They charged the Court with misreading the intent of Congress, eroding the rights of the states, and argued that the ruling represented the first time that the Court had interpreted an act of Congress as apportioning water rights to interstate streams. This untoward judicial prerogative threatened California, and Arizona leaders knew well that California would try to regain in the political arena what they had lost in the judicial decision. Roy Elson, Senator Hayden's administrative aide, described the situation on the heels of Arizona's Supreme Court victory: "We knew that California and Northcutt Ely would try some way to stop this through the legislative process, even though they had lost .... What they couldn't accomplish in court they would try in the field of politics."[46] Indeed, Elson's musings were on target. The Associated Press, on June 4, 1963, quoted California attorney general Stanley Mosk: "California's 38 member House delegation still could give Arizona substantial opposition in authorizing new Colorado River projects."[47] In short, California would oppose CAP as it had prior to the lawsuit.

Arizona's congressional delegation, keenly aware that Wilmer's legal handiwork had, by 1960, created an atmosphere for an Arizona victory in the case, began laying the political groundwork for another, and hopefully final, legislative push for CAP. The Arizona delegation, led by Senator Hayden, let it be known that it had supported several big reclamation packages for the upper basin states including the Colorado River Storage Act of 1956, which led to the construction of Glen Canyon Dam. Also, Arizona backed numerous individual state projects like New Mexico's San Juan Project, which passed Congress in 1962. In light of these palpable examples of support for regional development, Arizona's congressional leaders believed they deserved the same kind of consideration for CAP.

Yet between 1960 and 1963 the anticipation of a Supreme Court decision favorable to Arizona prompted federal administrators and representatives in the basin to begin formulating a regional plan for the entire basin—not just Arizona. In fact, in January 1962, Secretary of Interior Stewart Udall, a former Arizona congressman, encouraged Congressman Wayne Aspinall (D-Colorado), chairman of the influential House Interior and Insular Affairs Committee, to request a comprehensive study of water development in preparation for the authorization of individual state projects—including CAP—as soon as a decision in *Arizona v California* was rendered.[48]

The looming legislative fight in the last chapter of the quest for CAP notwithstanding, other aspects of the Court decision departed from past rulings. The secretary of the interior would allocate future surpluses and shortages among and within states. This dimension of the opinion marked, as one expert on the Colorado River has written, "an especially sharp break with tradition." Moreover, the Court majority ruled that Congress could invoke the navigation clause of the U.S. Constitution as well as the "general welfare" clause to divide the waters of non-navigable and navigable streams. This dimension of the ruling, as Justice William O. Douglas wrote in his tart dissent, increased drastically federal control over the nation's rivers. He wrote, in part: "Much is written these days about judicial lawmaking, and every scholar knows that judges who construe statutes must of necessity legislate interstitially ... the present case is different. It will, I think, be marked as the baldest attempt by judges in modern times to spin their own philosophy into the fabric of law in derogation to the will of the legislature. The present decision as Mr. Justice [John] Harlan shows, grants the federal bureaucracy a power and command over water rights in the seventeen western states that it has never had, that it has always wanted, that it could never persuade Congress to grant, and that this court up to now has consistently refused to recognize." In spite of the scathing dissent and charged rhetoric the ruling seemed to clear the way for Arizona to press forward legislatively for CAP.

Beyond the positive implications for Arizona and CAP, *Arizona v California* gave American Indians cause for hope. As noted earlier, when Arizona filed suit in 1952, the federal government intervened not only to protect its interests in the river, but also to defend the rights of American Indians living on the twenty-five reservations within the lower basin. Predictably, U.S. attorneys petitioned for water for all practically irrigable lands on Indian reservations as well as national parks, forests, recreation areas, and other federal lands. In their decision, the justices ruled for the government, although narrowly circumscribing the decision to include five reservations abutting the mainstream of the Colorado River—Fort Mohave, Chemehuevi, Cocopah, Yuma, and Colorado River. Basing its determination on *Winters v United States* (1908) that their rights extended to water to sustain their economies: "It is impossible to believe that when Congress created the ... Colorado Indian Reservation and when the Executive Department of the Nation created the other reservations they were unaware that most of the lands were desert .... and that water from the river would be essential to the life of the Indian people." In determining the amount the Indians were to receive, moreover, the Court adopted the government's position and awarded water based on practicable irrigable acreage. And, in a later supplemental decree, it added that the Indians were not restricted in the uses to which they would put their water. One scholar pithily observed, "Reason, rather than agriculture seemed to emerge as the ultimate test."[49]

Wilmer, like Arizona's leaders, expressed deep concern that the decision declared that Indian uses were to be charged against the state in which the reservation was located. Arizona, therefore, bore the majority of the burden of "Indian" water. Further, the justices ruled that Indian water rights dated from the establishment of a reservation and were thus superior to later, non-Indian rights, including those rights based on uses initiated before Indians had begun diverting water from the Colorado or its tributaries. Wilmer realized that *Arizona v California* left the tribes in a much stronger legal position than they previously maintained. The Court therefore reaffirmed *Winters,* asserting that Indian water rights existed whether or not they were actually using the water and continued unimpaired even if they should cease their uses. Some of the lands along the lower reaches of the Colorado had been set aside as early as 1865 and none later than 1917.[50]

Certainly, Wilmer's reading of the situation, his interpretation, and his arguments before Special Master Rifkind had paid Arizona substantial dividends. When he took over the position as special counsel in Arizona's water rights case against California in 1957, Wilmer understood his responsibility and that Arizona had little, if any, prospect of winning a case against California based upon a theory of equitable apportionment. Further, injecting a significant change in strategy late in the case—after Arizona had presented its case in full—was extremely risky. "Supposing we were wrong, and supposing the master throws this into the trash can—this theory we have," he recalled in a 1985 interview about the case, "Hell, we are going to have to go back to Phoenix and Arizona with not only egg on our face, we're going to be run out of the state."[51] Despite this risk and the possible dire consequences, Wilmer effectively convinced the special master and the Supreme Court of the value and veracity of his innovative legal theory. Because of that theory, Arizona has been enjoying its right to Colorado River water for nearly a half-century and will continue to do so into the future.

Wilmer's recollections and interpretations of what transpired 1957–1963 provide yet another relevant and personal perspective on these historic events. They also indicate the complexity and pressure that the attorneys faced amidst the grueling ordeal. During those six years, he recalled, the case devoured "a hell of a lot of time .... See, [Special Master] Rifkind went all through the rest of California's case" when he entered the trial in 1957. "Then he went through the cases of the California subsidiaries: Imperial

Frank Snell and Mark Wilmer at the wedding reception of Edwin and Genevieve Hendricks, August 10, 1963. Wilmer Family Photo Collection.

Valley, and up in the river and up to Indio and all of their cases. And then he went through the Nevada and the New Mexico cases. So it was August [28] 1958 when the Master finally closed the book and went to a briefing stage." By this time, however, Wilmer allowed that he thought his arguments had gained traction with the master, and he could tell that Ely and the California team were less confident than when he entered the case the previous year.

When questioned later about arguing the case before the U.S. Supreme Court he corrected, "Twice." When pressed why he went to the Supreme Court a second time to argue before the justices he said, "Well, I don't know, they don't state grounds, you know. We briefed it, Charlie [Reed], Burr Sutter ... Bill Meagher from a New York firm who was invaluable in briefing"; the case also participated between 1958 and 1960. "Anyway," Wilmer continued, "we spent the summer up in Prescott writing the brief to the Master and then of course we had to reply to California briefs and they replied to ours. And then it was all submitted to the Special Master but not argued to him. And then he ... announced his preliminary opinion.... This authorized us to file objections and so on, which we did. And, California, of course, filed a jillion of them. We went back to New York and argued that [the objections] for a day or two days. Then he took it back under advisement and then he filed his final report. And then we set about briefing that to the Supreme Court which was again another three months, four months job."[52]

Wilmer's reflections on his time arguing before the Supreme Court, especially the unusual process of a second hearing, added another fascinating dimension to the case. "Earl Warren was Chief Justice and because he was from California he recused himself and [Hugo L.] Black became acting Chief Justice. And we argued it the first time for three or four or five days, maybe .... They gave us an ungodly amount of time. And it was taken under advisement.... the labor lawyer [Justice Arthur] Goldberg was very friendly. We had a friendly court in one sense, except for this guy [Justice William O. Douglas], a horse's ass. The guy that was always going up to Oregon and dancing around with young girls .... but a capable lawyer. Douglas. But he gave us some trouble and ... apparently the Court was not satisfied and they took it under advisement .... So then it was resubmitted again in October [actually mid-November], I guess it was, for again a three or four or five-day argument."[53]

When asked later about opposition counsel for California, Wilmer was forthcoming with his opinions. "Oh, sure I remember him. He was an Arizona boy, Northcutt Ely. He was a hell of a lawyer; a hard worker, and a nitpicker .... They [California] had a whole goddamned building of engineers and lawyers back there at San Francisco. I went over one time to inquire as to somebody and they sent me down to the switchboard to find out where the hell he was, what office he was in ... there on Market Street .... We [Arizona's attorneys and engineers] had one floor on the Federal Building, which is about as wide as—well, it had two stories. California had a hell of a lot of help that didn't do them any good."[54]

The core arguments that Mark Wilmer brought to the *Arizona v California* case in the spring of 1957 altered the history of the Pacific Southwest. Wilmer transformed Arizona from a weak team playing ineffective defense into an offensive juggernaut that blew by California at the end of the game. Rifkind's musings in 1986 squared with the historical record; Wilmer turned around a situation that, in 1957, looked desperate and changed the course of regional history.[55]

In the course of eleven years, and at a cost of nearly $5 million, 340 witnesses and fifty lawyers produced 25,000 pages of testimony. When a sharply divided court announced its opinion on June 3, 1963, followed by its decree on March 9, 1964, it greatly modified the legal framework governing the apportionment and use of Colorado River water among the lower basin states (Arizona, California, Nevada, and part of New Mexico). Especially important for Arizona, the court awarded the Grand Canyon State a significant portion of Colorado River water previously claimed by California, thereby clearing the way for final legislative action on CAP.[56]

Chapter Seven

A Brave New Water World: Law, Politics, and CAP

The direct and enduring manifestation of Wilmer's legal genius before the Supreme Court was CAP. An indirect, and equally enduring, result was a generation of institutional ingenuity concerning water acquisition, distribution, conservation, use, and reuse of Colorado River water within Arizona. In the decision's aftermath, Arizona's eighty-five-year-old Senator Carl Hayden phoned Don Smith, a reporter for *U.S. News and World Report,* and placed the historic legal development in context while at the same time sounding the clarion call for another political battle against California: "The decision of the U.S. Supreme Court on the division of Colorado River water is the most significant federal action in history affecting the state of Arizona. This action must be followed by the construction of CAP." On June 4, 1963, one day after the Court's ruling, Arizona senators Hayden and Goldwater and the three House members of Arizona's delegation introduced legislation to authorize CAP. Indeed, Arizona's victory in the Supreme Court represented the end of one distinct phase in the century-long struggle with California over the Colorado River and the beginning of another.[1]

The new CAP bill, S 1658, though resembling similar measures of the 1940s and 1950s, was nevertheless more ambitious than its pre–*Arizona v California* predecessors. It provided for a diversion of 1.2 million acre-feet of water annually out of the Colorado River to supplement irrigation and municipal water to central and southern Arizona. In order to facilitate this transfer, the bill called for the construction of five dams and reservoirs, two power plants, and transmission and distribution facilities on the Colorado and its tributaries as well as in western New Mexico. A key feature of this version of the legislation was a 740-foot-high dam at Bridge Canyon on the Colorado River. If built, it would be the highest dam in the Western Hemisphere and its power plant would have an installed capacity of 1.5

million kilowatts. One-third of this capacity would be transmitted south to pump water over a canal and aqueduct system from the existing Parker Dam on the Colorado 219 miles to Phoenix and 341 miles to Tucson.

Significantly, in January 1962 the Bureau of Reclamation completed a second feasibility study on CAP. It estimated that CAP would provide additional water to irrigate 880,000 acres of land and would provide at least 303,000 acre-feet of municipal and industrial use water for 1.1 million people, primarily in urban centers Phoenix and Tucson. In the fifteen years that had elapsed between the two feasibility reports on CAP, Arizona's population had increased from 700,000 to 1.4 million, and irrigated acreage in central Arizona jumped from 566,000 to 1 million acres. Arizona's groundwater supplies raised questions of scarcity, and data indicated that Arizona had mined its groundwater basins at an alarming rate in recent years. In fact, the groundwater level in Maricopa County was dropping at the rate of ten feet per year; in Pinal County, twenty feet per year. In several areas of central Arizona wells were going dry or saline water was seeping into them, rendering these supplies useless. Worse, the ground was subsiding due to overpumping. C. A. Pugh, area engineer for the Bureau of Reclamation, was especially alarmed and estimated the overdraft of groundwater basins in the state totaled 2.2 million acre-feet annually. The net delivery of water from CAP amounted to what bureau engineers estimated at 1.07 million acre-feet per year. CAP could not possibly replenish more than half the water deficit in Arizona at that rate of use.[2]

Meanwhile, the John F. Kennedy administration, and particularly Secretary of Interior Stewart Udall, threw a wrench into the CAP political machinery. Udall introduced an enormous regional water resource development plan that he considered "constructive water statesmanship." In August 1963, after the Supreme Court case had been decided and CAP bills introduced, Udall unveiled a huge $8 billion plan—the Pacific Southwest Water Plan, which included projects in five western states—and sent it to the seven basin states and five federal departments for review. Udall, in his utopian endeavor, intended to erase what he considered "the outmoded concept of state lines" and address water issues on a comprehensive and regional basis. No state with water entitlements was left out of the ambitious PSWP scheme.

Seven of the proposed seventeen projects benefited Arizona, California, Nevada, New Mexico, and Utah. The plan, moreover, sought to harmonize the interests of Arizona and Southern California, the main battlefield in *Arizona v California,* with several projects designed to minimize California's concerns about Arizona withdrawals from the mainstream of the Colorado. Water transfer from northern to southern California, water salvage and conservation projects, and several new reclamation projects within the Golden State were included in order to mitigate California concerns. Beyond these attempts to assuage California water and power interests, Udall sought to exploit common ground among various regional stakeholders by proposing two huge hydroelectric dams, Bridge Canyon and Marble Canyon, to be located near Grand Canyon National Park. In essence, these were cash register dams that would underwrite the costs of the entire PSWP, thus guaranteeing the region's economic future. Udall framed his justification in almost urgent terms: "A critical need is at hand, a more critical period lies ahead for millions of people flocking to the Pacific Southwest to establish permanent homes. This burgeoning population will require vast quantities of additional water for industrial and municipal use; greater quantities of electricity and other basic services; and more irrigated lands. Piecemeal development can not do the job. Only regional planning and action will enable us to meet the growth of this area."[3]

Arizonans were incensed with the Kennedy administration and especially Secretary Udall. Over the next two years state leaders, in uncompromising language, let Udall know that the overdrawn PSWP was yet another method for delaying consideration of CAP, and it played directly into the hands of California. Paul Fannin, then Arizona governor, framed the situation in succinct terms: "PSWP is a plot against Arizona born in California and formalized in the Interior Department by California's undersecretary [Undersecretary of the Interior James Carr].... We must and will go it alone with the CAP as proposed by [Senator Carl] Hayden in S 1658.... It is already apparent that the report was cleverly written by someone in the Department of Interior to give California a logical excuse for delaying any and all favorable action on either a practical regional plan or the CAP which is now before Congress. In spite of a favorable Court decision...California can and will continue to use our share of the river until we obtain congressional authorization of CAP."[4]

Udall, in fact, took editorial abuse from virtually every newspaper, radio, and television station in Arizona. Moreover, younger brother and Arizona congressman Morris Udall was the focus of harsh and arguably unfair criticism. As the *Arizona Republic* opined: "Voters know where Stewart Udall stands.... Will Morris Udall align himself with the rest of the Arizona delegation, which unanimously supports the project. Or will he, in deference to his brother, sit on the sidelines and refuse to help Arizona?" Secretary Udall, shortly after this editorial, blinked and sent a conciliatory note to Senator Hayden. Conceding a "weekly horsewhipping from the Phoenix newspapers," Udall expressed resentment over what he termed a personal attack by Senator Goldwater and the unwarranted attacks on his younger brother. He sought a truce with Hayden's office, ending with the admonition, "It is largely up to the two of us to hold the whole thing together." As a result of Secretary Udall's attempt at reconciliation, both camps made a chilly pledge to confer on matters of CAP strategy; however, they agreed to disagree about a go-it-alone CAP bill versus a regional plan embodied in PSWP.[5]

Presidential politics, however, lay at the heart of Arizona's legislative frustrations in 1963 and 1964. According to several Capitol Hill insiders, President Kennedy and Secretary Udall, concerned that California's substantial electoral votes could be compromised in the 1964 general election, decided to minimize the impact of the Supreme Court decision as well as Arizona's attempts to secure CAP legislation. As Senator Hayden's administrative aide, Roy Elson, described the unwritten agreement, "Let's not rock the boat with anything that's going to cause a problem with California, especially southern California." *The Yuma Daily Sun* agreed and, on June 16, 1963, editorialized: "The mounting opposition of the politically powerful state of California is another obstacle. There is also the task of getting the approval of the Kennedy administration which will be ardently courting California's forty electoral votes in 1964, an election year."[6]

By 1964 California had grown into the largest state in the nation. It counted thirty-seven more electoral votes than increasingly Republican Arizona, and political pundits knew that President Kennedy would not dismiss the arguments of California's Democratic governor, Edmund G. "Pat" Brown or the state's forty-member congressional delegation. President Kennedy did not want it to appear that Udall was taking sides. Thus, CAP, in its long and tortured legislative journey, encountered yet another detour due to presidential politics. The political realities were evident: Arizona's three electoral votes, which would probably go to the Republican candidate—

its own junior senator, Barry Goldwater—were expendable. California's forty votes were not.

Though lacking in population and electoral clout Arizona still had formidable political capital. Senator Hayden, whose accumulated power and influence in the Senate was legendary, chaired the Senate Committee on Appropriations. He could, if necessary, hold up every other water project in the country. Further, an Arizona "task force" arrived in Washington to assist the congressional delegation in its efforts, drawing from the state's water establishment. The Arizona Interstate Stream Commission, Arizona Public Service, Salt River Project, and the Central Arizona Project Association each sent personnel to Capitol Hill to assist in the legal, engineering, and political nuances that needed legislative attention. Senator Hayden took the lead and, though elderly and frail, between 1963 and 1968 his parliamentary maneuverings and numerous testimonies before various committees and subcommittees were essential in building upon the legal victory in the Supreme Court.

Hayden testified on three key themes: that Arizona's efforts to obtain its full share of Colorado River water had been repeatedly opposed by the deliberate delaying tactics of California; that the simple and readily understood CAP, which had been before Congress for fifteen years was now being subsumed within one of the most controversial, complex, and confusing water resource plans ever presented; and that despite rumors to the contrary, there was enough water in the river for the CAP under the *Arizona v California* ruling.[7] What especially troubled Hayden was the obvious and continued effort of certain interests within California to delay CAP and nullify *Arizona v California*.

Indeed, for Hayden, whose statements in debate in 1928 concerning the Boulder Canyon Project Act aided Wilmer in his arguments before the Supreme Court, a lifetime of labor appeared to be coming to fruition. Earl Warren, the governor of California in 1948, had solemnly assured him that "whenever it is finally determined that water belongs to Arizona, it should be permitted to use that water in any manner or by any method considered best by Arizona," and CAP legislation should be acted upon with dispatch. To add to Hayden's glimmering hopes, California governor Pat Brown, shortly after the Court announced its decision, held a press conference and stated that California, having lost the Supreme Court case, would not try to accomplish by obstructionism what it had failed to accomplish by litigation.

As Hayden stated several times during the course of hearings on CAP, "For forty years I have witnessed the thwarting of Arizona's effort to put to use its share of Colorado River water. At every turn Arizona has encountered the delaying tactics of California and there is reason to believe that this plan of obstructionism will continue." "A small group of Californians," to his dismay, "notwithstanding previous commitments continued to nullify by delay the Supreme Court's decision." As he saw it, California had its water, Nevada had its water, the upper basin was developing its water, and Arizona had nothing.[8]

In countering California's recalcitrance, Arizona had other advantages. Between 1963 and 1968 Arizonans elected capable and bipartisan representation to the House and Senate. In the House, John Rhodes, a Republican, quickly became a respected and influential leader among House Republicans. George Senner, a Flagstaff Democrat from the newly created third district, lost his seat in 1966 to Prescott's inimitable Sam Steiger, a Republican. And Morris Udall, a member of the important Committee of Interior and Insular Affairs, held special responsibilities over the bill. This three-man team worked well together in the House and in the Senate, and Paul Fannin, former Arizona governor and CAP stalwart from the outset of his political career in the 1950s, filled Barry Goldwater's Senate seat when the latter won the Republican nomination for president in 1964. Fannin worked well with Hayden, knew the facts of the situation intimately, and continued to aid CAP legislation at every turn.[9]

Within the Senate, moreover, Hayden's close friendships with Senator Henry "Scoop" Jackson (D-Washington) and Senator Clinton Anderson (D-New Mexico), proved crucial to CAP. These powerful senators, who owed Hayden numerous favors for years of support, countered California's two senators, Thomas Kuchel and Claire Engle, both Republicans. The odious Engle, Arizonans remembered, helped defeat CAP in the House of Representatives in 1951.[10] The Senate appeared poised to pass CAP, but the House proved again to pose vexing challenges.

At the time that CAP was under consideration, nine out of every ten bills introduced in the House and referred to committee never saw a vote. Moreover, the power of congressional committees in the House, as well as the committee chairmen, could not be overstated. If a chairman opposed a bill, it rarely, if ever, saw a floor vote. The chairman, furthermore, controlled the schedule of hearings on legislation; more often than not, undecided members followed the chairman's lead. Since the principal obstacle to legislative passage of CAP remained in the House, the House Interior Committee—and its Irrigation and Reclamation Subcommittee, where the CAP bill was referred—held vital importance for the bill's supporters.[11]

This meant, of course, passing through the gauntlet of House Interior Committee chairman Wayne Aspinall, the former Colorado schoolteacher with the contrary disposition who viewed California and Arizona with equal disdain. In fact, the river ran directly under the window of his home, on Aspinall Drive in Palisade, Colorado, and Aspinall was concerned that Arizona's Supreme Court victory might somehow compromise Colorado's yet-to-be-developed upper basin allotment.[12]

In addition to Aspinall, CAP supporters had to contend with Congressman John Saylor from Pennsylvania, the ranking Republican on the House Interior Committee and the twentieth century's foremost congressional "Green Republican." An ardent conservationist in the mold of Progressive Republican president Theodore Roosevelt, Saylor, who hailed from Johnstown, Pennsylvania, supported the growth and expansion of the National Park system and advocated federal support for outdoor recreation programs. What concerned Arizona's House delegation specifically was that Saylor complained vigorously about the Bridge Canyon Dam provision of the CAP bill because, he said, it threatened to back water into Grand Canyon National Park. He looked skeptically at all reclamation projects, helped derail the CAP bill in 1951, and voted against the Glen Canyon Dam bill in 1956, thereby attracting favorable attention from environmental groups.[13]

Indeed, a force almost as powerful as California appeared in 1966 and 1967—environmental groups nationwide coalesced in opposition to the construction of dams in and around the Grand Canyon and threatened to derail CAP altogether. The previously fragmented environmental movement, representing a variety of interests, brought pressure to bear on Congress and the Lyndon Baines Johnson administration as news of "dams in the Grand Canyon," in the context of the CAP legislation, became public. Furthermore, a few groups, like the Sierra Club, National Parks Association, and the Arboretum were tracking the CAP bill and saw much to lose with the inclusion of hydroelectric dams in the proposed legislation. Clearly, the California-based Sierra Club, with a national membership of over 40,000 was the most prominent and potent of the anti-dam environmental groups.[14]

Its charismatic and controversial leader, David Brower, organized an impressive and effective public relations campaign against the construction of dams in or near the Grand Canyon. The strong emotional appeal of "saving" the Grand Canyon resonated throughout the country. Arizona leaders, as well as supporters within the Johnson administration, began receiving thousands of letters daily calling for a halt to dam building in the nation's scenic treasure, thus creating the need to revise legislative approaches to CAP.[15]

In the course of Sierra Club's advocacy campaign, Brower organized a series of well-attended public events that brought further attention to the issue. At a rally in Denver he quipped that he did not oppose dams in the Grand Canyon as long as the Bureau of Reclamation built a comparable canyon somewhere else. By early 1967 the public was convinced that the two proposed dams were the most controversial aspect of the legislation and they must never be constructed. In the spring of that year *Reader's Digest, Life,* and even the grade-school-age publication *My Weekly Reader* published articles attacking the Grand Canyon dams. In July 1967 the Senate Committee on Interior and Insular Affairs advised President Johnson that it had recommended passage of S 1004—another version of the CAP bill—and added that the legislation contained no new Colorado River dams. The elimination of dams from the proposed legislation reflected in part the acceptance of Brower's argument that within the region there were adequate amounts of alternative energy sources to hydroelectric power, notably low-grade coal. Yet, as environmental historian Donald Worster interpreted the Sierra Club's political victory in the debate, environmentalists lost something in the process. In exchange for Grand Canyon dams, energy required to pump CAP water was derived from coal strip-mined on Hopi land at Black Mesa and burned in the Navajo generating station outside Page, Arizona, thus polluting that portion of the Navajo Nation, Hopi Reservation, and Colorado River Plateau.[16]

Arizonans faced another necessary compromise in order to authorize CAP. From the start of congressional negotiations after Arizona's legal victory in 1963, California's senators and congressmen made it clear that its central demand for support of CAP was that it had first priority of 4.4 million acre-feet awarded to it in the Supreme Court decision. California sought to regain some of what it had lost due to Wilmer's advocacy. At first Arizona refused, but, by 1965, as tangential issues grew in number and complexity, versions of the CAP bill in the Eighty-eighth and Eighty-ninth Congresses carried provisions for twenty-five– and twenty-seven-year guarantees for the California priority. But in the end California won the point and the final version of the bill carried the provision that California had a 4.4 million acre-feet guarantee in perpetuity.[17]

The election of Ronald Reagan, a Republican, as governor of California in 1966 also played a noteworthy role in moving CAP forward. He began direct and constructive negotiations with fellow Republican governor of Arizona, Jack Williams. Reagan helped immensely in defrosting the icy political stalemate during a series of high-level discussions in 1967, voicing serious concern that the Colorado River controversy had an adverse impact on other programs in California and on reclamation throughout the West. Also, by the end of that year, the decades of political horse trading in Congress, feasibility studies, expert testimony, and post–*Arizona v California* legal posturing produced palpable results. CAP legislation, and its numerous pork barrel benefits for both lower and upper states, was ready to move.[18]

On September 12, 1968, when the Senate agreed to the House version of the Colorado River Basin Project Act, ninety-year-old Senator Hayden

Arizona federal officials at the time of the passage of the Colorado River Basin Project Act of 1968. Left to right, Congressman John Rhodes, Senator Barry Goldwater, Senator Paul Fannin, Congressman Morris Udall, Senator Carl Hayden, and Secretary of Interior, Stewart Udall. Author's files.

acknowledged the glowing tributes to his fifty-year record of tenacity with silent nods of appreciation. Three weeks later, on September 30, 1968, President Johnson signed CAP into law. At the time it was the most expensive single authorization in history, costing about $1.3 billion.[19]

Thus Wilmer's legal genius, as his contemporaries attest, led directly to passage of the Colorado River Basin Project Act in 1968. And, a new political and environmental calculus emerged on the heels of *Arizona v California* and the passage of CAP. After such a long period of dreaming, struggling, and planning, the actual turning of the first shovel in 1973 came as a kind of anti-climax. Arizona's new breed of municipal leaders stepped to the forefront as a new generation of champions for CAP because they viewed it as the best source of augmentation to address dwindling water supplies. In this way, what began as an agricultural rescue project was transformed into a lifeline to Arizona's growing cities.

Also, CAP was a substantial gain to the state's tribal residents. Ultimately, Arizona's tribes, cities, and, of course, farmers would play a major role in the use and distribution of the benefits of CAP. How these Arizona stakeholders managed their hard-won good fortune depended upon an efficient adminis-tration of CAP construction and finance as well as an enlightened and open relationship with the federal government.[20]

Moreover, there was a need for the U.S. Congress to appropriate monies for the Bureau of Reclamation to complete plans for construction of CAP. Additionally, the Department of Interior needed assurances from Arizona that the federal government would be repaid for construction. In 1970, Congress appropriated $1.2 million to begin CAP construction, but the U.S. Office of Management and Budget refused to release the money "until such time as a project cost repayment contract between the Secretary of the Interior and Arizona water users had been negotiated." Arizona leaders were forced to react. The governor and legislature considered several alternatives before enacting legislation that created the multicounty (Maricopa, Pinal, Pima) Central Arizona Water Conservation District on June 16, 1971, as the political and administrative agency designated to oversee repayment to the federal government.[21]

As Arizona developed its institutional infrastructure to administer the water won in *Arizona v California,* in 1977, President Jimmy Carter, in a polit-ical miscalculation of enormous proportions, commenced a campaign against nineteen western water projects, including CAP. Carter's mishandling of western water policy was one of a host of problems that beset the apparently naïve Democrat from Georgia; it further cemented a growing Republican domination of the inland West. Ultimately, the politically tone deaf Carter was forced to reverse his western water policy, but, even after the project was reinstated, Interior Secretary Cecil Andrus, on October 5, 1979, announced that Arizona must demonstrate a greater commitment to controlling groundwater use in the state before he issued final recommendations for CAP allocations.

Bruce Babbitt, Arizona governor, reputedly suggested using the federal government as a threat to unify Arizona water interests as a tactic to get groundwater use under control. The Carter administration reasoned that since CAP had been promoted as a rescue project to alleviate overdrafting of groundwater supplies to save irrigated agriculture, Arizona must demonstrate collective political will to curtail the use of groundwater in exchange for surface water deliveries from CAP.[22]

As a result of these political and fiscal realities, Democratic governor Babbitt and a cooperative Republican-led legislature adopted the Groundwater Management Act of 1980. The act established a timeline for reduction and elimination of groundwater pumping in certain areas of the state. It created Active Management Areas and Irrigation Non-Expansion Areas to facilitate the process. Within AMAs, it limited development to areas with an "assured water supply," an amount of water adequate for the needs of development for one hundred years. Further, any city with a CAP contract automatically had a hundred-year assured water supply designation. Wilmer approved these developments as he saw Arizona recast its water law and administration in response to changing needs. One development, the creation of a new agency of government, the Arizona Department of Water Resources, replaced the governor-appointed Arizona Water Commission. In fact, the series of proactive legislative initiatives, especially the Groundwater Management Act of 1980, prompted the federal government to put CAP in the reclamation forefront.

Serving as governor in 1986, Babbitt speculated what Arizona would have been like had Wilmer lost the case and there were no CAP. "It isn't so much what Arizona... would be like without CAP, but what sort of Arizona we'd be seeing in... 2000," he told a writer for *Arizona Highways*. "The absence of the Central Arizona Project would be terribly evident. We'd see an Arizona where agriculture had been ruthlessly eliminated by law—agriculture would be out of production to prevent an overdraft of the water supply. Sometime in the early twenty-first century, certainly by 2025, other things would begin to change. We'd have unacceptable water quality, earth fissuring, drastic groundwater problems. Ultimately, we would have to limit, progressively, certain types of water usage and impose dramatic limitation on growth."[23]

As the CAP neared completion in the early 1990s, a series of almost predictable problems appeared. First, the ultimate cost for CAP vastly exceeded the original estimates. Second, the exceedingly complicated repayment contract between CAP and the federal government was variously interpreted, and the State of Arizona and the U.S. government were at loggerheads. Thus in 1994 when the notice of completion triggered Arizona's obligation to repay its share of the construction costs the difference between the state and federal repayment calculations differed by nearly $1 billion.[24]

Underlying this complication, the original concept for charging CAP customers was that Arizona farmers would pay for any unused urban water. The farmers therefore entered into a series of contracts referred to as "take or pay" obligations that required them to pay for certain portions of the water supply. While agricultural water under the CAP contract bore no interest on the federal debt, the cost of repaying the principal amount to the federal government meant the water was far more expensive than originally conceived. Moreover, additional debt accumulated within those irrigation districts that had built CAP delivery systems to distribute the CAP water. At the same time, the value of cotton, CAP water's principal irrigated crop, had fallen precipitously in international markets. As a result, CAP deliveries to agriculture between 1993 and 1994 dropped from 500,000 acre-feet to 50,000 acre-feet, and agricultural customers were threatening to file bankruptcy.

The most widely reported problem with CAP waters concerned the City of Tucson. When Tucson, the largest municipal customer for CAP, commenced deliveries, the pipes emitted what consumers described as "brown gunk." Unfortunately, serious engineering and water quality issues arose because Tucson had switched from an entirely groundwater-based system to an entirely surface water–based system. Tucsonans responded with anger and used the voter initiative process to shut off all direct delivery of CAP water to Tucson consumers.

The little-known political institution of the CAWCD suddenly had to react to all three of these crises simultaneously. It attempted to negotiate a compromise with the federal government over the repayment cost. CAWCD officials, however, quickly discovered that the federal government was less interested in the amount of the repayment than in the question of how much CAP water might be reallocated to Arizona's Indian tribes. The claims of Arizona's Indian tribes to waters in central Arizona stemmed from the U.S. Supreme Court case *Winters v United States* (1908). *Winters* water rights claims, as noted earlier, were based on a doctrine under which the federal government was held to have reserved enough water to irrigate all practically irrigable acres on Indian reservations when those reservations were created. The claims in central Arizona were predominantly claims against the Gila River and its tributaries, the Salt and the Verde.

For these purposes, the Gila was non-negotiable—the Salt River Project had appropriated the vast majority of its flow. The federal government's plan, therefore, was to acquire some of Arizona's CAP appropriation and use it to satisfy Indian claims. In 1995, however, negotiations over Indian water and repayment collapsed. In one of several historical ironies concerning the struggle to put Colorado River water to beneficial use in central Arizona, Secretary of the Interior Bruce Babbitt and his assistant secretary for water and power, Betsy Rieke, the former director of the Arizona Department of Water Resources, represented the federal government.

In late 1995 the dispute with the federal government over the cost of CAP repayment and Indian water rights settlements resulted in CAWCD's filing suit against the United States. And in an echo of *Arizona v California*, in 2000, after hundreds of pages of depositions, interrogatories, motions, court hearings, and marathon negotiations, a tentative agreement was announced. Under that agreement, CAP's overall repayment obligation would be fixed at $1.65 billion, and a total of 653,000 acre-feet of water would be reallocated to satisfy the claims of Indian tribes, principally the Gila River Indian Community in central Arizona. In an agreement that would have confounded Wilmer, at the outset of the twenty-first century the Indians controlled 48 percent of the CAP water supply.

Criticized by many as a "give away" of huge quantities of water to a handful of Indian communities that would simply remarket the water to Arizona cities at a profit, the agreement is far more complex. Since *Winters*

(1908), courts have upheld claims of Indian communities to federally reserved water rights. Because of the senior status of Indian tribal claims to waters from rivers like the Gila, this reserved water rights doctrine could result in water being taken from the Salt River Project and the cities of central Arizona and given to the Gila River Indian Community.[25] Realizing this, Senator Jon Kyl of Arizona, himself an accomplished water rights attorney, took the lead in helping structure a settlement for the claims of the Gila River Indian Community and other Arizona Indian tribes. These settlements resulted in the Arizona Water Settlement Act, which President George W. Bush signed into law on December 10, 2004.[26] The agreement is one of the most complex and far-reaching water settlements in U.S. history. A few other legal, political, and institutional developments of note reflect the direct consequences of *Arizona v California*.

According to Gale Norton, then the secretary of interior, the settlement provided "a comprehensive resolution to some of the most critical water use issues facing Indian tribes and Arizona." As noted above, Arizona tribes control almost half of the water of the Colorado River coming through the CAP canal. The cities would be able to add a small amount of new water to their existing shares of the river and could bargain with tribes to get more. Central Arizona's farmers, long a part of Arizona's history and culture, face the prospect of losing water to tribal claims. Though rooftops will replace cotton fields throughout central Arizona, agriculture will survive primarily on Indian lands, in part, because of this water settlement.

Concerning agricultural water deliveries—Fife Symington, as governor, appointed a sixteen-member Governor's Task Force that met during the first six months of 1992. Its purpose was to propose strategies for use of the state's CAP entitlement. Unfortunately, this first task force was unable to develop any recommendations, and several members claimed they needed more information. Then, the governor's office and the Arizona Department of Water Resources requested another CAP study that resulted in "An Economic Assessment of Central Arizona Project Agriculture" authored by Professor Paul N. Wilson, of the University of Arizona's Department of Agricultural and Resource Economics. Wilson suggested, among other things, that CAWCD should restructure its economic formulas to recognize a "target price."[27] Essentially this meant that CAP would sell water to agriculture below even the marginal cost of delivery, with Arizona cities making up the difference. This program, implemented in 1995 had the net effect of agriculture's exchanging long-term CAP allocations for relief from the "take or pay" contracts. This creative response to the challenge proved successful: CAP agricultural deliveries bounced back to over 500,000 acre-feet annually in 2001.[28]

Tucson slowly worked through problems with its CAP water-quality issue. With the pronouncement "Start Your Pumps," on May 3, 2001, Mayor Bob Walkup announced delivery of "clean and safe" CAP water.[29] Because of these three issues, in part, Arizona did not use its full CAP allocation in the mid-1990s. California, meanwhile, vastly overused its 4.4 million acre-feet, because it had the right to take any water Arizona left in the river. This led Arizona to adopt additional innovative water management institutions, like "water banking," designed to encourage using as much Colorado River water as possible.

The concept of "banking" CAP water—putting it back underground in central Arizona—helped the state protect itself against its junior status in times of drought on the river. Also, groundwater banking was an effective mechanism to protect Arizona's allocation from California's hands. Thus SRP, CAWCD, and Arizona municipalities purchased excess Colorado River water from CAP and put it underground in central Arizona. This was done either through direct recharge—letting the water physically seep into the aquifers— or through a process called "indirect" recharge: the water would be sold to farmers at a heavily subsidized price and the groundwater that the farmers would otherwise have pumped would be counted as "recharged" surface water. This "recharged" water could then be used in the future.

In 1996, Governor Symington signed legislation establishing the Arizona Water Bank Authority as a separate state agency designed for the purpose of acquiring excess CAP water and banking it in central Arizona. In a brilliant innovation, the Arizona Water Bank was authorized to broker deals with neighboring states to allow them to bank water in Arizona for their future needs. This mechanism proved particularly effective with Nevada, thus creating a critical alliance in the always complex relationships over the Colorado River.

Three years earlier, in 1993, an additional innovative water-banking mechanism was created, the Central Arizona Groundwater Replenishment District. The CAGRD made it possible for developers to build housing subdivisions where they did not have direct access to CAP water or to a municipality with a CAP contract. The CAGRD, with legislative approval, expanded its powers and spheres of public policy influence in 1999. The CAGRD is a separate legal entity administered by the CAWCD, and it has the authority to acquire excess Colorado River water from CAWCD and store it underground on behalf of developers seeking to build subdivisions without direct access to CAP water. The subdivision joins the CAGRD, and each house is subject to an assessment to pay for the water put underground; thus, the subdivision is deemed to have the key criterion in establishing a hundred-year assured water supply.[30]

For the century prior to *Arizona v California*, water was the consummate shared experience in Arizona. Since 1963 the state has created institutions to secure, deliver, protect, and manage its hard-won supplies. Arizona has crafted laws, contracts, and decrees to organize the equitable sharing of its most precious resource. Arizonans should recall and celebrate the people like Wilmer, whose towering intellect triggered the brave new water world in the Southwest. Many focused their energies—even their entire professional careers—on this collective endeavor. Since the creation of Arizona Territory in 1863, water has provided Arizona's fundamental consensus. Arizona needs more water; it will take any legal steps to secure water; it will stretch its uses to the limit; and it will fight any entity that tries to take it away.

Chapter Eight

THAT LAWYER
FROM ARIZONA

When the Supreme Court announced its decision in 1963, Wilmer was a "happy guy," according to John Bouma, chairman of Snell & Wilmer's since 1983, but then a recently hired associate at the growing firm. Yet, Wilmer continued on his distinct and singular path, taking little, if any, time to bask in the glory of his legal victory. In fact, after the decision Wilmer decided to pursue a few days of what he loved best outside of law and family: hunting and fishing. Regarding these two recreational pursuits, if sons Bernie or Mark or one of his friends could not join him at Roosevelt Lake, San Carlos Lake, Lake Powell, or one of several secret spots in Gila County, he would just as readily go alone. Bouma, who fished and hunted with Wilmer on a regular basis, recalled hunting quail at the Big Sandy area near Florence, in Pinal County, where Wilmer had a long history trying cases.[1] To access the various desired rural locations, Wilmer fashioned a Jeep with a powerful Cadillac engine. The hybrid vehicle enabled him quick and assured access to his favorite haunts. And although he owned many boats, his favorite seemed to be a small aluminum one that he would use to go fishing by himself. "I'm a social fisherman," Bouma allowed, but "Mark would go hunting and fishing by himself."

Elder son Bernie confirmed that "hunting and fishing were his two great loves and to be honest with you, the hunting and fishing was probably second to his finding a good camp spot. And he'd go camping by himself. If he couldn't get me or my brother or my uncle or someone in the family to accompany him," he would head off to some remote location by himself. "He had a spot up in Winkelman—he had a rancher there that had worked out an agreement with him that if he would take care of his legal needs he would let my dad hunt and fish on his property any time he wanted and no one else could, and Dad loved that. He loved it." Wilmer preferred camping at

l-r, Charles Mark, Mark, and Mark Bernard, posing with prize catch (1956). Wilmer Family Photo Collection.

locations where cattle ponds created an attraction for wildlife. "We would duck hunt, and we would also quail hunt," recalled Bernie. "He had it all set up the way he wanted."[2]

Wilmer was known to enjoy an occasional drink, and he preferred bourbon. "We would go out hunting quail," Bouma reminisced, "and I remember a time going back to his house ... on Colter... We went in and he said bring the dog in. He and I were standing around drinking bourbon straight; he liked it straight as I recall... Mrs. Wilmer was so gracious about it all; she was cooking some steak, and she kept giving my dog bites of it, which I thought was quite unusual for such a woman to be so accommodating to my dog."

Another outcome of winning the lawsuit and earning a preeminent place in Arizona legal circles was an invitation for Wilmer to participate in the annual Highline Judicial Conference. This "conference," organized in the late 1950s and early 1960s, was actually a social gathering lasting several days. The original organizers—Frank X. Gordon, Arizona Supreme Court justice, and court of appeals judges Jack Ogg and Lawrence Wren—had, while sitting on superior courts in Arizona's northern tier of counties, invited their respective counties' attorneys to the early gatherings. Thus named for the electricity generated from the various highline dams along the Colorado

River, it featured fishing, partying, practical jokes, and storytelling on either Lake Mohave, Lake Havasu, Lake Mead, and later, Lake Powell. Over the years, the Judicial Highline Conference grew in numbers and social significance. The hosts decided that they ought to invite Wilmer because he was responsible for Arizona's securing rights to so much water. Soon, Cal Udall, Bouma, and others received prestigious invitations to the conference. In fact, in one instance, Bouma convinced a judge to recess a trial so he could attend the event. "We had this jury trial going on ... and I went to the judge and I said, 'You know, I gotta go on this fishing trip,' and the other attorney is just raising hell about me asking for the recess. The judge later told me that the line that persuaded him was when I said, 'You know, judge, there are a lot of trial days but there ain't many fishing days.' So he let me go; he recessed the trial."[3]

Mark Wilmer in 1970 . Wilmer Family Photo Collection.

In the late 1960s Wilmer and Bouma decided they needed to explore the San Carlos Indian Reservation and its various fishing lakes. Loading their rods, sleeping bags, and provisions into Wilmer's high-powered Jeep they left the valley and wound their way along Arizona Route 60. On this particular trip they miscalculated several times. Their first error in judgment was that they did not take a boat—they found that all the lakes had weeds ringing the shore lines, so "it was kind of tough fishing." As they proceeded east from Apache Junction, Bouma recalled, they stopped in Superior at one of Wilmer's favorite haunts to eat Mexican food at a combination bar and restaurant. As they left Superior, ash from Bouma's cigarette (he smoked in those days) blew to the back of the car and lit their sleeping bags on fire. They stopped, doused the flames, and continued to Globe near the border of the reservation. Then, deep in Apache land, car trouble on the "wrong road" to Dry Lake posed yet another challenge, so they were forced to make camp near the road for the evening. Wilmer, the camp cook, prepared dinner. As usual, the meal included generous amounts of garlic. Over whiskey, the two stranded attorneys began the standard philosophical discussion that ended with a debate about where to place their cots; either on the road in front of the car, where someone coming from Morenci on a dark night might not see it and run over them or find them or else just off the road in the tall grass where if a driver did see the car in the middle of the road it might swerve to go around it. Neither could sway the other to his opinion so one slept on the road in front of the car and the other off the road in the tall grass.

The next morning the car started, ran for a short distance, but sputtered to a stop. Through the day the pattern continued, until they decided to sit in lawn chairs and drink beer by the side of the road. Soon an Apache man came along in a pickup, stopped, looked under the hood, then jiggled and tightened some wires leading to the alternator. After thanking their Good Samaritan, Wilmer and Bouma were off and running again and lost only one day of fishing.

Meanwhile, the firm continued its strong, steady growth. During the 1960s it moved from the Heard Building to the Security Building in order to accommodate the increased number of attorneys required to staff its emerging practice areas, like complex business transactions, securities, and utility regulation. In fact, the number of attorneys—nineteen were pictured in the 1961 annual firm photo—had grown to forty-two by 1973. Some of the

John Bouma, Chairman of
Snell & Wilmer. Courtesy
of Snell & Wilmer.

junior members recognized the need to recruit young talent in spite of some
initial opposition to the idea. Still, in this ten-year period the firm's summer
clerkship program—the first in Arizona—took root and provided an innovative blueprint for recruiting the best young talent. Wilmer, Bouma, and Bud
Jacobson became an ad hoc recruiting committee and developed a recruiting
system that has served the firm well since its implementation.[4]

By the decade of the 1970s the law firm of Snell & Wilmer was a veritable
powerhouse. Beyond building a firm, garnering national praise for successfully arguing the lawsuit that Jack Pfister, like many others, calls "the most
important event in the history of the state of Arizona," the long, mutually
beneficial partnership between Snell & Wilmer continued unabated. Wilmer
was a loner, according to Bouma, and few contemporaries dispute that fact.
Pfister, who tried a few utility cases against Wilmer when he first started
practicing for Jennings, Strouss, and Salmon in the 1960s elaborated on
Wilmer's individualistic approach to law and life: "Mark was an individual
who did not want to be in the limelight. He listened carefully before he

uttered a word. He was a very self-effacing individual who operated under the radar screen. He was a ... very successful lawyer," who, unlike the other senior partner [Snell] in the firm, "was not involved politically in the higher echelons of society, and as a result of that he's often overlooked when people want to list the most important people in the ... history of Arizona."

Bouma's office was for many years located alongside Wilmer's, and they later shared a secretary. He offered a candid and practical view of Wilmer's "lone wolf nature": "Mark wasn't somebody that was easy to work with—not because of his personality, he was always very nice—but he wasn't interested in working with people... He wasn't the kind of guy who would call you into his office to sit down and discuss things." This description of how he approached his profession squares with how he executed the *Arizona v California* case. Wilmer tried the case, and Charlie Reed managed the team. Similarly, Wilmer had little interest in managing the firm, especially as it grew almost exponentially after 1960. "Mark was not involved in management," Bouma explained. "He loved to do his own research and that's where I think this reluctance to delegate comes from; he liked to be in the books, spending the time trying to figure things out."[5]

Snell, in contrast, maintained the consistently high profile of civic activism that marked his career. He remained prominent in social, political, and economic affairs and counseled the rich and powerful. He was a confidante to a generation of political leaders, Democrat and Republican. "He was very smooth," as Pfister and others recalled, but in a charming way that appealed to a broad range of people. "He was one of the best business getters or rainmakers in the legal community," according to C. Kimball Rose, former Maricopa County superior court judge, "and was the envy of almost all lawyers in the state because he really knew how to get business." Snell was always on the ground floor. When a new firm or business would arrive in Phoenix, somehow Snell would learn about it and throw a dinner party for the executives. Snell & Wilmer would end up representing them.[6] In fact, according to Pfister, who later became a leading member of the Phoenix 40, a group of business leaders dedicated to civic stewardship, Snell, a founding member of the group, was among the first three people mentioned when it came to those who were "decision makers" in the valley and state.[7]

William Rehnquist, who arrived in Arizona in 1953 and admitted to the bar in 1954, recalled that at that time Mark Wilmer and Elias Romley were the "recognized Deans of the Phoenix Trial Bar," and their courtroom battles were the stuff of legend. Rehnquist allowed that Wilmer bore little resemblance to some of the flamboyant performers that, thirty years later, were considered great courtroom litigators. "His manner," Rehnquist said, "while not folksy, was certainly down to earth, and I think jurors just naturally had confidence in what he told them."

Further, Rehnquist offered that Wilmer was an artist in the way he handled judges. "I remember once running into him as we both left the old courthouse on First Avenue and Washington Street. I commiserated with him because he was then trying a case before Judge X, who was generally regarded as one of the least competent of the superior court judges at that time. But he demurred, saying the question one ought to ask is not "how should I try my case before a good judge," but "how should I try my case before Judge X." Wilmer, Rehnquist concluded, "was probably even more successful before the Judge X's of the bench than he was before their abler counterparts, since they were generally bowled over by this reputation."[8]

Family and colleagues recall Wilmer's very dry sense of humor; various "Wilmerisms" punctuate his legacy. One of the most oft cited, "Blessed is he who has nothing to say and can't be persuaded to say it," sheds light on Wilmer and his values. At the same time, he carried a gentlemanly, almost stately, presence that secreted away opinions or feelings about people. Bouma reflected, "He always had this great persona of gentleness and not having any enemies and liking everybody. Well, he didn't like everybody by any means. He had pretty strong views but he was always a gentleman in how he dealt with people, and people didn't necessarily know how he felt about them." Also, judges, Snell & Wilmer employees, and opposing attorneys thought very highly of Wilmer. To the end of his career and well into his retirement he was considered, arguably, the best trial lawyer of his generation. "When I tried cases with him," said Bouma, "he was great; he was not always whispering in my ear or making comments." Wilmer, unlike some of the firm's litigators, would wait for a break in the trial then offer an appropriate word or two. A quiet mentor to those who were fortunate enough to work closely with him— and they were few—he was quick to bestow credit for work well done.

Wilmer also maintained a presence of selfless humility and genuine simplicity. Despite his accomplished career, virtually all who came in contact with him agreed that he remained modest, unpretentious, and down-to-earth. An intellectual of the first order, he was nevertheless a good listener, one of the keys to his ultimate success. Not surprisingly he was a voracious reader of the classics, poetry, and mystery novels. Material goods interested him little, and social status symbols were unimportant. His tastes were simple: he loved his family and his work, according to son-in-law Edwin F. Hendricks, also a distinguished trial lawyer, who frequently saw him in both roles.

When the Wilmer family was growing up in the 1950s, they spent weeks during the summer in the White Mountains at Pinetop where Genevieve and the children indulged the family cat "Wildflower." Liz Wilmer Sexson described Wildflower as "a very large and longhaired beautiful cat... wonderful markings... we were sure he wasn't a house cat." Older brother Bernie recalled Wildflower in slightly different terms. "We had a cat that was probably part wild Lynx or something... We used to spend our summers up there and it grew to be like thirteen pounds and a curly tail and I swear it killed dogs in the neighborhood. It was unbelievable... all muscle, and my mother loved that cat. Someone poisoned it. We all cried when we found it dead." Whether a bobcat mix, lynx hybrid, or an enormous cat, the Wilmer pet became a celebrity of sorts and inspired a newspaper story by longtime newspaper columnist Bert Fireman.[9]

Regarding Wilmer's family life Cal Udall, who worked closely with him for years on *Arizona v California*, reflected that many men who pursued careers as trial lawyers "neglected our wives and children because we thought it was required by our 'jealous mistress.' I am confident that Mark spent much more time with his children than most trial lawyers, but I know first hand his wife Genevieve was also his sweetheart. Arizona's lawyers in the "water case" in San Francisco often spent evenings together working and eating meals. Mark invariably found time to duck out to call 'Gen.'"[10]

From the opposing counsel's side, Jack Pfister, as an associate at Jennings, Strouss, and Salmon, encountered Wilmer in several utility-related trials during the mid- to late 1960s. His generous comments affirm those of other members of the bench and bar, like former Chief Justice Frank X. Gordon and well-known Arizona litigator Daniel Cracchiolo. "Some of the trial lawyers would act like Perry Mason, but that was not Mark Wilmer," Pfister recalled. "He was very gentle, easy going... almost gave the appearance of kind of stumbling along but, in fact, he was very clever in trying cases. One of the things that I concluded in watching him was that one of his major strengths was that he was always well-prepared. He really understood cases; he prepared at length and plotted out his course of action almost like a military campaign ... he was well-prepared and knew exactly where he wanted to go." Pfister corroborates the universal mantra regarding Wilmer's decorum: "Mark was a gentleman, really a first-class gentleman and though he could be extraordinarily intimidating to litigate against, there was never a personal thing and he was always pleasant." During recesses Wilmer and Pfister chatted about their families. It was during one of these periods that Pfister learned about Wilmer's passion for hunting and fishing on the lower Salt River as a way to relax.

Wilmer prevailed in other notable cases after *Arizona v California* and won numerous awards for his legal abilities and high standards of ethics and professionalism. In *Del Webb v Spur Feeding* (1972), Wilmer convinced the Arizona Supreme Court to require a developer that had expanded its residential subdivision toward a pre-existing cattle feeding operation—which they considered an unacceptable nuisance—that it must pay several million

Mark and Genevieve Wilmer in 1986. Wilmer Family Photo Collection.

dollars for relocating the business. Law students throughout the country have been required to study this case.[11]

In 1972 the Snell & Wilmer law firm reached an important milestone in its growth and development. Frank Snell, who had managed the firm since its formation in 1938, decided to reduce his administrative workload. As a result of this momentous decision, Wilmer, John Bouma, Joe Melczer, Jr., Don Corbitt, and Richard B. Snell, Frank's son, were elected to the firm's first Executive Committee and took over management of the firm. At this time the partners also agreed to invest in the future and commit partner earnings to building the infrastructure required to become a major law firm. Snell & Wilmer diversified its practice groups, developed significant non-attorney administrative support, and placed even more emphasis on recruiting the best talent available. Further, the firm stated its commitment to continuing legal education and community service. In 1973, Snell & Wilmer moved from the Security Building to the recently completed Valley Bank Center.[12]

Wilmer too began to reduce his case load in the mid-1970s. Increasingly, Bouma worked with him and as their lives blended at the office as well as at their favorite fishing holes. The younger attorney generously began relieving

Wilmer and Calvin Udall at ceremony honoring Wilmer's work for the Central Arizona Project (1986). Wilmer Family Photo Collection.

Edward "Bud" Jacobson and Wilmer in 1986. Wilmer Family Photo Collection.

Wilmer of his still considerable number of case files, particularly the insurance company work. It was not a simple or easy process for a man who, as he grew older, was still inclined to "do it himself" and not let go. As Bouma remembered, "I would go to his secretary, Mary Livingston, and say, 'Tell me about the files in there that aren't getting worked on.' She would tell me, and I would get them farmed out and make sure they were worked on.'" This unsolicited assistance was fine with Wilmer because he was never one to ask for help.

In 1983, Wilmer's daily activities at the firm officially ceased when John Bouma became chairman, succeeding Wilmer and Melczer. Then, incrementally, Wilmer "rolled out" of handling cases: he would arrive at the office, read his mail, and be available to talk to people. The firm kept an office for him, and after his secretary Mary Livingston moved on, he shared Bouma's secretary. Wilmer stopped visiting the office in the early 1990s when Genevieve, his wife for over fifty years, began having health problems.

Meanwhile, Snell & Wilmer commenced two decades of unprecedented and unrelenting institutional expansion. The firm's long history of conservative fiscal management was certainly a factor in the ability to increase its market share during the early 1980s contraction in the "law business," and

Arizona Governor Bruce Babbitt and Wilmer at the Central Arizona Project ceremony in 1986. Wilmer Family Photo Collection.

it attracted extremely capable attorneys from other prominent firms. Also, in 1989, Snell & Wilmer established a Tucson office. Shortly thereafter negotiations to combine with Tucson's largest and oldest law firm, Bilby and Shoenhair, were completed. With that merger, the first phase of geographic expansion was accomplished.

Then, during the early 1990s, the firm moved its Phoenix offices to the Arizona Center and opened offices in Irvine, California, and Salt Lake City, Utah. Offices in Denver, Colorado, and Las Vegas were opened in the early 2000s. With more than four hundred attorneys in six offices, Snell & Wilmer is now the largest firm headquartered in Arizona and one of the largest in the trans-Mississippi West.[13]

Throughout better than fifty years of practice, Wilmer distinguished himself as a litigator who could handle virtually any type of case at the trial and appellate levels. He was widely known as "the Dean of Arizona's trial lawyers," according to son-in-law and trial attorney Edwin F. Hendricks, and "he was a legal mentor, good friend, and wonderful man who touched the lives of many people in a special way." That legacy intact, Wilmer was no stranger to public service, well-deserved awards, and peer recognition for his numerous good works. A selective overview suggests a life of service to his community.

He was one of two Arizona trial lawyers first to be elected to be a fellow of the prestigious American College of Trial Lawyers. He was also elected a fellow of the International Academy of Trial Lawyers and in the International Society of Barristers. He found time to serve as president of the Phoenix Chamber of Commerce and served as president of the Maricopa County Bar Association. Not surprisingly he contributed time to various water conservation commissions and assisted with the incorporation of Scottsdale in 1963. Later, as chairman of the Arizona State Bar Committee of Examinations he was instrumental in adding a separate ethics examination that applicants had to pass prior to admission to the Arizona Bar. In 1985 he was a founding fellow of the Arizona Bar Foundation, served as a member of the Arizona State Bar Board of Governors and in 1987 he received that organization's Walter E. Craig Distinguished Service Award presented to "that attorney who has manifested adherence to the highest principles and traditions of the legal profession and service to the public which he lives." Other recognition of note included the Distinguished Citizen's Award in 1974 presented by the University of Arizona Alumni Association for outstanding service as a citizen, and the Board of Directors of the Central Arizona Project Association appropriately awarded Wilmer the Distinguished Contribution Award.[14]

Wilmer, at age 91, in his office at Snell & Wilmer (1994). Wilmer Family Photo Collection.

In his final years Wilmer took care of his wife, Genevieve, in north Phoenix, where they lived a quiet and sedentary existence. On occasion he would call Frank Snell, but as the years passed, their brief, pleasant conversations became less frequent. Snell died on September 5, 1994; three months later, on December 8, 1994, Wilmer passed away peacefully in Phoenix. A Who's Who of Arizona attended the memorial service, and the eulogy, presented by son-in-law Ed Hendricks, evoked strong emotions and at the same time celebrated an incredible life of accomplishment and contribution.

Son Bernie's reflections on his father during his final days were particularly poignant and compelling. When asked if there was anything he wanted to add to the record about his father, Bernie responded: "As a child, you are always going to speak highly of your father—and it would be terrible if you didn't—but he was just a neat person. I think we all got to understand him as we got older, and as he became older we realized what he stood for and what he had accomplished. But, just like everything else in life, it sometimes takes many years before you really understand what you had." As he continued, he carefully described a vivid memory: "In the afternoon I'd go in there and sit and watch him. He'd be sleeping, and I'd just watch TV and whatever. I'll never forget sitting next to him and holding his hand, because I knew I wouldn't be seeing him, and I held his hand. He opened his eyes and looked at me, and he had this big grin. Anyway, he had this big grin like he understood, and that was worth it all."[15]

On January 20, 1995, just weeks after the funeral, Edward "Bud" Jacobson, longtime friend and law partner, penned a short note to retired Arizona congressman John Rhodes, seeking to recognize Wilmer by naming some portion of the CAP for his longtime friend and colleague.[16] Rhodes apparently responded with enthusiasm because, within a week he and Jacobson had created a movement. Rhodes was assured "bipartisan support," from Senators Dennis Deconcini and John McCain, and he added in a missive to Jacobson, "Mark, after all, was the man who won the water in the first place."

Jacobson knew whom to contact. On February 7, 1995, he wrote Secretary of the Interior Bruce Babbitt, a former Arizona governor and water law reformer, informing him about an event two weeks hence at which he hoped to make an announcement. "On Saturday evening, February 25, 1995, at Camelback Inn, the Arizona Historical League of the Arizona Historical Society will award Mark Wilmer (posthumously) the title of 1995

Wilmer, in 1994, typing in his office. Wilmer Family Photo Collection.

Historymaker ... The principal jewel in Mark's crown as the lawyer's lawyer was winning *Arizona v California* in the United States Supreme Court which brought a portion of the waters of the Colorado to our State. How special the Historymakers' affair it would be if, in addition to receiving the Historymakers' award, an announcement could be made that some part of the Project would bear Mark's name."[17]

A "Post-it note" in Jacobson's files contained the interior secretary's response. "Bruce responded by voice mail and said, (1) great idea; (2) thinks John Rhodes is correct that he can name pumping station and has people looking into it, (3) would like it to come as a request from Central AZ Water Conservation District." A call to Grady Gammage, Jr., president of CAWCD, produced similarly prompt results, and, on February 17, 1995, Gammage wrote Babbitt that "Yesterday, the Central Arizona Water Conservation District authorized me, as President, to strongly request that you, as Secretary of Interior, name and designate the Havasu Pumping Station, 'The Mark Wilmer Pumping Station.'"

To add to the "perfect storm" that surrounded the pumping station naming effort, Gammage included in his letter, "It is the District's hope and mine that this might be accomplished on or prior to February 25, 1995," because on that evening, Gammage was to serve as master of ceremonies at the Historymaker event. "The reason for this request is compelling," Gammage confided to Babbitt, and "many aided and were critical to the final bringing of the waters of the Colorado to Arizona. But, without Mark's victory in the United States Supreme Court, there would not have been any water to bring. It seems uniquely fitting that the pumping station which pumps those waters from the River into our canals bears his name."[18]

On February 23, 1995, two days prior to the event at Camelback Inn, Babbitt's letter arrived at Gammage's office in downtown Phoenix. "It is with great pleasure that I write this letter to tell you that I have granted the request of the Central Arizona Water Conservation District and have this day officially designated the Havasu Pumping Station, 'The Mark Wilmer Pumping Station.' Liz Wilmer Sexson, the day after the Historymaker event at Camelback Inn, penned a heartfelt thank you to Jacobson for his efforts. Indeed, Babbitt's pronouncement regarding the naming of the pumping station had been kept secret—the announcement at the ceremony took all family members by surprise. "We know Dad liked his seat Saturday night and as he looked down on us all," Liz assured Jacobson, "I'm sure he was pleased to have you present his award."[19] Clearly, the immediate consensus and speed with which federal and local officials moved to complete the naming effort were truly remarkable and a fitting tribute to Wilmer and his career.

Shortly after the Interior Department named the pumping station in honor of Wilmer, his four children, Mark Bernard, Elizabeth, Charles Mark, and Genevieve, in 1994, created an endowment to provide an annual Mark Wilmer Family Scholarship at Arizona State University's Sandra Day O'Connor College of Law. Significantly, the student, selected by the four Wilmer children, must demonstrate integrity, high moral character, and financial need. Thus Wilmer's contributions and legacy will be recognized in the realm of legal education.

Most accounts of the political and legal history of CAP dutifully acknowledge Wilmer and the *Arizona v California* case. His most famous legal victory assured Arizona's access to Colorado River water and is widely considered the impetus for Arizona's spectacular growth into the twenty-first century. Yet the central influence of the case has often been obscured by the length of the process, and the thousands of pages of mind-bending technical and fiscal testimony that, in many instances, is mirrored in *Congressional*

Record. The hundreds of miles of canals, pumping stations—including the Mark Wilmer Pumping Plant—and water delivery systems that today wind their way through the desert stand as a testament to Mark Wilmer's intellect, discipline, and advocacy.[20]

The Byzantine legal odyssey that Arizona took to perfect title to its share of Colorado River water began with the Colorado River Compact of 1922, followed by the lawsuit *Arizona* v *California,* the hearings before the special master in San Francisco, the appeals briefs to the Supreme Court, and the final argument before the Supreme Court. The Central Arizona Project, which was the immediate and direct descendant of *Arizona v California,* similarly, was a concrete metaphor for the case. Authorization by Congress in 1968, the appropriation process, the letting of contracts, the physical impediments, the pump lifts, the boring through mountains, the flow gradients on the sides of foothills, and the hundreds of miles of canals to Phoenix and ending in Tucson, was in itself another odyssey. It literally took a lifetime.

Wilmer focused much of his considerable energy and legal acumen on the single most important factor confronting his arid state client—the search for large quantities of fresh water. Arizona, Wilmer knew, was a desert that discouraged human settlement and economic development, yet vividly defined the region as a unique place on the American landscape. From Wilmer's perspective, Arizona's most notable deficiency was legal title to water. What he considered the highlight of his legal career, exemplified in the fight for a specific allotment of Colorado River water, was devoted to rectifying this deficiency.

Underlying Wilmer's legal advocacy in *Arizona v California* was a peculiarly Southwestern obsession with economic growth and development. This obsession in the environmentally sensitive central Arizona desert has, understandably, come under close scrutiny and even criticism in recent years. As the next generation of scholars, lawyers, and politicians reassess and revise their interpretations of federal reclamation and water in the American West, Mark Wilmer will stand out as the man, who, in his quiet, gentlemanly, and understated way, gave order and meaning to the West's greatest challenge: delineating the region's water rights and constructing the legal framework for the use and distribution of this finite natural resource. Perhaps Judge Rifkind's words in the introduction of this volume provide the most cogent assessment of Wilmer's significance: "That attorney from Arizona, Mark

Wilmer, changed the course of the history of the American West."[21] Considering the source, that interpretation would be difficult to disprove.

Appendices

Appendix A: *Winters v United States*, 207 U.S. 564 (1908).

On May 1, 1888, the United States opened a large area of land in what would become the state of Montana. Previously, this land was reserved for various Indian tribes. However, the tribes ceded the land back to the United States, with the exception of the Fort Belknap Indian Reservation. The United States intended that the land be part of the public domain and open for settlement. The government's goal was that the land would be reclaimed, inhabited, cultivated, and communities established.

The Fort Belknap Indian Reservation remained for the Gros Ventre and Assiniboin bands or tribes of Indians in Montana. The Milk River, a non-navigable stream, was the northern boundary of the reservation. The reservation land, though dry and arid, was suitable for agriculture if a large quantity of water was available to irrigate. Thus, the Indians diverted the Milk River, the only possible water source, to irrigate the land and raise crops of grain, grass, and vegetables. The water supply was crucial not only for agriculture but also for the advancement and development of industry within their civilization.

Defendant/Appellant Winters and others entered on the land near the Milk River and acquired title to the property through the United States land office. Without notice of any claim on the river waters, appellants built large and substantial dams and reservoirs on the river, and used canals, ditches, and waterways to divert the river from its channel for agricultural and other purposes. Winters and others expended thousands of dollars for ancillary construction and improvements upon the land, such as building fences, structures, schools, and highways. Without the water supplied by the Milk River, the newly-developing communities, home to an increasing number of people, would be uninhabitable, and thus, the goal of the government opening the land would be wholly defeated.

The United States, on behalf of the Indians, brought suit to restrain Winters and others from constructing or maintaining dams or reservoirs on the Milk River, or otherwise preventing the river to flow to the Fort Belknap Indian Reservation. The Circuit Court of the United States for the District of Montana entered an interlocutory order, enjoining Winters and the other defendants from interfering in any manner with the reservation's use of 5,000 inches of the water. *See Winters v United States,* 143 F. 740 (C.C.A. Mont. 1906). The Ninth Circuit affirmed the order. *See Winters v United States,* 148 F. 684 (9th Cir. 1906).

On appeal to the United States Supreme Court, Winters (appellants) argued that the May 1, 1888, agreement that re-conveyed the land to the United States and delineated new borders for the reservation included the deliberate return of the rights to use the Milk River. The appellants reasoned that the lands that were ceded back to the United States were arid, and therefore, cession of the land necessarily included a cession of the waters. Further, they argued that the Indians made no affirmative reservation of the waters. *See Winters,* 207 U.S. at 577.

The Court did not accept these arguments. The Court noted that prior to cession, the Indians had command of all the reservation land and its waters for *any* beneficial purpose, whether for hunting and grazing of animals or for agriculture and "the arts of civilization." *See id.* at 576. Without the benefit of the water, the reservation land would be valueless and essentially uninhabitable. The Court applied the general interpretive rule that in agreements and treaties with Indians, ambiguities ought to be resolved in favor of the Indians. Thus, between two inferences, one which would support the purpose of the agreement (namely, that the Fort Belknap Indian Reservation continue to sustain Indian tribes) and another that would impair or defeat this purpose, the Court found the former. The Court declined to agree that the rights to the river water were ceded by the Indians. *See id.* at 576–77.

In the alternative, the appellants argued that even if the 1888 agreement reserved waters to the Indian Reservation, the admission of Montana into the Union on February 22, 1889, repealed the reservation. The Court found it would be impractical to hold that the agreement of May 1, 1888, was destroyed less than a year later and that Congress intended to destroy the reservation and take from the Indians their means of continuing their society. Importantly, the Court made clear that Congress retained the authority to reserve the waters—it was not automatically relinquished to Montana when she became a state. *See id.* at 577. "The power of the [federal] government to reserve the waters and exempt them from appropriation under the state laws is not denied, and could not be." *Id.* The Court dismissed this argument stating, "[O]ur construction of the [1888] agreement and its effect make it unnecessary to answer the argument in detail." *See id.* at 578. For the same reason, the Court declined to discuss the doctrine of riparian rights, urged by the government. *See id.*

Note: Justice Brewer dissented without opinion.

"An understanding of the [Colorado River] Compact and the [Boulder Canyon] Project Act is essential to an understanding of the decision of the United States Supreme Court June 3, 1963, in the case of *Arizona v California.*"

Mark Wilmer, *Arizona v California, A Statutory Construction Case,* 6 ARIZ. L. REV. 40 (1964–1965).

APPENDIX B: COLORADO RIVER COMPACT OF 1922

Congress passed an act on August 19, 1921, authorizing Arizona, California, Colorado, Nevada, New Mexico, Utah, and Wyoming, along with a representative of the United States, to convene and negotiate an agreement regarding the Colorado River.[1] In January 1922, the representatives of each state and the President's appointed representative, Herbert Hoover, met in Santa Fe, New Mexico, to draft what would become the Colorado River Compact ("Compact"). The Compact was completed and signed by the representatives on November 22, 1922.

Article I lists the Compact's purposes: 1) provide for the fair division and apportionment of the water's resources; 2) establish the relative importance of different beneficial uses for the water; 3) promote interstate relationships and remove present and future controversies; 4) secure expeditious agricultural and industrial development of the Colorado River Basin; 5) provide for the storage of its waters; and 6) protect life and property from floods.

Most importantly, the Compact divided land into two basins—the Upper Basin and the Lower Basin—with Lee Ferry as the point of division. Mark Wilmer commented on the natural division into two basins: "A canyon stretch of the river approximately 1,000 miles long in southern Utah and northern Arizona divides the basin of the Colorado River system into two natural parts, known as the upper and lower basins, respectively."[2] The Upper Basin states include Colorado, New Mexico, Utah, and Wyoming. The Lower Basin states include Arizona, California, and Nevada. Moreover, Article II defined the "Colorado River System" as the "portion of the Colorado River and its tributaries within the United States of America."

Critically, Article III(a) of the Compact apportioned 7.5 million acre-feet of water per annum for beneficial consumptive use to each Basin. Article III(b) granted the Lower Basin a right to increase its beneficial consumptive use by 1 million acre-feet per annum. As would ultimately be resolved by the Supreme Court, the Compact apportioned water *between* the two basins and did *not* apportion water among the states within each basin.

Article IV set forth priorities for use of the water. First, the Compact stated the use of the waters for navigation is subservient to domestic, agricultural, and power uses. Second, impounding the waters in order to generate electrical power is allowed, but such use is subservient to consumption for agricultural and domestic purposes. Additionally, Article VII of the Compact states that none of its provisions shall affect the obligations of the United States to Indian tribes.

Lastly, it was agreed the Compact would become binding and enforceable when approved by each of the seven state's legislatures and by Congress. By 1923, the state legislatures in six of the seven states—all but Arizona—accepted the Compact.

APPENDIX C: BOULDER CANYON PROJECT ACT
45 STAT. 1057 (1928); 43 U.S.C. § 617(A) (1958).

The Boulder Canyon Project Act ("Act") was approved by Congress on December 21, 1928. The stated purposes of the Act were 1) controlling floods; 2) improving navigation and regulating the flow of the Colorado River; 3) providing storage and for the delivery of the stored waters; and 4) generation of electrical energy. The Act accomplished three key goals: first, it extended congressional approval to the Colorado River Compact; second, it authorized the construction of Hoover Dam; and third, it authorized construction of the All-American Canal from the Colorado River to California's Imperial and Coachella Valleys.

Section 4(a) of the Act contained the critical and often disputed provisions. The section provided that in order for the Act to take effect, either a) all seven states that were party to the Colorado River Compact needed to ratify the Compact within six months of the passage of the Act; or if that did not happen b) six states (including California) needed to ratify the Compact *and* California. Additionally, California needed to agree that it would not exceed 4.4 million acre-feet of water of the 7.5 million acre-feet that the Compact apportioned to the Lower Basin States, plus not more than one-half of any water in excess of the allocated amount.

Additionally, Section 4(a) authorized the Lower Basin states (Arizona, California, and Nevada) to enter into an agreement to provide for the distribution of the apportioned 7.5 million acre-feet of water. The Act specified the agreement should contain the following distribution of the water for beneficial consumptive use: 300,000 acre-feet to Nevada, 2.8 million acre-feet to Arizona, and 4.4 million acre-feet to California. Additionally, the agreement would allow Arizona and California each one-half of any excess. The Act specified that the agreement should also include a provision that entitled Arizona to the exclusive beneficial consumptive use of the Gila River and its tributaries within the state. The agreement was subject to the provisions of the Colorado River Compact and was to take effect upon the ratification of the Compact by Arizona, California, and Nevada.

APPENDIX D: *ARIZONA V CALIFORNIA*, 376 U.S. 340 (1964)

The official published Supreme Court decision in *Arizona v California* is over ninety pages long—one of the longest in the history of the Court. *See* 373 U.S. 546 (1963). What follows is a summation of the Court's decree of findings and conclusions ("Decree") published in 1964.

The Decree defined "Mainstream" as including the mainstream of the Colorado River downstream from Lee Ferry and separately defined "Tributaries" as all stream systems that naturally drain into the mainstream of the Colorado River. As for the Tributaries, the Decree specifically enjoined New Mexico from diverting more than set amounts from the San Simon Creek, San Francisco River, and the Gila River. The Court recognized the Gila Decree, entered by the United States District Court of Arizona, which limited the diversion of the Gila River and in effect, preserved the Gila River for Arizona's exclusive use. *See United States v Gila Valley Irrigation District*, No. 19 (D. Ariz. June 29, 1935).

The Decree set forth the following priorities for the Colorado River Mainstream water: 1) river regulation, navigation, and flood control; 2) irrigation and domestic uses; and 3) generating power. Further, the Court recognized the United States was also authorized to release water to Mexico to satisfy its obligations under the Feb 3, 1944 Treaty.

But most importantly, the Court's Decree announced the distribution of the water among the Lower Basin States. The United States was to release Mainstream water to Arizona, California, and Nevada for irrigation and domestic uses, as follows:

Arizona:	2.8 million acre-feet
California:	4.4 million acre-feet
Nevada:	*300,000 acre-feet*
	7.5 million acre-feet

The Court affirmatively stated that "in no event shall more than 4.4 million acre-feet be apportioned for use in California, including all present perfected rights." *Arizona v California,* 376 U.S. at 342–43.

If sufficient Mainstream water was available, both Arizona and California would each receive one-half, unless the Untied States contracted with Nevada for excess water rights. In that case, Arizona would receive 46 percent of the excess and Nevada would receive 4 percent. Additionally, the Court apportioned varying acre-feet of water to Indian Reservations and Wildlife Refuges in the western states. The Court enjoined California, Arizona, Nevada and various water districts therein from interfering with the management and operation of the structures, interfering with releases and deliveries, diverting water from the Mainstream, and consuming the water in excess of their allocated amounts.

Notes

Introduction

1. Simon Rifkind oral history interview with Jack L. August, Jr., October 9 and 12, 1986, Ruidoso, New Mexico, author's files. Special Master Rifkind provided two interviews, one prior to the event and one afterward on the return trip to Albuquerque airport. The Honorable Simon H. Rifkind was born June 5, 1901, in Meretz, Russia, immigrated to the United States in 1910, and was educated in New York City public schools. He attended City College of New York, where he received his B.S. in 1922 and graduated from Columbia Law School in 1925. He was in private practice in New York City from 1926–1930; administrative assistant to Robert Wagner, U.S. senator, from 1927–1933; returned to private practice in New York City from 1933–1941; appointed to U.S. District Court, Southern District of New York, from 1941–1950; returned to private practice, 1950–1995, until he passed away on November 14, 1995. He was selected by the U.S. Supreme Court to serve as the special master in *Arizona v California* in 1955, after the first special master, George I. Haight, died suddenly.

2. *Arizona v California et al.*, 373 U.S. 564, 565 (1963); Simon H. Rifkind, *Special Master Report* (Washington, D.C.: Government Printing Office, December 5, 1960).

3. Rifkind, oral history with August, October 9, 1986.

4. Garret Hardin, "The Tragedy of the Commons," *Science,* 162 (1968): 1243–1248.

5. U.S. Senator Jon Kyl, Press Release, "Lifeblood of the West," August 14, 2006.

6. For a history of the Central Arizona Project see, Jack L. August, Jr., *Vision in the Desert: Carl Hayden and Hydropolitics in the American Southwest* (Fort Worth: Texas Christian University Press, 1999); T. Richmond Johnson, *The Central Arizona Project: 1918–1968* (Tucson: University of Arizona Press, 1977), 110–124; John Fowles to David Rauch, July 25, 2003, Snell & Wilmer Office Files, Phoenix, Arizona.

7. Senator Jon Kyl, "Tribute to Mark Wilmer," *Arizona State Law Journal* (1995), 411.

8. Three times prior to the 1952 filing Arizona had instituted actions in the Supreme Court concerning the Colorado River. *Arizona v California,* 283, U.S. 423, 51 S. Ct. 522, 75 L.Ed. 1154 (1931); *Arizona v California,* 292 U.S. 341, 54 S. Ct. 735, 778 L.ED. 1298 (1934); *Arizona v California,* 298, U.S. 558, 56 S.Ct. 848, 80 L.Ed. 1331 (1936). See also *United States v Arizona,* 295 U.S. 174, 55 S.Ct. 666, 79 L.Ed. 1371 (1935). The seven public agencies were the Palo Verde Irrigation District, Imperial Irrigation District, Coachella Valley County Water District, Metropolitan Water District of Southern California, City of Los Angeles, City of San Diego, and County of San Diego.

9. Robert G. Begam, interview with Jack L. August, Jr., November 28, 2006, Phoenix, Arizona, author's files.

10. Mark Wilmer, "Arizona v California: A Statutory Construction Case," *Arizona Law Review* 6 (1964): 40, 52, 58. Wilmer was quoting from Arizona's "Amended and Supplemental Statement of Position" (August 5, 1957).

11. See, for example, Johnson, *The Central Arizona Project,* 115.

12. Laura and George Danieli to Mark Wilmer, June 4, 1963, Mark Wilmer Collection, Box 1, Folder 3, Arizona Historical Foundation (hereafter AHF), Hayden Library, Arizona State University, Tempe (hereafter ASU).

Chapter One: Midwest to Southwest

1. Gregory Randall to Jack L. August, Jr., February 2, 2005, author's files; Richard Nelson Current, *Wisconsin: A History* (Champagne: University of Illinois Press, 2001). Both the Ringling Brothers' "World's Greatest Shows" and Barnum and Bailey's "Greatest Show on Earth" originated in Wisconsin. So too, did the typewriter and Johnson's Wax. Moreover, Wisconsin inventors contributed to the mechanization of American agriculture by developing harvesters, threshers, reapers, cultivators, and other machinery.

2. Mark Wilmer's father began his career as a school teacher in Wisconsin and later farmed in the state of Washington. He returned to Wisconsin because his wife preferred Wisconsin.

3. Honey Creek was a predominantly Baptist community and though the Wilmers were practicing Catholics, there was little, if any, religious tension within the close-knit community. See Mark Bernard Wilmer, oral history interview with Zona Davis Lorig, September 8, 1994, Phoenix, Arizona, Arizona Historical Society (hereafter AHS); Mark Bernard Wilmer, oral history interview with James McNulty, Arizona Bar Foundation Oral History Project, October 25, 1988, AHS.

4. Wilmer interview with Zorig; Wilmer interview with McNulty.

5. Elizabeth Sexson to Jack L. August, Jr., July 6, 2006; Mark Bernard Wilmer, Jr., oral history interview, August 18, 2004, Las Vegas, Nevada, AHF, ASU. According to "Bernie" Wilmer, his father read *Hiawatha* three or four times.

6. Wilmer interview with McNulty.

7. Wilmer revealed much in a few comments about his father and education in a 1988 oral history interview. In response to a question from the interviewer, former congressman Jim McNulty, concerning his father's education beyond high school, Wilmer said, "Well, I don't know that. All I know is that I learned as a boy that he started out as a school teacher. And then I suppose he met my mother. My father was not given to chatting about things like that. He believed in working. So I really don't know except that he was a learned person."

8. The law school at Marquette opened in 1908.

9. Edward Hendricks, Eulogy for Mark Bernard Wilmer, December 12, 1994.

10. Wilmer interview with McNulty.

11. Wilmer allowed, "I don't know whether they (Marquette administrators) would have let me in or not. But I don't think it was necessary to disclose that situation" to Georgetown law admissions staff. Wilmer interview with McNulty.

12. Wilmer interview with McNulty.

13. Iraan is located 135 miles west of San Angelo and 65 miles from Fort Stockton.

14. Wilmer was notified in September 1931 that he had passed the Arizona State Bar exam. See also, *Arizona Republic* (Phoenix), October 31, 1930, and February 21 and October 27, 1931.

15. Edward "Bud" Jacobson, oral history interview with Jack L. August, Jr., November 10, 2004, Phoenix, Arizona, Snell & Wilmer Law Firm.

16. *Arizona v California*, 283 U.S. 423 (1931); Simon H. Rifkind, Special Master, *Report In the Supreme Court of the United States*, October Term, 1960 (December 5, 1960), 7. This has been commonly called the *Special Master's Report*.

17. Douglas E. Kupel, *Fuel for Growth: Water and Arizona's Urban Environment* (Tucson: University of Arizona Press, 2003), 1–26.

18. The classic account on this topic is Emil Haury, *The Hohokam: Desert Farmers and Craftsmen: Excavation of Snaketown, 1964–1965* (Tucson: University of Arizona Press, 1965).

19. See Kupel, *Fuel for Growth*, 13; Michael Logan, "Head-Cuts and Check-Dams:

Changing Patterns of Environmental Manipulation by the Hohokam and Spanish in the Santa Cruz Valley, 200–1820," *Environmental History* 4 (July 1999): 405–430.

20. See, for example, Donald Worster, *Rivers of Empire: Water, Aridity and the Growth of the American West* (New York: Pantheon, 1985), 3–21.

21. Much of the Spanish water lexicon dates from the Moorish occupation of Spain from 711–1492.

22. For a cogent discussion of the prior appropriation doctrine in the regions see Michael Meyer, *Water in the Hispanic Southwest,* 54, 148–150. Though Spanish law recognized "first in use, first in right," in theory, Spanish settlers in many cases utilized a more pragmatic, communal approach to water that acknowledged the inherent value of the scarce resource in an arid region. For an account of this pragmatic approach, see Peter L. Reich, "The 'Hispanic' Roots of Prior Appropriation in Arizona," *Arizona State Law Journal* 27 (summer 1995).

23. "Appurtenant" indicates an incidental right attached to a principal property right and passing in possession with it.

24. Thomas Sheridan, *Arizona: A History* (Tucson: University of Arizona Press, 1996), 77–99.

25. For an account of the vicissitudes of flood and drought during this period see Jack L. August, Jr. "Carl Hayden: Born a Politician," *Journal of Arizona History* 26 (summer 1985): 127–130.

26. For an accessible institutional history of Salt River Project see **www.srpnet.com/history**.

27. For a city to take delivery it required modifications of the 1902 Reclamation Act.

28. Later, when the Reclamation Service conducted an analysis of the lands in the Salt River Project area, project officials designated urban acres as "Townsite Lands" based upon provisions of the 1906 Townsite Act.

29. And, as Wilmer navigated the course of his early legal career during his first two decades in Arizona he witnessed the construction of five additional dams on the Salt and Verde Rivers and by 1949 the creation of a special municipal power district (Salt River Project Agricultural Improvement and Power District) which was formed to sell hydroelectric power and other types of energy to citizens of the emerging metropolis of Phoenix.

30. Karen L. Smith, *The Magnificent Experiment: Building the Salt River Reclamation Project* (Tucson: University of Arizona Press, 1986), 1890–1917; Grady Gammage, Jr., *Phoenix in Perspective: Reflections on Developing the Desert* (Phoenix: Arizona State University, 1999); Joel Garreau, *Edge City: Life on the New Frontier* (New York: Doubleday, 1991).

CHAPTER TWO: THE FIRM AND THE RIVER

1. Wilmer interview with McNulty.

2. *Snell & Wilmer: The First Sixty Years, 1938–1998* (Phoenix: Snell & Wilmer, 1998), 8.

3. *First Sixty Years,* 8; Wilmer interview with McNulty; "Outtakes," *The Phoenix Two: The Fiftieth Anniversary of Snell & Wilmer,* Documentary Film, Snell & Wilmer, Phoenix, Arizona.

4. Wilmer interview with McNulty.

5. They were married on October 1, 1934. The *Arizona Republic* reported on October 8, 1934, "Mr. and Mrs. Mark Wilmer returned Monday from a five day's wedding trip to the Pacific Coast to the home of Mrs. Wilmer's mother, Mrs. Fareda Tibshraeny, 32 N. Robson Street, where the young couple will reside during the absence of Mrs. Tibshraeny and her son, Iser."

6. Mark Bernard Wilmer, Jr., interview with Jack L. August, Jr., August 18, 2004, Las Vegas, Nevada; Elizabeth Wilmer Sexson, interview with Jack L. August, Jr., August

24, 2004, Phoenix, Arizona; Charles Mark Wilmer, interview with Jack L. August, Jr., August 26, 2004, Phoenix, Arizona; Edwin Francis Hendricks and Genevieve Wilmer Hendricks, interview with Jack L. August, Jr., August 30, 2004, Phoenix, Arizona, Mark Wilmer Collection, AHF, ASU.

7. *First Sixty Years,* 8; Wilmer interview with McNulty. The deputy county attorney position was a full-time job at the time, though Wilmer allowed, "If you could scrounge up a divorce or something like that they didn't complain about it." In the spring of 1936, Wilmer was promoted to the post of chief civil deputy county attorney.

8. *Arizona Republic,* January 18, February 4, May 17, October 1, November 18, 1937; *First Sixty Years,* 8, Wilmer interview with McNulty.

9. *First Sixty Years,* 8. Snell was born December 23, 1899, in Kansas City, Missouri. Snell's unpublished biography is located in the Frank L. Snell Collection, AHF, ASU. See, also, Snell & Wilmer LLP Law Offices, Snell & Wilmer, *http://www.swlaw.com/aboutus/history.asp*; "Frank Snell Dies; Longtime Civic Leader: Civic Giant was Arizona's most powerful man ever," *Phoenix Gazette,* September 7, 1994.

10. Memorandum of Agreement, Fred J. Elliott and Frank L. Snell, September 1, 1927, Snell Collection, Box 13, Folder 1, AHF.

11. *First Sixty Years,* 8; Wilmer interview with McNulty. The Snells had two children, Kathryn and Richard. Snell's numerous achievements are well-documented. In time, Snell became friends with Eugene Pulliam, owner of the *Phoenix Gazette* and *Arizona Republic,* and Walter Bimson, president and CEO of the Valley National Bank. These men comprised "The Big Three" and would later found the "Phoenix 40." These relationships, and Snell's acquisitiveness, contributed significantly to Phoenix civic affairs during the middle decades of the twentieth century. Additionally, he helped found the American Graduate School of International Management and served as chairman of the Civic Plaza Art Enrichment Committee. He also served as president, director, committee member, and volunteer for many prominent Arizona organizations. His numerous awards include being one of the first inductees to the Arizona Business Hall of Fame in 1987. In 1992, Snell received the Arizona Heritage Award from the Arizona Chamber of Commerce. In 1983 Snell lost his beloved wife, Betty, to cancer. He married Jean Thompson in 1987 and welcomed her daughter, Kirstin, into the family. Frank L. Snell passed away on September 5, 1994, at age 94. He was survived by his wife, Mary Jean, children Kathryn and Richard, step-daughter, Kirstin, six grandchildren, and two great-grandchildren. After World War II Joseph T. Melczer, Jr., and James Walsh, Wilmer's former roommate and partner in Mesa, joined the firm that became known as Snell, Wilmer, Walsh, and Melczer. Soon thereafter, Edwin Beauchamp joined the firm and the firm's name became the cumbersome Snell, Wilmer, Walsh, Melczer, and Beauchamp. Recognizing the need to streamline the name and letterhead, Walsh, in 1950, suggested shortening the firm's name to just Snell & Wilmer. Walsh left the firm about that time to become a renowned U.S. district court judge.

12. Memorandum of Agreement, Charles Strouss, Frank Snell, Mark Wilmer, August 1, 1938, Snell Collection, Box 11, Folder 1, AHF, ASU.

13. "Outtakes," *The Phoenix Two,* 1988.

14. Ibid.

15. Today, the Snell & Wilmer firm maintains offices in Phoenix, Tucson, Las Vegas, Salt Lake City, Denver, and Irvine.

16. Wilmer interview with McNulty; "Outtakes," *The Phoenix Two,* 1988.

17. The interstate and international stream possesses other noteworthy characteristics. It flows on a ridge above sea level and in ages past, it tore through its banks and poured into the lower lying valleys. Important consequences of these intermittent floodings were the creation of a large lake of fresh water, the Salton Sea, and the depositing of

rich alluvial soil that reached hundreds of feet deep. Also, the Colorado was one of the heaviest silt carriers in the world, carrying five times that of the Rio Grande and seventeen times that of the Mississippi. Toward the Mexican delta, its speed decreased, dropping much of its load of silt, thereby causing the channel to rise above the surrounding countryside. By the twentieth century, these periodic floodings had created a rich delta in a climate conducive to year-round agricultural production. See Jack L. August, Jr., *Vision in the Desert: Carl Hayden and Hydropolitics in the American Southwest* (Fort Worth: Texas Christian University Press, 1999), 70; Committee on Water of the National Research Council, *Water and Choice in the Colorado River Basin* (Washington, D.C.: Academy of Science Publications No. 1689, 1968), 1–47; Norris Hundley, Jr., *Water and the West: The Colorado River Compact and the Politics of Water in the American West* (Berkeley: University of California Press, 1975), xiv–xvi; Norris Hundley, Jr., "The Colorado River Waters Dispute," *Foreign Affairs* 42 (April 1964): 495; Beverly Moeller, *Phil Swing and Boulder Dam* (Berkeley: University of California Press, 1971), x–xi; Phillip Fradkin, *A River No More* (New York: Alfred A. Knopf, 1981), 15.

18. Richard Hinton, a widely read western journalist, carried Powell's arguments further. In uncompromising terms Hinton urged massive federal spending for devising comprehensive irrigation works in the region. Famed scientist and army engineer Hiram Chittendon added that "a comprehensive reservoir system in the arid regions of the United States is essential." Hinton and Chittendon agreed that the federal government was the only agency suited to act on these recommendations. Mark Wilmer, Historical Notes, n.d., Mark Wilmer Legal Files, Snell & Wilmer Law Firm, Phoenix, Arizona; August, *Vision in the Desert,* 72; John Wesley Powell, "Report on the Lands of the Arid Region of the United States, *House Executive Document 73,* 45 Congress, 2 Session (1878); John Wesley Powell, "Reservoirs in Arid Regions of the United States," *Senate Book of Arizona* (San Francisco: Payot, Upham, and Company, 1876), 66; Hiram Chittendon, "Preliminary Examination of Reservoir Sites In Wyoming and Colorado," *House Document 141, 55* Congress, 2 Session (1897).

19. Rockwood's scheme required huge sums of money from American and European investors.

20. Barbara Ann Metcalf, "Oliver Wozencraft in California," (M.A. Thesis: University of Southern California, 1963), 81–96; *Weekly Arizona Miner* (Prescott), June 13, 1879; *Arizona Citizen* (Tucson), June 13, 1879. Indeed the introduction of water to the valley precipitated a land rush. Thousands of settlers formed mutual water companies that purchased and distributed water from Rockwood's company. By 1909 over 15,000 people farmed approximately 160,000 acres of the Imperial Valley. Of immediate concern was the delivery system that tapped the river just north of the international border and fed water into the Alamo Channel that skirted the California sand dunes through the Republic of Mexico for fifty miles before turning north again into the United States. International legal problems, questions over the control of the diversion route below the border, troubles related to the Mexican Revolution (1910–1921), and the presence of American speculators in Mexican lands who often worked at cross-purposes to Imperial Valley interests, made life for Rockwood, the Colorado Development Company, and valley residents a series of crises.

21. Engineer Chaffey, relying largely on Wozencraft's earlier designs, was responsible for the problematic situation that placed large stretches of the canal in Mexico.

22. Hundley, *Water and the West,* chapters 1 and 2; Norris Hundley, Jr., "The Politics of Reclamation: California, the Federal Government, and the Origins of the Boulder Canyon Act," *California Historical Quarterly* 52 (winter 1973): 301–306.

23. Hundley, *Water and the West,* 17–21; August, *Vision in the Desert,* 74.

24. The vision for reclaiming lands in the American West became a reality on June 17, 1902, when Congress passed the Newlands Reclamation Act. The act created a federal

reclamation fund supported by the sale of public lands in sixteen Western states and
territories, including Arizona. And while the original bill restricted federal support to
the sale of public lands, Arizona lobbyists Benjamin Fowler and George Maxwell persuaded President Theodore Roosevelt to eliminate the restriction. Soon afterward
Secretary of Interior Ethan Hitchcock created a new agency within the U.S.
Geological Survey called the Reclamation Service and appointed Frederick Newell as
its first director. Davis Dam, located on the lower Colorado River just north of
Bullhead City, Arizona, is named after Arthur Powell Davis. In fact, the modern origins of Bullhead City are tied to the construction of Davis Dam, which began in
1942, but had to be halted because materials necessary for construction were being
consumed by World War II efforts. Construction resumed in 1946 and the dam was
completed in 1950.

25. *San Diego Union,* January 20, 1918; Rufus Von Klein Smid, "The League of the
Southwest: What it is and Why," *Arizona: The State Magazine* 11 (May 1920);
Hundley, "Politics of Reclamation," *California Historical Quarterly,* 297–301; Arthur
Powell Davis to J. B. Lippencott, "October 10, 1902, Bureau of Reclamation Papers,
File 187, Colorado River Project, 1902–1919, Record Group 115, National Archives
and Records Service (NARS); U.S. Geological Survey, *First Annual Report of the
Reclamation Service, 1902* (Washington, D.C.: Government Printing Office, 1903),
106–107, 109; U.S. Department of the Interior, *Fourteenth Annual Report of the
Reclamation Service, 1914–1915* (Washington, D.C.: Government Printing Office,
1915), 323; House Committee on Irrigation of Arid Lands, "Hearings on All
American Canal in Imperial Valley, California, H.R. 6044," 66 Congress, 1 Session
(1919), 98–99. For the best short essay on Arthur Powell Davis see Gene Gressley,
"Arthur Powell Davis, Reclamation, and the West," *Agricultural History* 42 (July
1968): 241–57. Proponents of comprehensive development received much-publicized
support from the League of the Southwest, a regional booster organization. Largely a
California-sponsored group, the league, founded in 1917, nevertheless claimed that it
represented businesses and local governments dedicated to the commercial and social
interest of the southwest quarter of the country. At its initial convention at the Hotel
Del Coronado in San Diego, representatives from the seven basin states, Oklahoma,
and Texas joined envoys from Washington, D.C., and even Europe to discuss the
region's future. Rufus Von Klein Smid, an Arizonan and president of the University of
Arizona, was elected the league's first president. During 1917 and 1918 the group met
at San Diego and Tucson where discussions centered on tourism, commercial development, and transportation. By 1920 the League of the Southwest became an organization with virtually one purpose which was reflected on its newly adopted letterhead:
"The League of the Southwest holds as axiomatic that the development of the
resources of the Colorado River Basin fundamentally underlies all future progress
and prosperity of the Southwest."

26. The best account of these activities, especially Phil Swing's actions in the IID before his
election to Congress from California's Eleventh District, are discussed in Moeller, *Phil
Swing and Boulder Dam,* 3–19 and Hundley, *Water and the West,* 38–39.

27. August, *Vision in the Desert,* 76; Wilmer, Historical Notes, n.d., Box 1, File 4, Snell
& Wilmer Law Firm; *Congressional Record,* 65 Congress, 3 Session (1919), 2647,
2934, 3738; 66 Congress, 1 Session (1919), 22, 24, 1258. See also House Committee
on Irrigation of Arid Lands, "Hearings on the All-American Canal in Imperial Valley,
California," H.R. 6044 (1919), 7–8, 48, 51, 94, 142, 285–87.

28. Though Hayden drafted this bill, it was submitted later under Kettner's name.

29. Jack L. August, Jr., "Water, Politics, and the Arizona Dream: Carl Hayden and the
Modern Origins of the Central Arizona Project, 1922–1963," *Journal of Arizona
History* 40 (winter 1999): 393; *Mohave County Miner* (Kingman), December 1, 1894,
January 12, 19, 1895.

30. *Congressional Record,* 66 Congress, 2 Session (1920), 7360; Hundley, *Water and the West,* 51. Kettner relied heavily on Congressman Hayden and Phil Swing to draft added provisions to his 1920 bill. See also, Carl Hayden to B.F. Fly, Box 600, Folder 6, Carl Hayden Congressional Papers Collection (hereafter CHCP), ASU.

CHAPTER THREE: A QUESTION OF RELEVANCE

1. *Tombstone Epitaph,* June 8, 1922. Upper basin fears crystallized at a meeting of the League of the Southwest in Denver, Colorado. At this August 1920 meeting, just four months after a harmonious gathering in Los Angeles, upper basin representatives raised serious questions about California and its motives concerning the Colorado River. Governor of Colorado Oliver Shoup sounded the clarion call: "It is not time for any of the western states holding the headwaters to lose any of the rights for any reason whatever." His state engineer, A. J. McCune, echoed these remarks and added, "Our main fear is that Los Angeles and the people of the Imperial Valley will get the government committed to a policy that will interfere with our development." Furthermore he reiterated the warning that construction of the reservoir and beneficial use of the water would give California prior rights over upper basin states. Like Arizona, the upper basin expressed great trepidation regarding California and called for some form of protection.

2. For an excellent biography of Carpenter see, Ron Tyler, *Silver Fox of the Rockies: Delphus E. Carpenter and Western Water Compacts* (Norman: University of Oklahoma Press, 2003).

3. Carpenter believed in the preservation of states rights in order to preserve the constitutionally mandated balance between state and federal authority.

4. *Wyoming v Colorado* 259 U.S. 419 (1922); Hundley, *Water and the West,* 76, 78, 105, 106. Carpenter's role in subsequent Colorado River affairs was especially noteworthy. Although he called for federal cooperation in river development, he shared the long-cherished, jealously guarded position many westerners held concerning the supremacy of state's rights. The Coloradan vigorously resisted the claim, argued in *Wyoming v Colorado,* that the U.S. government owned all the unappropriated waters in non-navigable streams. "There should be no super-government imposition established," he wrote western congressmen, and he saw the federal government as an arbiter, not a dictator, in Colorado River affairs.

5. Moeller, *Phil Swing and Boulder Dam,* 29; Hundley, *Water and the West,* 105, 110, 111. According to Moeller, Hoover's appointment came after Phil Swing protested the rumored appointment of "a Denver man," doubtlessly Delph Carpenter. Secretary of Interior Albert Fall, according to Moeller, persuaded President Harding to appoint Hoover.

6. The Boulder Canyon site, moreover, held other advantages; most important among them was that the dam site was closest to the power markets in the areas where year-round irrigated agriculture took place. In addition to this advantage, a high dam would create a reservoir that controlled flooding, regulated flow, and allowed silt to settle, eliminating that problem without compromising storage capacity. See also, *Senate Doc. 142,* appendix, "Problems of Imperial Valley and Vicinity," 67 Congress, 2 Session (1922), 238, 239; Hundley, *Water and the West,* 119–134; Moeller, *Phil Swing and Boulder Dam,* 21, 24, 25.

7. Hydroelectric power generation, previously an incidental byproduct of reclamation endeavors, suddenly emerged as one of the most emotional, bitterly contested, and complicated issues of the entire effort. Davis, in a preliminary version of the Fall-Davis Report, left open the possibility that a private, municipal, or state agency might build the proposed dam and sell the power generated at the site. Almost immediately private power companies, like Southern Sierras Power and Southern California Edison, saw the potential for enormous profits, and quickly filed with the recently created Federal

Power Commission (FPC). Likewise, the City of Los Angeles, seizing upon public sentiment that private power companies were already charging unfair rates, and eager to secure affordable power for a burgeoning population, also applied to build a power-generating dam at the proposed site. The subsequent conflict over the merits of private versus municipally operated power raged for months, polarizing contending interests, and as a consequence, hastened the demise of the League of the Southwest. Secretary Fall, however, closed this chapter of the power debate and ended preliminary speculation over who would build and operate the dam when, at the public hearings in San Diego, he announced that the U.S. government had the ultimate authority to deal with that issue. Arizona's needs, while not as immediate as California's, nevertheless required hydroelectric power. It would be needed for groundwater pumping, Arizona's world-renowned copper industry, and meeting increasing domestic demand. Moreover, power was needed to pump water from the Colorado to the central portions of the state, the illusory dream of many Arizonans at the time.

8. Ultimately, Wilmer would minimize the compact's influence in determining Arizona's rights to mainstream water.

9. See August, *Vision in the Desert*, 85–86; William S. Norviel to Carl Hayden, May 1, October 5, 1922, CHCPC, ASU; Jack L. August, Jr., "Carl Hayden, Arizona, and the Politics of Water Development in the Southwest, 1923–1928," *Pacific Historical Review* 58 (May 1989): 195, 196; *House Doc. 605, 67* Congress, 4 Session (1923), 8–12.

10. August, "Carl Hayden and the Politics of Water," *Pacific Historical Review*, 197; Hundley, *Water and the West*, 142, 149, 200–203; Norviel to Hayden, February 26, 1926, CHCPC, ASU.

11. August, *Vision in the Desert*, 84; Hayden to G.E.P. Smith, February 17, 1923, Box 598, Folder 10; Hayden to F.T. Pomeroy, December 22, 1924; Box 600, Folder 9; CHCPC, ASU; House Committee on Irrigation of Arid Lands, "Hearings on Protection and Development of Lower Colorado River Basin, H.R. 11449," 67 Congress, 2 Session (1922), 18, 19; *Arizona Republican*, November 25, 1922; Hundley, "Colorado River Waters Dispute," *Foreign Affairs*, 195–200.

12. Other basin leaders expressed optimism similar to Hamale. Delph Carpenter, for example, placed the compact signing in broader perspective when he wrote, "This is the exemplification of interstate diplomacy on so large a scale." Fellow Colorado water law expert F. Ward Bannister called the pact "a great document ... a product of two years of labor by the best minds the states and nation had to give." In Arizona, newspaper editor, businessman, and politician Dwight Heard hailed the compact as a broad and necessary foundation for the erection of machinery that would ultimately determine the rights of the basin states and expedite development of the river.

13. *Congressional Record*, 70 Congress, 2 Session, (1928), 459, 466–472; Hundley, *Water and the West*, 268–270; Moeller, *Phil Swing and Boulder Dam*, 118–119; August, "Carl Hayden and the Politics of Water," *Pacific Historical Review*, 207.

14. For an analysis of Arizona's debates over the ratification of the Colorado River Compact see August, *Vision in the Desert*, chapter 5.

15. *Congressional Record*, 69 Congress, 2 Session, (1926), 5822; Dwight Mayo, "Arizona and the Colorado River Compact" (M.A. Thesis: Arizona State University, 1964), 30–34.

16. *Arizona Republican*, January 22, 1927; *New York Times*, January 22, 1927; House Committee on Rules and Administration, *Hearings on H.R. 9826*, 69 Congress, 2 Session (1927), 61–62.

17. House Committee on Rules, *Hearings on H.R. 9826*, 64–70; *Arizona Republican*, January 22, 1927; *Imperial Valley Farmer* (El Centro), January 13, 1927.

18. *Los Angeles Times*, May 29, 1928; *Los Angeles Examiner*, May 30, 1928; *Arizona Republican*, May 29, 1928; Moeller, *Phil Swing and Boulder Dam*, 115, 120;

Hundley, *Water and the West*, 275–276; *Congressional Record*, 70 Congress, 2 Session, (1928), 823, 836. The Boulder Canyon Project Act was signed into law on December 21, 1928.

19. August, *Vision in the Desert*, 136.

20. Ibid., 137.

21. Norris Hundley, Jr., "Clio Nods: *Arizona v California* and the Boulder Canyon Act— A Reassessment," *Western Historical Quarterly* 3, no. 1 (1972): 17–51.

CHAPTER FOUR: ARIZONA ADRIFT

1. *Arizona v California*, 283 U.S. 423 (1931). The bill was dismissed without prejudice to a future action for relief in the event that the dam was so operated as to interfere with Arizona's rights.

2. August, *Vision in the Desert*, 140. Black Canyon was often publicly misidentified as Boulder Canyon. Also, Simon Rifkind, oral history interview with Jack L. August, Jr., October 9, 1986, author's files; *Arizona v California*, et al. 373 U.S. 546 (1963); *Congressional Record*, 70 Congress, 2 Session (1928), 459, 466–472.

3. August, *Vision in the Desert*, 140–141. Arizona's Colorado River Commission provides a case in point. A. H. Favour, a veteran of several commissions wrote Senator Carl Hayden about that agency's lack of effectiveness: "We haven't formulated any definite water policy pertaining to the Colorado." In 1935 the editor of Tucson's *Arizona Daily Star* noted that for over a dozen years, "factional disputes within the state have cost it a pretty price." And, in 1939, Favour, briefing newly elected Governor Robert T. Jones, again commented that "Arizona has gone through various administrations since 1922 with no very definite water policy." Thus, the Arizona Colorado River Commission, often inefficient, usually unprofessional, and with little political power, further reflected the state's problems within the context of evolving federal reclamation policy.

4. Norris Hundley, Jr., "The West Against Itself: The Colorado River—An Institutional History," in Gary D. Weatherford and F. Lee Brown, eds., *New Courses for the Colorado River: Major Issues for the Next Century* (Albuquerque: University of New Mexico Press, 1985), 22–23. Hundley points out that construction of the dam, under the terms of the new law, could not begin until the federal government had obtained contracts for the hydroelectric power needed to pay for the project. Nevada had no market at the time; Arizona had neither the desire, nor the market. Thus California, in 1930, agreed to purchase all of the electricity to underwrite the cost of the dam and the power plant. Also, the contracts provided that the government could buy back 36 percent of the power for use in Arizona and Nevada any time during the fifty years required to pay for the project, thus protecting potential future power needs of the two states.

5. In his *Report* of December 5, 1960, Rifkind wrote, "On February 14, 1934, Arizona moved for leave to file a bill to perpetuate the testimony of the negotiators of the Colorado River Compact. The parties named were the other six states of the Colorado River Basin, the California agencies which are defendants in the present action and the Secretary of the Interior. A unanimous Court, speaking through Mr. Justice Brandeis, denied the application. One of the alternate grounds for decision was the incompetence of the evidence sought to be perpetuated. It was held that oral statements of negotiators of a treaty or compact not communicated to the ratifying body were not admissible to establish meaning." Rifkind, *Special Master's Report*, 7. See also, *Arizona v California* 292 U.S. 341 (1934).

6. Craig Lowell Whetten, "The March on Parker Dam: Why Governor B. B. Moeur Declared Martial Law, The Consequences Thereof, and its Place in Arizona Water Rights History," unpublished manuscript, 2005; Benjamin B. Moeur to Ray Lyman Wilbur, February 16, 1934; Ray Lyman Wilbur to Carl Hayden, February 28, 1934, Box 601, Folder 19, CHPC, ASU; Hundley, *Water and the West*, 285–288. For fur-

ther accounts see *Tucson Daily Citizen,* July 1, 1931; *Arizona Daily Star,* May 29, 1931.

7. *U.S. v Arizona* 295 U.S. 174; 79L. Ed. 1374 (1935); *Tucson Daily Citizen,* November 10, 11, 1934; *Arizona Daily Star,* March 7, November 10, 11, 12, 1934; *Arizona Republic,* November 10–14, 1934. MWD officials issued a statement the day after Arizona declared martial law: "We are taking no part in the controversy—our job is to build the Colorado River Aqueduct to receive water when it is impounded by the Bureau of Reclamation at Parker Dam." Ida Tarbell, the Progressive Era muckraker, covered the colorful affair for her readers in an article, "Arizona's Threat to Secede," in the *New York Tribune* of November 25, 1935. Tarbell defended Arizona's actions, claiming the state had "suffered outrageous injustice at the hands of California and the federal government. She labeled the conflict a "miniature war." Special Master Rifkind wrote, "On January 14, 1935, the United States sued to enjoin Arizona's interference with construction of Parker Dam, Arizona having threatened to use military force to prevent work at the dam. The Court, per Mr. Justice Butler, dismissed the complaint on the ground that there was no showing that the Secretary of the Interior was authorized to construct the dam. Subsequently, the Congress, by Act of August 30, 1935, specifically authorized erection of Parker Dam for the purpose, *inter alia,* of improving navigation.

8. 49 Stat. 1039.

9. *Arizona v California* 298 U.S. 558 (1936).

10. Rifkind, *Special Master's Report,* 8.

11. Parker Dam was completed in 1938 at a cost of approximately $8.8 million. The original bid by the Six Companies, who constructed Hoover Dam, was $4.2 million. As it turned out, Parker Dam was one of the deepest in the world; the crest reached 320 Fort and the excavation required digging to bedrock 235 feet below the river bottom.

12. August, *Vision in the Desert,* 147–148.

13. California planned to increase its annual use by 2 million acre feet through a proposed project at Pilot Knob. Even more disturbing for Arizonans, the Pilot Knob Project included selling additional water to Mexico at $1 per acre foot. Additionally, the drought prompted farmers to pump groundwater in unprecedented quantities. By 1940 most of the state's water storage reservoirs were nearly empty. In fact, hydroelectric power generation dwindled to the point that, in 1939 state leaders faced a severe power shortage. In response to the pleas of Governor Jones and other lawmakers, Senator Hayden contacted the interior department and the Bureau of Reclamation officials, who hastily constructed a transmission line on wood poles from Parker Dam. Thus Hoover Dam power, through a connecting link at Parker Dam, brought much-needed electricity to the Salt River Valley in 1940–1941. The irony of the situation was not lost on close observers who realized that the decision to accept Hoover power represented a sharp reversal of Arizona policy. The drought, and its immediate consequences—overdrafting of groundwater supplies and power shortages—forced state leaders to distance themselves from state's rights policies.

14. By the outbreak of World War II state leaders realized that they faced the possibility of water and power shortages if current demographic trends continued and these factors provided yet another impetus for reconsideration of state water policy. See Margaret Finnerty, "Sidney P. Osborn, 1884–1940: The Making of an Arizona Governor," (M.A. Thesis: Arizona State University, 1883); *Arizona Republic,* February 25, 1944; September 8, 1950; U.S. Bureau of the Census, *Sixteenth Census of the United States: 1940 Population,* Vol. 1, *Number of Inhabitants* (Washington, D.C.: Government Printing Office 1942), 89–91; *Journal of the Senate, Sixteenth Legislature of the State of Arizona, 1943* (Phoenix 1943), 89–90; *Journal of the Senate, Sixteenth Legislature of the State of Arizona, First Special Session, 1944* (Phoenix 1944), 1–39.

15. Hundley, *Water and the West,* 295–297; Carl Hayden to Jack Gavin, n.d., Box 614, Folder 7, CHPC, ASU. The implications of the Mexican Treaty were abundantly clear.

Unless Arizona took steps to put mainstream water to beneficial use within the state, California and Mexico could claim a prior right to Arizona's claimed share. Moreover, Bureau of Reclamation engineers, during hearings on the Mexican treaty, underscored the point when they reported that supply figures were significantly less than previously believed.

16. Senate Committee on Foreign Relations, *Hearings on Water Treaty with Mexico,* 79 Cong. 1 Sess. (1945), 1760; "Water Supply Below Boulder Dam," *Sen. Doc. 39,* 79 Cong. 1 Sess. (1945), part 1, 5–8; Hundley, *Water and the West,* 297; Carl Hayden to Sidney P. Osborn, February 15, 1943, Box 616, Folder 2, CHPC, ASU.

17. The short-term historical context of these developments is significant and shed light on the Arizona senator's relationship with the Bureau of Reclamation. As a result of the water shortage emergency in Arizona during the late 1930s and early 1940s, Secretary of Interior Harold Ickes supported Hayden's request to have Bureau of Reclamation engineers survey various routes to direct water from Parker Dam to central Arizona. In fact, on October 4, 1940, Hayden met with President Roosevelt to discuss the desperate need for new sources of water. Although the wet year of 1941 eliminated the need for emergency surveys, these steps anticipated later developments. In connection with these preparations, and the resumption of the drought a year later, the Arizona legislature, in early 1943, approved $200,000 for use by the Bureau to conduct investigations on various routes for an aqueduct from the Colorado to central Arizona. Also, according to Marc Reisner, a critic of the Bureau of Reclamation activities in the American West, Hayden supposedly exercised "near-despotic rule" over the Bureau's authorizing committees by World War II. During the war, moreover, Hayden was the ranking member of the Senate Committee on Post-War Economic and Policy Planning. Arizonans viewed their senator's position on this Committee as crucial in their quest for water from the Colorado River. See Marc Reisner, *Cadillac Desert: The American West and its Disappearing Water,* rev. ed. (Vancouver: Douglas and McIntyre, 1993), 118; Gerald Nash, *The American West Transformed: The Impact of World War II* (Bloomington: Indiana University Press, 1985).

18. U.S. Senate, "Authorizing with Respect to Present and Future Need for Development of Projects for Irrigation and Hydroelectric Power," (1943), *passim.*

19. Of great help to Arizona during these hearings was Harold Ickes, the Secretary of Interior. By this time Hayden and Ickes had developed a close personal and working relationship. Ickes recalled the pleasant talks on matters of interest to the West and marveled at Hayden's persuasive powers in committee. On July 11, 1943, for example, Ickes, ruminating over a recent budget battle in one of the subcommittees on appropriations, confided to his diary: "Senator Hayden has never shown himself as much a useful friend to my department as he has shown in recent fiscal legislation. As chairman for the Sub-committee on Appropriations for the Interior, he succeeded in restoring many items that had been cut out . . . And he put in additional items, especially for reclamation projects." In turn, Hayden received from Ickes special consideration for programs he favored. "Ickes Diary," entries July 11, 1943, Vol. 49, 7970–7971; July 20, 1941, Vol. 39, 5592; May 9, 1943, Vol. 47, 7705, Library of Congress, Washington, D.C.; Ernest McFarland, *Mac: The Autobiography of Ernest McFarland* (Phoenix: Ernest McFarland, 1979), 200–207. McFarland recalled the significance of these hearings in his autobiography: "Looking back, I consider this to have been the most important move because it created an interested Arizona which had never existed before. We held five days of hearings in Phoenix, Florence, Safford, Yuma, and Kingman. Eighty-three persons appeared before the subcommittee, some representing different industries and including almost all sections of the state of Arizona, particularly those representing irrigation, electrical power districts, land corporations, and farmers."

20. August, *Vision in the Desert,* 161.

21. Hearings, *Sen. Res. 304*, 12–15; *Arizona Republic*, August 22, 1944.

22. This portion of the hearings was held in Florence, Arizona. Hearings, *Sen. Res. 304*, 50–54; *Arizona Daily Star*, August 4, 1944.

23. U.S. Bureau of Reclamation, *Comparison of Diversion Routes, Central Arizona Project Planning Report, Project Planning Report No. 3–8b 4–0* (Washington, D.C., 1945), 4–6; *Arizona Republic*, August 22, 1944.

24. Bureau of Reclamation, *Report on the Central Arizona Project*, 13; *Arizona Republic*, February 6, 1948; Arizona Daily Star, February 6, 1948; Jack L. August, Jr., "Carl Hayden's 'Indian Card': Environmental Politics and the San Carlos Reclamation Project," *Journal of Arizona History* 33 (winter 1992), 397–422.

25. Bureau of Reclamation, Report on the Central Arizona Project, 43; Walter Rusinek, "Bristor v Cheatham: Conflict Over Groundwater Law in Arizona," *Arizona and the West* 24 (summer 1985): 143–162. Indeed much remained to be resolved, including the groundwater issue which resulted in a long series of State Supreme Court decisions that had the effect of limiting the right of private ownership of groundwater while increasing the power of the state government in controlling withdrawals.

26. McFarland, *Mac*, 207; Carl Hayden to Forrest Donnell, June 20 1947, Box 662, Folder 4, CHPC, ASU. In the House of Representatives, John Murdock (D-Arizona) submitted a companion bill to accompany S 433. HR 1598 was offered on February 3, 1947.

27. August, *Vision in the Desert*, 165.

28. *Newsweek Magazine*, March 6, 1950, described this aspect of the political process in vivid terms for its readers: "Carl Hayden, who almost never speaks to newsmen but is articulate enough in the cloakrooms, had a couple of helpful talking points. As chairman of the Rules Committee he is in charge of Capitol patronage in the Senate wing. This strategic spot enables him to block funds for any special committee investigations voted by the Senate. In addition, Hayden is the ranking members and de facto chairman of the Appropriations Committee, which passes on specific projects, sometime legitimate, sometimes porkbarrel, upon which the political life of many senators depends." *Arizona Republic*, February 22, 1950; U.S. Senate, *Congressional Record*, February 21, 1950, 81 Cong., 2 Sess., 2101–2102; Walter Bimson to Carl Hayden, February 22, 1950, Box 19, Folder 10, CHPC, ASU.

29. August, *Vision in the Desert*, 167. Engle told several California audiences that "Hayden is the most powerful man in the U.S. Senate . . . and as a top ranking member of the Senate Appropriations Committee—Hayden had done favors for everyone."

30. *Phoenix Gazette*, October 25, 1950; Johnson, *Central Arizona Project*, 60, 67.

31. Sims Ely, *The Lost Dutchman Mine* (New York: William Morrow and Company, 1953); Dennis McBride, "Sims Ely (1862–1954): The Boulder City Dictator," Stephens Media Group, 1999, 2.

32. Northcutt Ely, "Doctor Ray Lyman Wilbur: Third President of Stanford and Secretary of the Interior," The Fortnightly Club, Redlands, Calif., December 16, 1994.

33. "Overseer Northcutt "Mike" Ely Dies at age 93," *Hoover Institution Newsletter* (summer 1997). As executive assistant to Wilbur during the Hoover administration, Ely chaired a technical advisory commission to the Federal Oil Conservation Board in Washington from 1931–1933. Other significant legal benchmarks in his career: he was counsel to the Governor of Oklahoma when he was negotiating the Interstate Oil Compact of 1935–35 and counsel to the governments of Saudi Arabia, Turkey, The People's Republic of China, Algeria, Malagasy Republic, Ethiopia, Grenada, and Thailand on mining and petroleum issues. He was also a member to the U.S. delegation to the United Nations Conference on the Application of Science and Technology for the Benefit of Less Developed Areas in 1963 and the United Nations Conference on mineral legislation held in Manila in 1969 and Bangkok in 1973.

34. Roger Ernst interview with Jack L. August, Jr., March 23, 1983, Oral History Collection (OHC), Department of Archives and Manuscripts, Hayden Library, ASU; *Arizona Republic,* September 7, 1950, Johnson, *Central Arizona Project,* 59–71.

35. Representatives Murdock and Patten introduced HR 1500 and HR 1501, to support construction of CAP in the first session of the Eighty-second Congress. See also, August, *Vision in the Desert,* 170.

36. Howard Pyle interview with Jack L. August, Jr., November 9, 1982, Tempe, Arizona, OHC, ASU; House of Representatives, Interior and Insular Affairs Committee, *Hearings on H.R. 1500, 1501,* 82 Cong., 1 Sess., 741–63; *Arizona Republic,* April 19, 1951, *Arizona Daily Star,* April 19, 1951, *Los Angeles Times,* April 19, 1951.

37. *Arizona Daily Star,* May 31, 1951; U.S. Senate, *Congressional Record,* 82 Cong., 1 Sess., 5974–6210. This version of S 75 not only authorized a Supreme Court test of water rights but also provided that construction could not begin while any suit was pending before the Court.

38. For an analysis of the tempestuous legislative history of the CAP bills from 1947–1952, see August, *Vision in the Desert,* 159–174.

CHAPTER FIVE: ARIZONA V CALIFORNIA

1. Perry Ling and Burr Sutter, who each served as special counsel to the Arizona Interstate Stream Commission, were associates at Snell & Wilmer.

2. *Arizona Republic,* April 14, 1952.

3. Moeur was the son of former Arizona Governor B. B. Moeur. *Arizona Daily Star,* August 14, 1952; *Arizona Republic,* August 14, 1952; Wayne Akin oral history interview with Jack L. August, Jr., September 18, 1982, Oral History Collection, Department of Archives and Manuscripts, Hayden Library, ASU; Hundley, "The West Against Itself," in Weatherford and Browns, eds., *New Courses for the Colorado River,* 30; Donald Worster, *Rivers of Empire: Water, Aridity, and the Growth of the American West* (New York: Pantheon, 1985). At the start of the suit, Governor Pyle signed the motion and complaint in which the Arizona Interstate Stream Commission asked the Supreme Court to take jurisdiction in the battle over the Colorado River. With Pyle at the signing were Moeur, Secretary of State Wesley Bolin, AISC Executive Secretary Ray Killian, Arizona Attorney General Fred O. Wilson, Chief Assistant Attorney General Alexander B. Baker, and Perry M. Ling, of Snell & Wilmer who served as Special Counsel to AISC.

4. *Arizona Republic,* August 14, 1952; *Los Angeles Times,* August 14, 1952.

5. Apparently, California was caught completely by surprise by the timing of Arizona's suit filing. Although the suit was filed at 2:50 P.M. the Californians failed to reach the clerk's office before the 4:30 P.M. closing time to get copies of the Arizona pleadings.

6. Frank Snell and Mark Wilmer met Senator McFarland in the late 1930s, when he was serving as Pinal County superior court judge, admired his legal and political skills, and campaigned vigorously for him in the Democratic Senate primary of 1940, when he upset the incumbent Democrat, Henry Fountain Ashurst. McFarland went on to win the general election and entered the Senate in 1941.

7. *Los Angeles Times,* August 3, 1952.

8. *Arizona Republic,* August 14, 1952; J. H. Moeur, Special Counsel, Arizona Interstate Stream Commission, "The Colorado River Controversy," memorandum, February 1, 1951, Arizona Interstate Stream Commission (AISC), Arizona State Library, Archives and Public Records, Phoenix, Arizona. Nixon had been recently tapped as the Republicans' vice presidential candidate with General Dwight D. Eisenhower.

9. Arizona's 3.8 million acre-feet claim included the 1 million acre-feet of Gila River water put to beneficial use within Arizona under the San Carlos Irrigation Project. Rich Johnson, *The Central Arizona Project, 1918–1968* (Tucson: University of

Arizona Press, 1977), 84, 94–95. See also, the Boulder Canyon Project Act [45 Stat. 1057 and the California Limitation Act [Laws of California 1929, ch. 16, 38–39]; John G. Will, "Law and Water," *Project Rescue: A Seminar on the Central Arizona Project* (Tempe: Arizona State University, 1964), 19–23.

10. The solicitor general advised the Court on October 17, 1952, that the federal government would move to intervene in the case. T. Richmond Johnson oral history interview with Jack L. August, Jr., March 20, 1985, Phoenix, Arizona, OHC, DAM, Hayden Library, ASU; *New York Times,* June 4, 1963; *Los Angeles Times,* May 21, 1953; *Arizona Republic,* May 21, 1953.

11. *Arizona v California,* et al., 373, U.S. 564, 565 (1963); Johnson, *Central Arizona Project,* 88–97; August, *Vision in the Desert,* 178–179.

12. Rifkind, *Special Master's Report,* 2.

13. While case transcripts document this phase, Governor Ernest McFarland's unique role in the final phases of the preliminary hearings is described in the recent biography of James E. McMillan, Jr., *Ernest W. McFarland* (Prescott, Ariz.: Sharlot Hall Museum Press, 2004), 310–313.

14. John P. Frank, Partner, Lewis and Roca, *www.lrlaw.com/professional_bio.asp.* See also, United States Courts for the Ninth Circuit, News Release, "New Ninth Circuit Award Honors Memory of Renowned Attorney John P. Frank," June 11, 2003. Frank was involved in hundreds of appeals in his years with Lewis and Roca and his professional activities, political activism, and scholarly output—eleven books and over one hundred scholarly articles—was impressive in scope. His awards and special recognitions were without peer.

15. Ibid., 310–311.

16. *Arizona Republic,* June 9, 1984. Avery reflected on this instance and others upon McFarland's death.

17. For an excellent overview of this interpretation see Robert Hoffman, "Wilmer Strategy Key to Water Rights," *Maricopa Lawyer* 4, no. 7 (August 1985).

18. U.S. Supreme Court, *Arizona v California,* 350 U.S. 114 (1955). Court records indicate that John P. Frank and Ernest W. McFarland argued the cause for the State of Arizona, complainant. On the brief were Robert Morrison, Attorney General of John H. "Hub" Moeur, John Geoffrey Will, Burr Sutter, Perry Ling, and Theodore Kiendl.

19. McMillan, *Ernest W. McFarland,* 311–313. *Arizona v California,* 350 U.S. 114 (1955).

20. Rifkind interview with August, October 9, 12, 1986.

21. Ibid.

22. Rifkind interview with August, October 9, 12, 1986; Norris Hundley, Jr., *The Great Thirst: California and Water, 1770–1990* (Berkeley: University of California Press, 1992), 300–301; *Arizona Republic,* August 15, 1955.

23. *Arizona Republic,* July 7, 1985; John Fowles to David Rauch, Memorandum, July 29, 2003, Snell & Wilmer Law Offices.

24. *Arizona Republic,* July 7, 1985.

25. See Sidney Kartus, "Report to the Arizona Legislative Committee On Trial Proceedings Before the Hon. Simon Rifkind, Special Master, in the Case of Arizona v California, et al. (No. 10, Original, U.S. Supreme Court, October 1952 term) Held at San Francisco, California, February 10–18, 1957, in the Mater of the Colorado River," Arizona Interstate Stream Commission Papers, Box 27, Arizona State Library, Archives, and Public Records, Phoenix.

26. Ibid.

27. *See Ickes v Fox,* 300 U.S. 82 (1937). In this case, cited in the California brief, the U.S. Supreme Court held that water rights vested in water users in accord with state laws and not contracts with the United States or its agents such as the Secretary of Interior (23–24).

28. *Arizona Republic,* July 7, 1985.

29. "Outtakes," *Phoenix 2,* 1988.

30. Minutes, "Joint Conference of House-Senate Appropriations Committee members with members of the Arizona Interstate Stream Commission," March 11, 1997, Arizona Interstate Stream Commission Collection, Box 27, Arizona State Library, Archives, and Public Records, Phoenix, Arizona.

31. Ibid.

CHAPTER SIX: ENTER MARK WILMER

1. Wilmer, much like Frank Snell learned from Maricopa County judges in 1938, was the consensus choice as the best litigator in Arizona available.

2. McNulty interview with Wilmer, 1988. See also, Columbus Giragi, "Our Amazing Arizona: State Bar Lauded in Water Case," n.d., Wilmer Notebooks. According to Giragi, a noted political journalist in the 1940s and 1950s, "The method of selecting such an attorney presented a problem and it was not easy. It was finally decided to heave the problem at the Arizona State Bar Association. As a result, a special committee was named by the president of the bar association. This committee unanimously endorsed Mark Wilmer, of Phoenix, one of the senior members of the firm of Snell and Wilmer. The bar association did not lay out the silk gloves of request. Wilmer was drafted."

3. Elizabeth Sexson oral history interview with Jack L. August, Jr., February 12, 2005, Phoenix, Arizona, Snell & Wilmer Archives.

4. *Snell & Wilmer, The First Sixty Years,* 8. Ultimately, James Walsh left the firm to become a U.S. district court judge, and Melczer, who joined the firm in 1946, became the dean of Arizona's tax and estate planning bar. Celebrities from throughout the country, like John Wayne and Senator Barry Goldwater, frequently visited Melczer, who assisted these prominent figures and many others in their legal affairs.

5. *Snell & Wilmer, The First Sixty Years,* 8–9. In 1950 Edward "Bud" Jacobson joined the firm and began a career that spanned five decades that exemplified Snell & Wilmer's commitment to excellence and public service.

6. Calvin Udall oral history interview with John Bouma, February 18, 2000, Snell & Wilmer, Phoenix, Arizona.

7. *Arizona Republic,* April 3, 1957. According to Calvin Udall, who worked closely with Wilmer and Reed on the case, "The Interstate Stream Commission, which was charged by statute with conducting the litigation, had only two full-time lawyers, Burr Sutter and Geoff Will." See, Calvin Udall, "Tribute to Mark Wilmer," *Arizona State Law Journal* 27, no. 2 (summer 1995): 421.

8. In the 1988 documentary, "The Phoenix 2," Wilmer made clear that he made a "deal" with Reed that he would litigate and Reed would take care of related details surrounding the case.

9. *Arizona Republic,* July 7, 1985.

10. Ibid.

11. McNulty interview with Wilmer, 1988.

12. For a comprehensive account of the various pleadings, briefs, and orders of the court see Rifkind, *Special Master's Report,* Appendix 1, 363–370.

13. "Amended and Supplemental Statement of Position by Complainant, State of Arizona," U.S Supreme Court, October Term 1956. Arizona's lawyers listed on the document, Charles H. Reed, Chief Counsel, Colorado River Litigation, Arizona Interstate Stream Commission, Mark Wilmer, John Geoffrey Will, Burr Sutter, John E. Madden, Robert Begam, Calvin Udall, For the Interstate Stream Commission, Robert Morrison, Attorney General of Arizona. According to Begam, this filing was Plan B in the Arizona legal arsenal. "You know," he recalled in November 2006, "I remember

we called it Plan B and we spent a lot of time on our witnesses and putting on our use of water, the equities, but we didn't abandon that we knew we had to persuade the court that you've got equities on your side, so that was the thrust of Plan A, as I recall. I don't know why we called it Plan B but Plan B was simply the Statute Case." See Begam interview with August, November 28, 2006.

14. Outtakes from "The Phoenix 2," 1988; Rifkind, *Special Master's Report,* Appendix 1, 365.

15. *Arizona Republic,* July 7, 1985.

16. *Arizona Republic,* August 6, 1957.

17. "The Phoenix 2," 1988; Wilmer interview with McNulty.

18. *Colorado River Compact,* 1922.

19. See Article 8, *Colorado River Compact,* 1922.

20. Outtakes from "The Phoenix 2," 1988. (author's files); Wilmer interview with Lorig.

21. Wilmer interview with McNulty.

22. Indeed, Rifkind concluded, "that the claims of Arizona, California, and Nevada to water from Lake Mead and from the mainstream of the Colorado River below Hoover Dam are governed by the Boulder Canyon Project Act, 45 Stat. 1057 (1929), the California Limitation Act, Act of March 4, 1929, and several water delivery contracts which the Secretary of Interior made pursuant to the authority vested in him by Section 5 of the Project Act. The Colorado River Compact, the doctrine of equitable apportionment, and the law of appropriation are irrelevant to the allocation of such water among the three states." See, Rifkind, *Special Master's Report,* 138.

23. *Arizona v California,* et al., 373, U.S. 564, 565 (1963). The Court cited a quote from HR Doc. No. 717, 80 Cong. 2 Sess. (1948), 22, "Participants (in the Compact negotiations) have stated that the negotiations would have broken up but for Mr. Hoover's proposal: that the Commission limit its efforts to a division of water between the upper basin and the lower basin, leaving each basin the future internal allocation of its share."

24. Wilmer also expressed his profound thanks to Governor McFarland, who traveled to San Francisco to publicly announce his support for the amended pleading.

25. Outtakes, "The Phoenix 2," 1988. "Response to Arizona," Northcutt Ely, n.d., Northcutt Ely Papers, Box 241, File 17, Special Collections, Stanford University, Stanford, California.

26. Mark Wilmer, holograph notes, n.d., Snell & Wilmer Archives.

27. He stated that after six months of studying the Colorado River Compact, "it had nothing to do with the case." See Outtakes, "The Phoenix 2," 1988.

28. *Congressional Record,* 70 Cong., 1 Sess. (1928), 466–467.

29. Ibid., 467; August, *Vision in the Desert,* 184–186.

30. Rifkind, *Special Master's Report,* 54.

31. See *Arizona v California* 292 U.S. 341 (1934).

32. Wilmer, "*Arizona v California:* A Statutory Construction Case," *Arizona Law Review,* 55.

33. *Arizona Republic,* May 10, 1960.

34. Northcutt Ely to Mark Wilmer, May 7, 1960, Box 1, Folder 3, Mark Wilmer Collection, AHF, ASU.

35. *Arizona Republic,* January 18, 1962, July 7, 1985.

36. Elizabeth Wilmer Sexson, oral history interview with Jack L. August, Jr., October 5, 2004, Phoenix, Arizona, Mark Wilmer Collection, AHF, ASU.

37. *Arizona v California* 373 U.S. 546 (1963).

38. Wilmer interview with McNulty, 1989.

39. Ibid.

40. Calvin Udall, "Tribute to Mark Wilmer," ASLJ, 422.

41. August, *Vision in the Desert,* 183–184; *Arizona Republic,* June 4, 1963. The five justices upholding the recommendations of the special master were Byron R. White, Arthur J. Goldberg, Tom C. Clark, William Brennan, Jr., and Hugo L. Black, author of the opinion, Justice William O. Douglas wrote a strongly worded dissent, and Justice John H. Harlan drafted a separate dissent that had the concurrence of Justice Potter Stewart.

42. *Arizona Republic,* June 4, 1963; *Los Angeles Times,* June 4, 1963.

43. *Arizona Republic,* June 5, 1963.

44. *Arizona Republic,* June 4, 1963. The *Republic* added, "The victory itself actually would have to be credited to relief pitchers Charley Reed of Coolidge and Mark Wilmer of Phoenix, along with their backup staff of lawyers and engineers."

45. Theodore Kiendl to Mark Wilmer, June 4, 1963, Box 1, Folder 3, Mark Wilmer Collection, AHF, ASU.

46. Roy L. Elson, administrative aide to Senator Carl Hayden and candidate for the U.S. Senate, 1955–1969, "Oral History Interviews, July 27 to August 21, 1990," Senate Historical Office, Washington, D.C., 103.

47. *Arizona Republic,* June 4, 1963.

48. John Rhodes to Carl Hayden, January 25, 1963, Box 3, Folder 8, CHPC; Wayne Aspinall to Stewart Udall, November 27, 1962, Box 3, Folder 10, CHPC, ASU; *Washington Post,* January 22, 1962; *Arizona Republic,* January 22, 1962, *New York Times,* January 22, 1962; U.S. Secretary of the Interior, "News Release: Secretary Udall Announces Study for Regional Solution of Water and Power Problems of the Pacific Southwest," January 22, 1963. See also, Helen Ingram, *Water Politics: Continuity and Change* (Albuquerque: University of New Mexico Press, 1990), 46–48.

49. See Norris Hundley, Jr., "'The Winters Decision' and Indian Water Rights: A Mystery Reexamined," *Western Historical Quarterly* 13 (1982): 17–42; *Arizona v California,* et al., 373, U.S. 587, 596, 598–601 (1963); *Winters v United States,* 207 U.S. 564 (1908); *Arizona v California,* et al., 439 U.S. 422 (1979). Arizona, where most of the Indian land under the ruling was located, therefore, bore the burden of this "Indian" water. Additionally, the justices ruled that these rights dated from the establishment of a reservation and were superior to later non-Indian rights, including those rights based on uses initiated before Indians had begun diverting water from the Colorado or its tributaries. Clearly, the case left the Indians in a much stronger legal position than they had previously maintained.

50. See Norris Hundley, Jr., "The Dark and Bloody Ground of Indian Water Rights: Confusion Elevated to Principle," *Western Historical Quarterly,* 9 (1978), 478–479. Also, the U.S. Supreme Court decree in 1964 gave Arizona the right to use 2.8 million acre-feet of water but with a junior priority. When the Colorado produces less than what is allocated to the three lower basin states, Arizona suffers reductions first. In 2005 the basin states agreed to an operational framework that reduces the risk of a shortage trigger. Yet, Arizona still takes the shortage first, though the probabilities are much less due to the recent agreement. Indeed, this is good news for the more than 5 million people living in Maricopa, Pinal, and Pima Counties as well as cities like Bullhead City, Yuma, and Lake Havasu City—all of which rely on the river.

51. *Arizona Republic,* July 7, 1985.

52. Wilmer interview with McNulty, 1989.

53. Ibid.

54. Ibid.

55. Rifkind interview with August, October 9, 12, 1986.

56. The Supreme Court voted 5–3 in favor of Arizona. *Arizona v California,* et al. 373 U.S. 564, 565 (1963); Hundley, "The West Against Itself," *New Courses for the Colorado River,* 375, *Washington Post,* June 4, 1963; *Arizona Republic,* June 4, 1963.

CHAPTER SEVEN: A BRAVE NEW WATER WORLD: LAW, POLITICS, AND CAP

1. Anticipating Wilmer's legal victory, on April 10, 1963, Senator Hayden sent a memorandum to his fellow Arizona senator, Barry Goldwater, and the three congressmen, George Senner, Morris Udall, and John Rhodes indicating, "I feel that our bill should be as simple as possible, and as similar as practicable to the bill considered by Congress in the late 1940s and early 1950s that twice passed the Senate." See Carl Hayden, "Memorandum," April 10, 1963, Box 2, Folder 4, CHPC, ASU; "Arizona Seeks Billion Dollar Water Project," *Congressional Quarterly Fact Sheet,* June 5, 1963. The bill numbers were S 1658 in the Senate and HR 6796, HR 6797, and HR 6798 in the House.

2. C.A Pugh to Carl Hayden, January 15, 1963; Roy Elson to Paul Fannin, June 3, 1963; Memorandum to File, "Statement Made by Secretary of Interior Udall to Senator Hayden," July 11, 1963, Box 2, Folder 15, CHPC, ASU, "Arizona Seeks Billion Dollar Water Project," *Congressional Quarterly Fact Sheet,* June 5, 1963.

3. U.S. Department of Interior, "News Release," January 22, 1963; Ingram, Water Politics, 48, Ernest Englebert, *Policy Issues of the Pacific Southwest Water Plan,* (Boulder: University of Colorado Press, 1965), 130–135; Carl Hayden, "Fact Sheet on Interior's Pacific Southwest Water Plan," n.d., Box 2, Folder 14, CHPC; Carl Hayden to Stewart Udall, February 20, 1964, White House Central Files (WHCF), NR 7, University of Texas, Lyndon Baines Johnson Presidential Library (LBJ), Austin, Texas.

4. In extensive correspondence over the next two years Udall suggested to Arizona leaders that CAP, did, in fact, fit into his broader regional program. To one of these missives, dated December 19, 1963, in which Udall alerted Senator Hayden that he could not file a favorable report on a separate CAP bill, Hayden replied, "I vigorously protest the failure to keep your commitment to me and to the other officials of this state. I insist that language be included in PSWP which will be a clear endorsement of the CAP as embodied in S 1658 and/or as a separate first segment in any regional program." See, for example, Stewart Udall to Carl Hayden, December 19, 1963, Box 2, Folder 14, CHPC. Paul Fannin, "News Release," December 27, 1963, in Box 2, Folder 14, CHPC, ASU.

5. Stewart Udall to Carl Hayden, "Personal," August 20, 1963, Box 2, Folder 14; Hayden to Udall, December 5, 1963, Box 2, Folder 1, CHPC, ASU; *New York Times,* June 13, 1963; *Arizona Republic,* August 14, 1963. In his August 20, 1963, letter to Senator Hayden, Secretary Udall declared, "From this point on I intend to give Goldwater and Pulliam blow for blow if that is what they want. I may be 1000% wrong but on the basis of my knowledge of the art of the possible in the House and my conversations with Chairman Aspinall and others, it has been my best judgment that some kind of regional approach will be absolutely essential if a Central Arizona Project is to pass in the House.... In my opinion, Governor Fannin and the Arizona water people have made a grievous mistake in failing to have any consultation whatsoever with the members of the House concerning basic strategy. The Pulliam-Goldwater tactics of attempting to bludgeon my brother and Representative [George] Senner into line with their strategy is outrageous and indefensible."

6. *Yuma Daily Sun,* June 16, 1963; Roy Elson to Jack L. August, Jr., January 18, 2006, author's files.

7. Hayden also reminded various committees that before any water could be conveyed through proposed PSWP facilities the federal government had to construct the Auburn-Folsom South Unit ($400 million) the East Side Division of the Central Valley Project ($1 billion) and the State of California needed to complete the aqueduct system

under the California State Water Plan. He allowed that he opposed any proposals that would permit consideration to these California projects in preference to consideration of CAP. See, Carl Hayden, "Statement Upon Resumption of Hearings on S 1658," n.d., Box 3, Folder 9, CHPC, ASU.

8. Hayden detailed ten methods in which California obstructed Arizona from putting water to beneficial use between 1924 and 1963. He included, for example, California's refusal to accept the division of water recommended by the Colorado River Basin Governors conference in 1924 and its insistence on endless negotiations among the lower basins states. Hayden also pointed to California's strenuous resistance to the Mexican Water Treaty of 1944 and the state's consumption of eleven months instead of ninety days required by law in commenting on the Department of Interior's Central Arizona Project Report in 1947.

9. Ingram, *Water Politics*, 52; August, *Vision in the Desert*, 194–195.

10. Ingram, *Water Politics*, 52–53. For a thorough discussion on Senator Jackson and Senator Anderson and their respective support of CAP see August, *Vision in the Desert*, 194–195.

11. It should be noted that the House Interior Committee had the heaviest workload of any committee in Congress. In fact, nearly three in ten bills in the House were referred to this committee. At the time of CAP consideration, the committee was generally favorably disposed to reclamation bills since a majority of its members were from districts that had receive benefits from reclamation legislation. In the years just prior to CAP consideration, reclamation projects had met with increasing resistance both in committee and in the House itself due to the marginal quality of projects and the reluctance of eastern and urban congressmen to put water to additional lands because of farm product surplus. In addition to these drawbacks, CAP was not the only reclamation bill before the Subcommittee on Irrigation and Reclamation. Since January 1963, no less than fifteen other projects had been proposed and these bills awaited action. This backlog was a critical problem. Morris Udall, "Congressman's Report," June 21, 1963; Ingram, *Water Politics*, 48–50.

12. Two recent books assess and interpret the life and career of Wayne Aspinall. See Stephen C. Schulte, *Wayne Aspinall and the Shaping of the American West* (Boulder: University of Colorado Press, 2002), and Stephen C. Sturgeon, *The Politics of Western Water: The Congressional Career of Wayne Aspinall* (Tucson: University of Arizona Press, 2002).

13. See Thomas G. Smith, *Green Republican: John Saylor and the Preservation of America's Wilderness* (Pittsburgh: University of Pittsburgh Press, 2006). Smith's volume chronicles the life of Congressman John Saylor who believed that wilderness was intrinsic to the American experience and that our concepts of love of country, conservation, and independence were shaped by our wilderness experiences. Through his unyielding efforts to protect national parks and his efforts to add new areas to the park system, Saylor, the author argues convincingly, helped propel the American environmental movement in the three decades since World War II.

14. August, *Vision in the Desert*, 197.

15. See Roderick Nash, *Wilderness and the American Mind*, 3d ed. (New Haven: Yale University Press, 1982), 209–235; Henry M. Jackson to Carl Hayden, August 15, 1963; Hayden to Jackson, February 18, 1964, Box 2, Folder 15, CHPC, ASU; See David Brower to President Lyndon Johnson, , to Stewart Udall, to Henry Jackson, January 30, 1967, Box 19, Folder NR 7–1, WHCF, LBJ, Austin, Texas.

16. Senator Hayden and the Arizona delegation took the defeat of the Grand Canyon dams in stride. The senior senator wrote a friend, "I was aware of this future need [hydroelectric power] when Grand Canyon National Park was created by Act of Congress in 1919 when I was a young congressman from Arizona and for that reason made certain that the reservation for future reclamation development was clearly

understood. The same question arose when Grand Canyon National Monument was created in 1932 and a letter exists in the Department of Interior files from then-Director of the National Park Service Horace Albright to the Commissioner of Reclamation Elwood Mead, stating positively that creation of the monument would not interfere with construction of Boulder Canyon Dam or other dams." See Carl Hayden to Oakes, n.d. Box 5, Folder 9 CHPC; Carl Hayden to President Lyndon B. Johnson, "Statement of Carl Hayden of Arizona, July 26, 1967, Accompanying the filing of the Majority Report of the Senate Committee on Interior and Insular Affairs on S 1004 authorizing the Central Arizona Project," Box 1967, NR 7 1/6 FG 145, WHCF, LBJ, Austin, Texas. Donald Worster, *Rivers of Empire: The American West and Its Disappearing Water* (New York: Random House, 1985).

17. Ingram, *Water Politics*, 60–65; August, *Vision in the Desert*, 199. Another political frustration emerged within Arizona. As CAP remained stalled in the House Interior Committee despite numerous concessions, impatient elements within state leadership triggered a minor, but serious, complication. Rumors of an "Arizona-Go-It-Alone" CAP, promoted by conservatives and elements within the Arizona Power Authority surfaced shortly after Arizona's victory in the Supreme Court. A prominent feature of the state-financed and operated project included included an application to the Federal Power Commission in order for APA to finance, construct, operate, and manage a hydroelectric dam on the Colorado River. Senator Hayden and Congressman John Rhodes quickly thwarted this effort by ushering through Congress S 502 that preserved the jurisdiction of Congress over the construction of hydroelectric power works below Glen Canyon Dam. With passage of S 502 on June 23, 1964 Arizona "Go-It-Alone" advocates were effectively neutralized though they kept threatening to take action throughout the course of the legislative process. John Rhodes interview with Jack L. August, Jr., November 4, 1985, Tempe, Arizona, Oral History Collection, Department of Archives and Manuscripts, ASU; Carl Hayden to Lawrence Mehren, August 14, 1964, Box 4, Folder 10, CHPC, ASU.

18. Besides CAP, the legislation included authorization of several other controversial reclamation projects, including Hooker Dam in New Mexico, an aqueduct from Lake Mead to Las Vegas, the Dixie Project in Utah, and the Uintah unit of the Central Utah Project. The act also authorized the San Miguel, Dallas Creek, West Divide, Dolores, and Animas La Plata projects in Congressman Aspinall's state of Colorado. Additionally, it authorized the creation of the Lower Colorado River Basin Development Fund to build a still-yet-to-be determined augmentation project. Finally, the bill made delivery of Mexico's 1.5 million acre-feet of water annually a national, not regional, responsibility.

19. Ronald Reagan to Raymond R. Rummonds, November 28, 1967, Box 600, Folder 6, CHPC, ASU; Barefoot Sanders to Lyndon Johnson, August 1, 1968; James R. Jones to Carl Hayden, August 19, 1968, Central White House File (CWHF), LBJ Presidential Library, Austin, Texas. See also House Committee on Interior and Insular Affairs, *Hearings on the Lower Colorado River Basin Project, H.R. 4671 and Similar Bills*, 89 Cong. (1965–1966); *Hearings on Colorado River Basin Project*, 90 Cong. 1 Sess. (1967); *Hearings on Colorado River Basin Project: Part II*, 90 Cong. 2 Sess. (1968). For a narrative/chronological history of Arizona's struggle for CAP see Rich Johnson, *The Central Arizona Project, 1918–1968* (Tucson: University of Arizona Press, 1977).

20. Doug Kupel, *Fuel for Growth: Water and Arizona's Urban Environment* (Tucson: University of Arizona Press, 2003), 154.

21. See Earl Zarbin, "Central Arizona Water Conservation District: A Miracle of Unity," *www.cap-az.com*.

22. Kupel, *Fuel for Growth*, 176; Central Arizona Water Conservation District, "Chronological History of the Central Arizona Water Conservation District," unpublished manuscript, Central Arizona Water Conservation District, Phoenix, Arizona, 1992, 6–8.

23. Don Campbell, "An Interim Report: Central Arizona Project, *Arizona Highways,* (November 1968): 9.

24. Grady Gammage, Jr., was president of CAWCD 1995–1999. See Jack L. August, Jr., and Grady Gammage, Jr., "Shaped by Water: An Arizona Historical Perspective," in *Water Management Innovations for Arid Regions: Policy and Practice,* edited by Bonnie Colby and Katherine Jacobs (Baltimore, Md.: Resources for the Future Press, 2006).

25. See Jack L. August, Jr., "Hopis Seek Their Water Rights," Special to the *Arizona Republic,* September 21, 2003; Michael Pearce, "Indian Water Rights Settlements: The Arizona Landscape," *Western Water Law and Policy Report* (May 2003).

26. See Patti Jo King, "Bush Signs Water Settlement Act," *Indian Country Today,* January 17, 2005. Prior to the passage the legislation was known as S 437. The measure encompassed three settlements: two with Indian communities and one with the federal government. Through this settlement the Gila River Nation will receive approximately 155,700 acre-feet of water while the Tohono O'odham will receive approximately 37,800 acre-feet. The Gila River tribe will also lease another 40,000 acre-feet of their allotment as per the settlement agreement. Some 67,000 acre-feet of water that had been previously unclaimed will be distributed among several Arizona cities, with an additional 96,000 acre-feet held in reserve for future allocation.

27. Joe Gelt, "Long Awaited CAP Water Delivers Trouble for State," *Arroyo* 6, no. 3 (fall–winter 1993).

28. Michael Hanneman, "The Central Arizona Project, Working Paper No. 397," *Department of Agriculture and Resource Economics,* University of California, Berkeley (October 2002).

29. *Arizona Daily Star* (Tucson), May 4, 2001. In 1995 a well-financed "anti-CAP/anti-Tucson Water" campaign spearheaded by auto dealer Bob Beaudry, used images of dying women in wheelchairs linked to "CAP Chemical Soup" to instill fear in the community. Independent experts and community leaders who privately supported delivery of CAP water were unwilling to set themselves up as targets. The campaign resulted in the passage of the 1995 Water Consumer Protection Act, which is still in effect and bans the direct delivery of CAP water unless it is treated to a quality far beyond the Safe Drinking and Water Act standards. The current deliveries are a mix of Colorado River water that has been recharged through the aquifer and recovered through wells and groundwater from Avra Valley.

30. Not surprisingly, the CAGRD has been heavily criticized as opening a "loophole" in the Groundwater Management Act's link between renewable water supplies and urban development. It has proved far more popular than originally anticipated with more than 165,000 lots enrolled in the CAGRD mechanism as of 2005, and many thousands more likely to come.

CHAPTER EIGHT: THAT LAWYER FROM ARIZONA

1. John Bouma oral history interview with Jack L. August, Jr., March 13, 2006, author's files. Bouma, who joined Snell & Wilmer in 1962, also noted that they used to hunt dove in the area of northwest Phoenix that is now between Twenty-seventh Avenue and Thirtieth Avenue and Bell Road.

2. Mark Bernard Wilmer, Jr., interview with August, August 18, 2004.

3. According to Bouma, "There were a lot of stories and a lot of partying, a whole lot of tricks and stunts and things like that, such as putting something on somebody's out-board so that when they started the motor, it exploded and blew smoke, making them think it blew up, or throwing water on their boat at night so they thought it was sinking…. they were the things you never talked about when you got to town. Your hair was down but everybody understood it was off the record."

4. *First Sixty Years,* 9–14.

5. Bouma interview with August.

6. Pfister interview with August. C. Kimball Rose to Jack L August, Jr., February 18, 2006, author's files.

7. In the same sentence Pfister included Eugene Pulliam, Walter Bimson, Tom Chauncey, and Sherman Hazeltine.

8. William H. Rehnquist, "Tribute to Mark Wilmer, *Arizona State Law Journal* 27, no 2 (summer 1995): 411.

9. Mark Bernard Wilmer, interview with August; Liz Wilmer Sexson to Jack August, August 11, 2006, author's files.

10. Calvin Udall, "Tribute to Mark Wilmer," 420.

11. Edwin F. Hendricks, "Tribute to Mark Wilmer," *Arizona State Law Journal* 27, no. 2 (summer 1995): 420.

12. *First Sixty Years,* 9; Daniel Cracchiolo, oral history interview with Jack L. August, Jr., February 2, 2004.

13. *First Sixty Years,* 9. Snell & Wilmer's client base and practice areas have broadened and deepened in the last decade. Among the larger clients are Apollo Group, Inc., Arizona Public Service, Bank of America, Bank One, Ford Motor Company, Mayo Clinic, Mercury Marine, Prudential, Salt River Pima-Maricopa Indian Community, and the Tucson Airport Authority. Moreover, many of the firm's attorneys practice in the realms of small business, emerging businesses, and entrepreneurial enterprises. For further information about the firm's awards and nationally recognized benevolent activities see website *www.swlaw.com.*

14. Edwin F. Hendricks to Jack L. August, Jr., August 15, 2006, author's files. Hendricks, "Tribute to Mark Wilmer," 417–419.

15. Mark "Bernie" Wilmer interview with August.

16. Edward Jacobson to Honorable John J. Rhodes, January 20, 1995, Snell & Wilmer, Phoenix, Arizona. The note read, in part, "On Saturday evening, February 25, 1995, Mark Wilmer will be posthumously given the Historymaker's award. The family has requested that I present the award to Mark's eldest (Bernie). I thought it would be an appropriate and wonderful surprise if, at the same time, the Arizona Project Canal (or any portion thereof that is not already named), could be named after Mark. Do you have any idea whether the idea might fly and how and with whom I might get it started?"

17. Edward Jacobson to Honorable Bruce Babbitt, February 7, 1995, Snell & Wilmer, Phoenix, Arizona.

18. Grady Gammage, Jr., to Honorable Bruce Babbitt, February 17, 1995, Snell & Wilmer, Phoenix, Arizona.

19. Liz Wilmer Sexson to Bud Jacobson, February 26, 1995, Snell & Wilmer, Phoenix, Arizona.

20. August, *Vision in the Desert,* 175–213.

21. Philip L. Fradkin, *A River No More: The Colorado River and the West* (New York: Alfred A. Knopf, 1981); Walter Prescott Webb, "The American West: Perpetual Mirage," *Harper's* 214 (May 1957); Rifkind interview with August.

APPENDICES NOTES

1. 42 Stat. 171 (1921).

2. Wilmer, *Arizona v California* at 41.

SELECTED BIBLIOGRAPHY

BOOKS

Abbott, Carl. *The New Urban America: Growth and Politics in Sunbelt Cities.* Chapel Hill: University of North Carolina Press, 1982.

Arizona Highline Reclamation Association. *The Highline Book.* Phoenix: The Arizona Highline Reclamation Association, 1923.

August, Jack L. Jr. *Vision in the Desert: Carl Hayden and Hydropolitics in the American Southwest.* Ft. Worth: Texas Christian University Press, 1999.

Berkman, Richard L. and W. Kip Viscusi. *Damming the West.* New York: Grossman Publishers, 1973.

Byrkit, James W. *Forging the Copper Collar: Arizona's Labor Management War of 1901–1921.* Tucson: University of Arizona Press, 1982.

Current, Richard Nelson. *Wisconsin: A History.* Champagne: University of Illinois Press, 2001.

Davis, Arthur Powell. *Irrigation Near Phoenix, Arizona.* Washington, D.C.: Government Printing Office, 1897.

Etulain, Richard, ed. *The Twentieth Century West: A Bibliography.* Norman: University of Oklahoma Press, 1994.

Farish, Thomas Edwin. *Arizona History.* Phoenix: Phoenix Manufacturing Company, 1920.

Fradkin, Philip L. *A River No More: The Colorado River and the West.* (New York: Alfred A. Knopf, 1981.

Gammage, Grady, Jr. *Phoenix in Perspective: Reflections on Developing the Desert.* Tempe, Arizona: Herberger Center for Design, 1999.

Gates, Paul W. *History of Public Land Law Development.* Washington, D.C.: Zenger Publishing Company, 1968.

Goff, John F. *George W. P. Hunt and His Arizona.* Pasadena, California: Socio-Technical Publications, 1973.

Graebner, Norman. *Manifest Destiny.* New York: Bobbs-Merrill, 1968.

Gressley, Gene. *The Twentieth Century American West: A Potpourri.* Columbia: University of Missouri Press, 1977.

Haber, Samuel. *Efficiency and Uplift; Scientific Management in the Progressive Era, 1890–1900.* New York: Oxford University Press, 1981.

Haury, Emil. *The Hohokam: Desert Farmers and Craftsmen—Excavations at Snaketown, 1964-1965.* Tucson: University of Arizona Press, 1965.

Hays, Samuel P. *Conservation and the Gospel of Efficiency: The Progressive Conservation Movement, 1890–1920.* New York: Atheneum Press, 1975.

Ingram, Helen. *Water Politics: Continuity and Change.* Albuquerque: University of New Mexico Press, 1990.

Hundley, Norris, Jr. *Water and the West: The Colorado River Compact and the Politics of Water in American West.* Berkeley, University of California Press, 1975.

_____. *The Great Thirst: Californians and Water: 1770s-1990s.* Berkeley: University of California Press, 1992.

Johnson, Rich. *The Central Arizona Project, 1918–1968.* Tucson: University of Arizona Press,1977.

Kupel, Douglas. *Fuel for Growth: Water and Arizona's Urban Environment.* Tucson:

University of Arizona Press, 2003.

Lamar, Howard R. *The Far Southwest, 1846–1912: A Territorial History.* New Haven: Yale University Press, 1966.

Layton, Edwin T., Jr. *The Revolt of the Engineers: Social Responsibility and the Engineering Profession.* Cleveland: Case Western University Press, 1971.

Leuchtenburg, William E. *The Perils of Prosperity.* Chicago: University of Chicago Press, 1958.

Lowitt, Richard. *The New Deal and the West.* Bloomington: University of Indian Press, 1984.

Luckingham, Bradford. *The Urban Southwest: A Profile History of Albuquerque, El Paso, Phoenix, and Tucson.* El Paso: Texas Western Press, 1982.

Meyer, Michael. *Water in the Hispanic Southwest: A Social and Legal History, 1550–1850.* Tucson: University of Arizona Press, 1984.

Moeller, Beverly. *Phil Swing and Boulder Dam.* Berkeley: University of California Press, 1971.

Mowry, George. *The Era of Theodore Roosevelt and the Birth of Modern America, 1900-1912.* New York: Harper and Sons, 1958.

Nash, Gerald. *The American West in the Twentieth Century: A Short History of an Urban Oasis.* Albuquerque: University of New Mexico Press, 1973.

_____. *The American West Transformed: The Impact of World War II.* Bloomington: University of Indiana Press, 1985.

_____. *World War II and the West: Reshaping the Economy.* Lincoln: University of Nebraska Press, 1990.

Pisani, Donald. *To Reclaim a Divided West: Water, Law, and Public Policy, 1848- 1902.* Albuquerque: University of New Mexico Press, 1992.

_____. *Water and the American Government: The Reclamation Bureau, National Water Policy, and the West, 1902–1935.* Berkeley: University of California Press, 2002.

Pomeroy, Earl. *The Pacific Slope: A History of California, Oregon, Washington, Idaho, Utah, and Nevada.* New York: Alfred A. Knopf, 1965.

Reisner, Marc. *Cadillac Desert: The American West and its Disappearing Water.* New York: Viking, 1986.

Richardson, Elmo. *Dams, Parks, and Politics: Resource Development in the Truman-Eisenhower Era.* Lexington: University of Kentucky Press, 1973.

Sheridan, Thomas. *Arizona: A History.* Tucson: University of Arizona Press, 1995.

Smith, Karen. *The Magnificent Experiment: Building the Salt River Reclamation Project, 1890–1917.* Tucson: University of Arizona Press, 1984.

Starr, Kevin. *Americans and the California Dream, 1850–1915.* New York: Oxford University Press, 1973.

Tyler, Daniel. *Silver Fox of the Rockies: Delphus Carpenter and Western Water Compacts.* Norman: University of Oklahoma Press, 2003.

Wiebe, Robert. *The Search for Order, 1877–1920.* New York: Hill and Wang, 1967.

Wiley, Peter and Gottlieb, Robert. *Empires in the Sun: The Rise of the New American West.* New York: G. P. Putnam and Sons, 1982.

Worster, Donald. *Rivers of Empire: Water, Aridity, and the Growth of the American West.* New York: Pantheon, 1984.

_____. *Under Western Skies: Nature and History in the American West.* Albuquerque: University of New Mexico Press, 1994.

Zarbin, Earl. *Roosevelt Dam: A History to 1911.* Phoenix: Salt River Project, 1984.

JOURNAL ARTICLES

August, Jack, L. Jr. "Carl Hayden: Born a Politician." *Journal of Arizona History* 26 (Summer 1985).

_____. "A Sterling Young Democrat: Carl Hayden's Road to Congress, 1900–1912." *Journal of Arizona History* 28 (Autumn 1987).

_____. "Carl Hayden, Arizona, and the Politics of Water Development in the Southwest,

1923–1928." *Pacific Historical Review* 58 (May 1989).

————. "Carl Hayden's Indian Card: Environmental Politics and the San Carlos Reclamation Project." *Journal of Arizona History* 34 (Winter 1993).

————. "A Vision in the Desert: Charles Trumbull Hayden, Salt River Pioneer." *Journal of Arizona History* 36 (Summer 1995).

————. "Desert Bloom or Desert Doom? Carl Hayden and the Origins of the Central Arizona Project, 1922–1952." *Cactus and Pine* 8 (Summer 1996).

————. "Water, Politics and the Arizona Dream: Carl Hayden and the Modern Origins of the Central Arizona Project, 1922–1963," *Journal of Arizona History* 40 (Winter 1999).

Caughey, John. "The Insignificance of the Frontier in American History." *Western Historical Quarterly* 5 (January 1974).

Conkin, Paul. "The Vision of Elwood Mead." *Agricultural History* 34 (April 1960).

Day, Juliet. "A Dam for Arizona's Indians." *Arizona Highways* 6 (July 1930).

Ganoe, John T. "The Origin of a National Reclamation Policy." *Mississippi Valley Historical Review* 18 (June 1931).

Gressley, Gene. "Arthur Powell Davis, Reclamation and the West." *Agricultural History* 42 (July 1968).

Hardin, Garret. "The Tragedy of the Commons." *Science* 162 (1968).

Hendricks, Edwin F., "Tribute to Mark Wilmer." *Arizona State Law Journal* 27, 2 (Summer 1995).

Houghton, N. D. "Problems of the Colorado River as Reflected in Arizona Politics." *Western Political Quarterly* 4 (December 1951).

Hundley, Norris. "The West Against Itself," in *New Courses for the Colorado River: Major Issues For the Next Century.*" Weatheford, G. D. and Brown, F.L. eds. Alburquerque: University of New Mexico Press, 1986.

————. "Clio Nods: *Arizona v California* and the Boulder Canyon Act—A Reassessment." *Western Historical Quarterly* 3 (January 1972).

————. "The Colorado Waters Dispute." *Foreign Affairs* 42 (April 1964).

————. "The Politics of Reclamation: California, the Federal Government, and the Origins of the Boulder Canyon Act." *California Historical Quarterly* 52 (Winter 1973).

James, George Wharton. "In the Egypt of America: The Salt River Project." *Twentieth Century Magazine* 4 (April 1911).

Kyl, Jon. "Tribute to Mark Wilmer." *Arizona Law Review* 27, 2 (Summer 1995).

Lamar, Howard, R. "Persistent Frontier: The West in the Twentieth Century." *Western Historical Quarterly* 7 (January 1973).

Logan, Michael. "Head-Cuts and Check-Dams: Changing Patterns of Environmental Manipulation by Hohokam and Spanish in the Spanish Santa Cruz Valley, 200–1820." *Environmental History* 4 (July 1999).

Luckingham, Bradford. "Urban Development in Arizona: The Rise of Phoenix." *Journal of Arizona History* 22 (Summer 1981).

Meredith, H. L. "Reclamation in the Salt River Valley, 1902–1917." *Journal of the West* 7 (January 1968).

Moore, Hal. "The Salt River Project: An Illustrious Chapter in U.S. Reclamation." *Arizona Highways* 37 (April 1961).

Murphy, Ralph. "Arizona's Side of the Question." *Sunset Magazine* 56 (April 1926).

Newhall, Richard. "Arizona and the Colorado: How Not to Win a River by Trying Very Hard." *Phoenix Point West Magazine* 6 (March 1965).

Parsons, Malcolm. "Origins of the Colorado River Controversy in Arizona Politics, 1922–1923." *Arizona and the West* 4 (Spring 1962).

————. "Party and Pressure Politics in Arizona's Opposition to Colorado River

Development." *Pacific Historical Review* 19 (February 1950).

Pearce, Michael. "Indian Water Rights Settlements: The Arizona Landscape." *Western Water Law and Policy Reporter* (May 2003).

Reich, Peter L. "The Hispanic Roots of Prior Appropriation in Arizona." *Arizona State Law Journal* 27, 2 (Summer 1995).

Rehnquist, William. "Tribute to Mark Wilmer." *Arizona State Law Journal* 27, 2 (Summer 1995).

Pomeroy, Earl. "Toward a Reorientation of Western History: Continuity and Environment." *Mississippi Valley Historical Review* 41 (March 1955).

Rusinek, Walter. "*Bristor v Cheatham*: Conflict Over Groundwater Law in Arizona." *Arizona and the West* 27 (Summer 1985).

Shadegg, Stephen. "The Miracle of Water in the Salt River Valley, Part 1." *Arizona Highways* 18 (July 1942).

_____. "The Miracle of Water in the Salt River Valley, Part II." *Arizona Highways* 18 (August 1942).

Smith, Karen. "The Campaign for Water in Central Arizona, 1890–1903." *Arizona and the West* 23 (Summer 1981).

Smith, Thomas G. "Lewis Douglas, Arizona Politics, and the Colorado River Controversy." *Arizona and the West* 22 (Summer 1980).

Trelease, Frank. "*Arizona v California*: Allocation of Water Resources to People, States, and Nation." *The Supreme Court Review* (1963).

Van Petten, Donald R. "Arizona's Stand on the Colorado River Compact." *New Mexico Historical Review* 17 (January 1942).

Udall, Calvin. "Tribute to Mark Wilmer." *Arizona State Law Journal.* 27, 2 (Summer 1995).

Von Klein Smid, Rufus B. "The League of the Southwest: What It Is and Why." *Arizona: The State Magazine* 11 (May 1920).

Wilmer, Mark, "*Arizona v California*: A Statutory Construction Case," *Arizona Law Review* 40, 4 (1964).

Woodward, F. A. "Arizona Resources." *Arizona Magazine* 13 (November 1928).

COURT CASES

Arizona v California, 298 U.S. 558; 80 L. Ed. 1331, 1332–33 (1936).

Arizona v California, 299 U.S. 341; 78 L. Ed. 1298 (1934).

Arizona v California, et. al. 283 U.S. 423; 75 L. Ed. 115 (1931)

Arizona v California et. al., 373 U.S. 546 (1963) (opinion); 376 U.S. 340 (1964) (decree).

Bristor v Cheatham I, 240 P.2d 185 (Arizona 1952).

Bristor v Cheatham II, 255 P.2d 173 (Arizona 1953).

Hurley v Abbott, Maricopa County Territorial Court Case No. 4564 (1910).

United States v Arizona, 295 U.S. 174; 79 L. Ed. 1374 (1935).

Winters v United States 207 U.S. 564 (1908).

Wyoming v Colorado 259 U.S. 419 (1922).

NEWSPAPERS AND PERIODICALS

Arizona Blade Tribune (Florence)

Arizona Citizen (Tucson)

Arizona Daily Star (Tucson)

Arizona Democrat (Phoenix)

Arizona Gazette (Phoenix)

Arizona Miner (Prescott)

Arizona Republic (Phoenix)

Arizona Republican (Phoenix)

Calexico Chronicle

The Daily Silver Belt (Globe)

Denver Times

Graham County Guardian (Safford)

The Imperial Valley Farmer

La Voz Del Pueblo

Los Angeles Examiner

Los Angeles Times

New York Times

Newsweek Magazine (New York)

Phoenix Gazette

Prescott Daily Courier

Prescott Journal-Miner

Salt River Herald

San Diego Union

San Francisco Chronicle

San Francisco Daily News

Tempe Daily News

Time Magazine (New York)

Tombstone Epitaph

Tucson Citizen

Washington Post

Washington Star

Weekly Arizonan

Yuma Examiner

GOVERNMENT DOCUMENTS

Arizona Engineering Commission. *Reports Based on Reconnaissance Investigation of Arizona Land Irrigable from the Colorado River.* Arizona Department of Library, Archives and Public Records, 1923.

Chittenden, Hiram. *Preliminary Examination of Reservoir Sites in Wyoming and Colorado.* 55 Cong., 2 sess., 1897, H. Doc. 141.

Colorado River Commission of Arizona. *Official Report of the Proceedings of the Colorado River Conference.* Phoenix: State of Arizona, 1925.

_____. *Second Report to the Eighth Legislature, December 21, 1928.* Phoenix, Arizona, 1928. *Congressional Record.* 62 Cong., 2 sess., 1912.

_____. 63 Cong., 2 sess., 1914.

_____. 65 Cong., 3 sess., 1919.

_____. 66 Cong., 1 sess., 1919.

_____. 66 Cong., 2 sess., 1920.

_____. 69 Cong., 2 sess., 1926.

_____. 70 Cong., 2 sess., 1928.

_____. 90 Cong., 2 sess., 1968.

Powell, John Wesley. *Report on the Arid Region of the United States.* 45 Cong., 2 sess., 1878. H. Ex. Doc. 73.

_____. *Reservoirs in Arid Regions of the United States.* 50 Cong., 1 sess., 1888. S. Ex. Doc. 163.

Rifkind, Simon. *Special Master's Draft Report, May 5, 1960: Arizona v California,* Washington, D.C., Government Printing Office, 1960.

_____. Special *Master's Final Report and Recommended Decree, December 5, 1960.* Washington, D.C.: Government Printing Office, 1960.

State of Arizona. House of Representatives. *Journal,* 1923.

_____. *Journal,* 1925.

_____. *Journal,* 1927.

_____. *Journal,* 1928.

_____. *Journal,* 1944.

_____. *Journal,* 1957.

State of Arizona. Senate. *Journal,* 1923.

_____. *Journal,* 1957.

United States Congress. House. *Boulder Canyon Reclamation Project.* 69 Cong., 2 sess., 1926.

H. Rept. 1657, Part 3.

_____. *Colorado River Compact.* 67 Cong., 4 sess., 1923. H. Doc. 605.

_____. Committee on Irrigation and Reclamation. *Hearings on Protection and Development Of the Lower Colorado River Basin, H. R. 2903.* 68 Cong., 1 sess., 1924.

_____. Committee on Irrigation of Arid Lands. *Hearings on All-American Canal for Imperial Valley and Coachella Valleys, California, H.R. 6044.* 66 Cong., 1 sess., 1919.

_____. Committee on Irrigation of Arid Lands. *Hearings on Protection and Development of Lower Colorado River Basin, H.R. 11449.* 67 Cong., 2 sess., 1922.

_____. Committee on Rules. *Hearings on H.R. 9826.* 69 Cong., 2 sess., 1927.

_____. *Report of the Colorado River Board on the Boulder Dam Project.* 70 Cong., 2 sess., 1928. H. Doc. 446. United States Congress. Senate. *Problems of Imperial Valley and Vicinity.* 67 Cong., 2 sess., 1922. S. Doc. 142, appendix.

United States Department of Agriculture. *Silt in the Colorado and its Relation to Irrigation.* Technical Bulletin no. 67. Washington, D.C., 1928.

United States Department of the Interior. *Fourteenth Annual Report of the Reclamation Service, 1914–1915.* Washington, D.C., 1915.

_____. *Report on the Central Arizona Project, United States Department of the Interior Planning Report no. 3–8B, 4–2.* Washington, D.C.: Government Printing Office, 1948.

United States Geological Survey. *First Annual Report of the Reclamation Service, 1902.* Washington, D.C., 1903.

MANUSCRIPT COLLECTIONS

Arizona Colorado River Commission Papers. Arizona Department of Library, Archives and Public Records, Phoenix, Arizona.

Arizona Interstate Stream Commission Papers. Arizona Department of Library Archives and Public Records. Phoenix.

Bureau of Reclamation Papers. National Archives and Records Administration, Washington, D.C.

Central Arizona Project Association Papers. Department of Archives and Special Collections, Arizona State University, Tempe, Arizona.

Ely, Nortcutt. The Northcutt Ely Papers. Stanford University, Stanford, California.

Fireman, Bert. Bert Fireman Collection. Arizona Historical Foundation. Arizona State University, Tempe, Arizona.

Goldwater, Barry. The Personal and Political Papers of Barry Goldwater. Arizona Historical Foundation, Arizona State University, Tempe, Arizona.

Hayden, Carl. Carl Hayden Papers Collection. Department of Archives and Special Collections, Arizona State University, Tempe, Arizona.

Hunt, George. W. P. George W. P. Hunt Diaries. Department of Archives and Special Collections, Arizona State University, Tempe, Arizona.

Pyle, Howard. Howard Pyle Papers. Arizona Historical Society, Tempe, Arizona.

Snell & Wilmer Law Firm Papers. Snell & Wilmer Law Firm, Phoenix, Arizona.

Wilmer, Mark. The Mark Wilmer Papers, Arizona Historical Foundation, Arizona State University, Tempe, Arizona.

Maxwell, George. George Maxwell Papers. Arizona Department of Library, Archives and Public Records. Phoenix, Arizona.

INTERVIEWS

Akin, Wayne. Interview with author. Phoenix, Arizona, September 15, 1982, Oral History Collection, Department of Archives and Special Collections, Arizona State University.

Begam, Robert. Interview with author. Phoenix, Arizona, November 26, 2006. Author's Files.

Bouma, John. Interview with author. Phoenix, Arizona, March 13, 2006. Author's files.

Chilton, James. Interview with author. Los Angeles, California, June 18, 19, 1992. Author's Files.

Cracchiolo, Daniel. Interview with author. Phoenix, Arizona, April 12, 2004. Author's Files.

Elson, Roy. Interview with author. Washington, D.C., September 27, 1987. Author's Files.

Hayden, Carl. Interview with Joe Frantz. Old Senate Office Building 133. Washington, D.C., October 28, 1968. Oral History Collection, Lyndon Baines Johnson Presidential Library, Austin, Texas.

Hendricks, Genevieve. Interview with author. Phoenix, Arizona, November 18, 2004.

Jacobson, Edward. Interview with author. Phoenix, Arizona, November 10, 2004. Author's Files.

Pfister, Jack. Interview with author. Phoenix, Arizona, October 29, 2005. Author's Files.

Rifkind, Simon. Interview with author. Albuquerque, New Mexico. October 9, 1986. Author's Files.

Rose, C. Kimball. Interview with author. Phoenix, Arizona, February 18, 2006. Author's Files.

Sexson, Elizabeth. Interview with author. Phoenix, Arizona, February, 12, 2005. Author's Files.

Steiner, Fred. Interview with author. Phoenix, Arizona, February 22, 2006. Author's Files.

Udall, Calvin. Interview with John Bouma. Phoenix, Arizona, February 18, 2000. Snell & Wilmer, Phoenix, Arizona.

Wilmer, Bernard Mark. Interview with author. Las Vegas, Nevada. August 18, 2004. Author's Files.

Wilmer, Charles Mark. Interview with author. Phoenix, Arizona, February 18, 2005. Author's Files.

Wilmer, Mark. Interview with James McNulty, October 25, 1988, Arizona Bar Association Oral History Project, Arizona Historical Society, Tucson, Arizona.

Wilmer, Mark. Interview with Zona Davis Lorig, September 8, 1994, Phoenix, Arizona. Arizona Historical Society, Tucson, Arizona.

UNPUBLISHED MATERIALS

Kluger, James R., "Elwood Mead: Irrigation Engineer and Social Planner." Ph.D. dissertation, University of Arizona, 1970.

Mawn, Geoffrey P. "Phoenix, Arizona: Central City of the Southwest, 1870–1920." Ph.D. dissertation, Arizona State University, 1979.

Mayo, Dwight. "Arizona and the Colorado River Compact." Master's Thesis, Arizona State University, 1964.

Metcalf, Barbara Ann. "Oliver Wozencraft in California, 1849–1887." Master's Thesis, University of Southern California, 1963.

Smith, Karen. "The Magnificent Experiment: Building the Salt River Reclamation Project, 1890–1917." Ph.D. dissertation, University of Southern California, Santa Barbara, 1982.

Wilson, Marjorie Haines. "The Gubernatorial Career of G.W.P. Hunt of Arizona." Ph.D. dissertation, Arizona State University, 1973.

INDEX